V & W DESTROYERS
A Developmental History

John Henshaw

Frontispiece
HMS *Vimiera* in heavy weather on North Sea convoy duty, common conditions that small destroyers had to take in their stride. (vandwdestroyerassociation.org.uk)

First published in Great Britain in 2020 by
Seaforth Publishing,
A division of Pen & Sword Books Ltd,
47 Church Street,
Barnsley S70 2AS

www.seaforthpublishing.com

British Library Cataloguing in Publication Data

A catalogue record for this book is available from the British Library

ISBN 978 1 5267 7482 8 (hardback)
ISBN 978 1 5267 7483 5 (epub)
ISBN 978 1 5267 7484 2 (kindle)

Pen & Sword Books Limited incorporates the imprints of Atlas, Archaeology, Aviation, Discovery, Family History, Fiction, History, Maritime, Military, Military Classics, Politics, Select, Transport, True Crime, Air World, Frontline Publishing, Leo Cooper, Remember When, Seaforth Publishing, The Praetorian Press, Wharncliffe Local History, Wharncliffe Transport, Wharncliffe True Crime and White Owl

Designed by Neil Sayer

Printed and bound in India by Replika Press Pvt Ltd

Contents

ACKNOWLEDGEMENTS AND NOTES ON THE DRAWINGS

One can only begin to write a book such as this from reading many other books. The hard-to-obtain *British Destroyers: A History of Development 1892-1953* by Edgar J March was a gold mine of basic information and drawings. Norman Friedman's several books were, as always, useful beyond measure. Both authors' works were constantly being referred to for the sort of detail I needed or to cross-check information gleaned from other sources. As always, thank you Norman. The many authoritative books of David K Brown (ex-Deputy Chief Naval Architect of the Royal Corps of Naval Constructors) were also a frequent and reliable reference. Source material, indeed inspiration, came from Antony Preston's *V & W Class Destroyers 1917-1945* and *'V' and 'W' Class Destroyers* by Alan Raven and John Roberts. Narratives of life on board 'V & Ws' at war came particularly from Captain Donald Macintyre's *U-Boat Killer*, Robert Moore's *A Hard Fought Ship; The Story of HMS Venomous* and John Moyes' *Scrap-Iron Flotilla*. For information on camouflage I am most indebted to Malcolm Wright's incomparable book, *British and Commonwealth Warship Camouflage of WWII: Destroyers, Frigates, Escorts, Minesweepers, Coastal Warfare Craft, Submarines & Auxiliaries*. The notes relating to each camouflage drawing also provided additional historical information which was useful. Two websites that were most helpful were thedreadnoughtproject.org, and I thank Tony Lovell for his help, and the very thorough research of u-boat.net which has been responsible for updating many incorrect wartime records of U-boat losses.

But the forty drawings in this book did not come from books written by others. That's why I wrote this book. I wanted to gather in one place all the information about the 'V & W' destroyers I could find – well, all the technical type information that I considered relevant to the average reader – and present this with my own drawings at constant scales, in a consistent format so that the evolution of the breed could be examined, so that one could visualise in one volume the designs that led up to them, the variations in the generic 'V & W' class itself, the modifications and conversions they went through to extend their service life, the designs of other navies influenced by them and, lastly, the fanciful conversions that were proposed but which never took place.

The basis of the drawings of the 'V & Ws' – the starting point, indeed the very genesis of the project itself – was a somewhat unusual drawing prepared for and by the Australian Department of Defence as late as 28 June 1990. It is titled HMAS V & W CLASS DESTROYERS, Profile Upper deck & Sections and is numbered A015521 drawn to a scale of 1:100. I say it is unusual only in that a drawing of a ship built in 1918 is drawn 72 years later. For what conceivable reason? My only explanation is that it was probably as some sort of exercise for a trainee draftsman – the signatures and counter-signatures of those who have checked and approved the drawing (despite the error that the whaler is noted as being 21ft and not 27ft!) are just readable but, for obvious reasons, I do not wish to quote them here. The point is, this gave me a very good, reasonably detailed drawing from which I could prepare my own drawing on AutoCAD. With CAD you draw in 1:1 scale. That is, you draw the actual dimensions – or what you reckon to be the actual dimensions. If you had a printer and paper big enough, you could reproduce the plans full size.

I was able to scale off it and produce my own profile and deck plan with all of the basic elements in place – especially knowing the frame spacing. So, why was the frame spacing important? Ships are constructed on a modular basis – the frame spacings dictate where bulkheads and other structural elements are located. Because I have to create my drawings by scaling off other drawings, when I establish what I think is a scaled dimension and transfer it to my drawing, its relationship to the framing grid determines the final location. For instance, deckhouses and masts will line up with a frame because they will be supported on the beam that spans the frame or will be a continuation of the bulkhead beneath. Deck openings will fit between deck beams. Scuppers, ventilators and portholes always fit between frames.

While I work solely in the metric system, I have chosen to write the book using measurements in the Imperial system as this was the system of the time. Yes, I could have placed all the metric equivalents in brackets after the Imperial measurements but this becomes very messy appearance-wise and since everyone has a pocket calculator or access to one via their mobile phones, it is a simple matter to convert any Imperial measurement as and when needed.

The purpose of the drawings is not to provide a definitive set of drawings, or a reference work for modelmakers who, having been one, tend to be a pedantic lot. To some, absolute and total accuracy is an obsession. My drawings should be viewed, therefore, as a means of making comparisons of one ship with another, as examples of the progression of the design from its beginnings and to identify what basic changes occurred – not as a factual record, for example, as to the exact number and placement of portholes, or the precise separation of wireless aerials. As such, the amount of detail on the drawings is by no means all-embracing. At, say, 1:500 scale, a lot of that detail is lost anyway as, no matter how good a printer may be and using the finest line possible, it is simply not possible to distinguish all the detail so the purists will, undoubtedly, find fault. If I had the original drawings from the Ships' Covers, I would have used them. In some instances, indeed in many instances, because the drawings or the photographs I have had to work from have been basic to say the least, I have had to make calculated guesses as to what sort of detail to include to give an overall impression rather than a definitive drawing. In order to give some idea of the likely arrangement of flag and signal halyards and radio aerials, I have chosen to draw all yards at 15° from the horizontal.

I trust readers will regard my drawings as descriptive rather than prescriptive – as a means of making comparisons between types rather than thinking of any one of them as being an absolutely factual representation. If I was ever fortunate to come across the builders' drawings it would give me great pleasure to make good all inaccuracies in a later edition.

John Henshaw
Cape Schanck 2019

INTRODUCTION

Why a book on the 'V & W' destroyers when there are already so many words written about them – and good ones at that? Well, that's a question I asked myself until I realised that no-one had put together a comprehensive study of these fine warships with what I regarded as the three missing ingredients: the 20 years of destroyer development that led up to their design, the influence of their legacy on future designs and – most importantly for me – all illustrated with detailed drawings to assist in telling this story. My previous work on the *Town Class Destroyer: A Critical Assessment*, had been well received largely due to the number and type of drawings which augmented the narrative – as had *Liberty's Provenance: The Evolution of the Liberty Ship from its Sunderland Origins*. So, I figured a similar approach would fit well with this important story.

I think I have always been interested in destroyers since as a young boy I remember seeing one of the Royal Australian Navy's 'Tribal' class destroyers at Melbourne's Station Pier. I can't remember which one she was – *Arunta*, *Bataan* or *Warramunga* – but she looked like she was moving forward, even while tied firmly to the pier: the rake of the stem, the way the superfiring guns stepped up to the bulk of the bridge with its gunnery directors, the towering lattice mast then the rake of those well-proportioned funnels sweeping back to the lesser height of the armament towards the stern. They were truly handsome and inspiring ships viewed from any angle. If ever a warship deserved the title 'Racehorse of the sea', it was the 'Tribal' class destroyer – a perfect example of form and function combined.

The 112 single-funnelled War Emergency Programme Classes ('O' to 'Cr' classes which formed the 1st to 13th Flotillas) were the last of any British destroyer designs which made any pretence at maintaining a handsome appearance. The classes which followed – the 'Battles', the 'Weapons' and the *Daring*s – were decidedly designed around function first and form second (a distant second!) and it was only the very much larger 'County' class guided-missile destroyers which offered some sense of style being re-introduced with a reasonable blend of form and function.

Such could not have been said of the 'V & Ws', because they were certainly not handsome ships. Functional – yes. Indeed, very much so. But attractive – no. Well, not in the sense that looking at them stirred any sense of an appreciation of aesthetics. On the other hand, they were in the same mould as the classes which preceded them except, perhaps for the smaller 'R' and 'S' class which did have a certain rakish look to them with their long forecastles and low, two-level bridges. Certainly, the preceding 'M' class – disparate as it was – and the *Marksman*/*Lightfoot*/*Kempenfelt* type leaders and the *Parker* class had that 'look', with raked, thin funnels behind a raised forecastle introduced with the 'River' class. Yet, one tall, skinny funnel forward tucked behind a tall spindly bridge made to look even more ungainly by one short squat funnel amidships was not exactly shipshape and Bristol-fashion to many eyes. Certainly not to John I Thornycroft & Company. They produced a more handsome version with slightly higher freeboard and two more even-height and flat-sided funnels. But, of course, one should not judge a book by its cover. Underneath that better-looking exterior there was more horsepower, a wider beam and, generally, a better version of the basic design. Thornycroft's were mavericks in many respects and had a do-it-their-own-way attitude when it came to interpreting the Admiralty requirements, somewhat at their peril at times. Yet, more often than not, they were ahead of the curve and their designs were superior in principle, execution and appearance. If Thornycroft's had a failing, it was in delivery time and price. But you got what you paid for.

Readers unfamiliar with the 'V & W' story will already have begun to realise that these sixty-seven destroyers weren't one homogenous class if one shipyard can interpret the Admiralty's requirements with a certain amount of discretion. There were in fact seven definable categories – some major, some minor: 'V' class leaders, Thornycroft 'V' class, Admiralty 'V' class, Admiralty 'W' class or 'Repeat V' class, Admiralty 'Modified W' class 1st Group, Admiralty 'Modified W' class 2nd Group and Thornycroft 'Modified W' class.

The 'V & Ws' developed from a series of small, flush-decked torpedo boat destroyers through to slightly bigger 'whalebacks', to the raised forecastle design – all in less than 30 years. Propulsion went from coal-fired boilers with reciprocating engines, through turbines with high-revving direct drive and multi-propellers to oil-fired boilers and geared turbines. Weapons increased from small, quick-firing guns and single or twin fixed torpedoes to four 4in guns then the heavy-hitting 4.7in guns and six trainable torpedoes, all in that 30-year period. Yet, in that next 30-year period – certainly in the first 20 or so years of it – the fundamentals that came together in the 'V & Ws' remained basically unchanged in destroyer design. When one compares how much advancement there was, for instance, in aircraft – from fragile, slow, wood and canvas biplanes in 1918 to intercontinental, all-metal, much faster monoplanes in the mid-1930s and the beginnings of jet aircraft five years later – destroyer design was still following the basic principles established by the 'V & Ws'.

We can rightfully put the 'V & W' class destroyers on a pedestal as being ground-breaking, the peak of destroyer design for their time. They set a trend in destroyer design that lasted – in basic principle, subject to varieties of interpretation – for over 20 years.

So, a hundred years after all but the very last of these destroyers were commissioned, this book tells that step-by-step story.

HMS *Vanoc* on convoy duty. Note the QF 12-pounder 12 cwt mounting in the foreground which has replaced the aft bank of torpedo tubes.

1: Background

There are only two classes of warship whose descriptors evoke real emotion – destroyer and battleship. The latter is, of course, a relic – made redundant by the aircraft carrier. It has faded from our lexicon except for news journalists who think that anything that's painted grey with guns on it is a 'battleship'. But the destroyer lives on, in many guises. It alone has a title that denotes menace, that states what it was designed to do, which underlines its very purpose. Cruiser, frigate, corvette as descriptors carry little of the inherent threat of DESTROYER, even if prefixed by something like guided missile. Somehow that threatening air of peril or danger just doesn't ring as true as it does to the naval destroyer.

The name originated from the need to create warships to counter the threat posed by the Whitehead self-propelled torpedo which gave rise to small, agile and fast torpedo boats in the 1880s. The torpedo provoked the arms race of the time. Suddenly, the Royal Navy's total dominance of the sea, which had been firmly reasserted with Nelson's success at Trafalgar, was threatened. Sea control was expensive and only the British Empire could sustain the largest fleet in the world. But the advent of the torpedo meant that any small insignificant navy could possess what amounted to the equivalent of today's cruise missile. The torpedo, crude as it was to begin with, was potentially a one-hit-wonder that could disable if not destroy the most powerful warships afloat – of which the Royal Navy then possessed not only the most but also the best. Britain was, at the time, the world leader in naval ship design and construction. But big ships – and lots of them to boot – with powerful but slow-firing guns almost became irrelevant. The Royal Navy's deterrent factor was very much at risk. The concept of *Pax Britannica* was under threat. The control of the sea and the denial of the sea to one's enemies was in jeopardy – basic tenets of Alfred Thayer Mahan's doctrine as espoused by his 1890 thesis, *The Influence of Sea Power Upon History, 1660–1783*. Mahan emphasised that naval operations were chiefly to be won by decisive fleet-on-fleet battles and by blockades.

The Naval Defence Act of 1889 provided for the expansion of the RN in order that the number of battleships should be equal to those of the next two largest navies combined (France and Russia) and, specifically, for the construction of ten battleships, forty-two cruisers and eighteen torpedo boats and four fast gunboats. Some sources refer to only thirty-eight cruisers and omit the reference to the four gunboats. An amount of £20 million was set aside and a four-year time frame was specified.

Old enmities die hard and the greatest threat to Britain's empire was still France – not so much world-wide but in the home waters of Britain and in the English Channel in particular. In France, the *Jeune École* (Young School) proposed that technologies emerging from the Industrial Revolution could be harnessed by a weaker fleet to offset the strengths of a superior maritime foe. Fast torpedo-carrying vessels perfectly fitted their policy. Torpedo boats could sally forth from defended ports and wreak havoc on enemy commercial shipping, particularly at choke points – such as the English Channel – or simply attack enemy warships blockading ports or in their own ports using stealth (due to their small size and low silhouette) and speed. To counter this, the torpedo boat destroyer evolved armed with light, quick-firing guns – up to fifteen rounds per minute out to a range of 2,000 yards which was well beyond that of current torpedoes. Warships responded to the threat by fitting the same quick-firing guns and new large warships had anti-torpedo bulges fitted below the waterline or suspended anti-torpedo nets from booms.

As tube-launched torpedoes became more efficient, the torpedo boat destroyers grew in size and carried torpedoes of their own becoming offensive as well as their defensive weapons. However, they were still very small warships, albeit termed boats, of between 125ft and 160ft in length and between 70 and 185 tons' displacement. They were powered by coal-fired boilers delivering steam to reciprocating engines which, no matter how sophisticated, limited speed – eventually – to a maximum of 27 knots, and only then in the calmest of waters. These were not ocean-worthy craft. They were limited in range because of their size. That is, the delicate balance of a sufficiently powerful power plant to achieve the requisite speed plus carrying the appropriate amount of coal plus the crew size necessary to tend the hungry boilers. Bigger power plants meant more steam which required bigger boilers, meant more crew to tend them, meant more length, meant more weight which then required more power. Back to square one. It was a vicious circle. Railway-type boilers were used to reduce weight and increase efficiency. These drew heat through horizontal tubes surrounded by water. The French Belleville boiler reversed the procedure by putting the water in small tubes exposed more surface area to the heat source, thereby increasing the efficiency.

The Parsons turbine-engined *Turbinia* of 1897 made such ships obsolete by achieving 37 knots. These turbines drove smaller propellers at much higher revolutions than the slow-revving reciprocating engines. But these direct-drive turbines were only efficient at high speed, the opposite of reciprocating engines. While suited to making short, fast forays, they were not suited to loitering to maintain the blockade of an enemy port.

The major change in operational strategy and tactics came when the size of the torpedo boat destroyer had increased sufficiently for them to accompany the fleets rather than operate separately from them. Their role then became one of offence against the enemy's fleet and defence against the enemy's own torpedo boat destroyers. However, their design was such that these were still, essentially, vessels to operate close to bases and in the restricted waters of the North Sea, the Irish Sea and English Channel. They also found uses such as despatch vessels and guard ships. Offensive action was night-oriented, approaching at low speed so as to not produce a white bow wave and reducing, if at all possible, embers from coal-fired boilers before accelerating when spotted – made more difficult by being painted black – or ready to attack. However, one of the characteristics of reciprocating steam engines as compared with the later turbines is that they are slow to accelerate. These vessels were scaled-up torpedo boats rather than scaled-down torpedo cruisers – the latter being an in-between design that was, in essence, a small sloop-type warship mounting guns (QF 3-pounders) and torpedoes (18in) but with a maximum speed of 25 knots.

A characteristic of the torpedo-boat destroyer designs up to the turn of the century was the 'turtleback' forecastle – in effect a humped foredeck which contained a bow-firing torpedo and, at its highest point, a 12-pounder (or similar) gun sitting atop what was termed a conning tower – a small, cylindrical citadel with little more than portholes of very limited visibility from which the ship was 'conned' – or directed – when in action. Otherwise, for normal navigation, there was a rudimentary open bridge aft of the gun. Two other torpedoes were on revolving mounts on the iron deck. Needless to say, they were very 'wet' and could not be driven hard in a heavy sea. This issue of seaworthiness was overcome in 1903 by introducing the raised forecastle in the 'River' class, which became mandatory in all future designs.

But first we need to examine the genealogy of the destroyer types starting with the turtleback types. While there had been previous classes of torpedo-boat destroyers before these, the turtleback types could be reasonable regarded as the last of the genus of 'boat' (often unnamed and distinguished by a pennant letter and number only) and what followed them represented the beginning of 'ships' with some, albeit limited, ocean-going potential.

Turbinia, at speed, 1897. (*Grace's Guide to British Industrial History*)

2: Destroyer types of the late 1800s

THE TWENTY-SIX AND TWENTY-SEVEN KNOTTERS

One fundamental aspect of the torpedo boat destroyers was the fact that the designs were not produced in-house by the Admiralty but exclusively by private enterprise. The leaders in this particular type of vessel were Yarrow and Company Limited (Poplar, then Isle of Dogs, London) and John I Thornycroft & Company Limited (Chiswick, London, later Woolston, Southampton).

Yarrow's specialty was in water-tube boilers to their own, then quite revolutionary, design while Thornycroft was the more adventurous in overall ship design with certain trademarks that set them apart from the more conservative, follow-the-leader type of shipbuilder. We will revisit the Thornycroft penchant for thinking outside the box several times in this book. In order to obtain Admiralty contracts, it was standard procedure for these shipbuilders – and for others slightly less entrepreneurial – to design and build their own warships to meet somewhat vague Admiralty specifications. However, there was one quite specific criterion: speed. The Admiralty wanted destroyers with a 27-knot speed. This was largely at the behest of Rear Admiral 'Jacky' Fisher as Third Naval Lord and Controller of the Navy via the Director of Naval Construction (DNC). The 1892–3 Estimates design brief, if it could be called that, was expanded by the DNC to include what had become the normal bow-mounted torpedo, two other torpedo tubes (one each side) with reloads and a QF 12-pounder gun forward, and the QF 6-pounder as the secondary armament. The anti-torpedo boat version would lose its side torpedo tubes for additional QF 6-pounders. The Admiralty circulated this brief with a basic general arrangement drawing which merely confirmed what was already known from current designs. However, a legend accompanied the documents as to expected displacement (226.1 tons), expected power and coal capacity and crew size.[1] Apart from Yarrow and Thornycroft, Palmers Shipbuilding & Iron Co (Ltd) (Jarrow), Laird Bros Ltd (Birkenhead), J Samuel White & Co (Ltd) (Cowes), Hanna, Donald & Wilson (Paisley) responded with proposals.[2]

HMS *Daring*, Thornycroft's contribution and a name perpetuated in the current Type 45 air defence destroyer of the Royal Navy. (photoship co.uk)

Needless to say, there were large variations in the shipbuilders' interpretation of the Admiralty's requirements. Yarrow submitted *Havoc* and a near sister-ship *Hornet* (differently boilered). Thornycroft submitted *Daring* and *Decoy* – the former's name perpetuated in the current, but controversial, *Daring* class Type 45 air defence destroyers. Laird's contribution was *Ferret* and *Lynx*. The other builders' models were rejected for a variety of reasons although Palmers and White's were successful in building follow-on orders in the 1893–4 Estimates – three and four ships respectively.

Norman Friedman credits Yarrow with designing and building the first British destroyer in 1895: *Havoc*.[3] According to the official

HMS *Ardent* at Malta as tender to the flagship, HMS *Ramillies*. She was completed in March 1895 but scrapped in 1911. Note the absence of a bow-mounted torpedo. (sudomodelist.ru)

Yarrow history, it was Alfred Yarrow who, in 1892, visited Admiral Fisher and acquainted him with the exceptionally fast French torpedo boats and, as a result, Fisher wanted a ship 180ft LOA by 18ft beam with 4,000 horsepower (IHP) with heavier armament, speed and greater ability to stand up to rough weather to chase torpedo boats and destroy them.[4]

Alastair Borthwick – Yarrow's biographer – then goes on to affirm Friedman's statement that this – meaning Fisher's requirements – was the world's first destroyer. Many sources attribute Fisher with using the term 'destroyer' on its own without reference to torpedo or boat. Others credit Alfred Yarrow. Either way, the terms torpedo boat destroyer (commonly abbreviated to TBD) continued on and both it and destroyer were both in common use at the same time until, at some indeterminate time probably early in the First World War, the single word 'destroyer' simply took over.

On trials, *Havoc* attained 26.1 knots (locomotive boilers) and *Hornet* 27.3 knots (water-tube boilers).[5] The difference in speed put paid to locomotive boilers and established water-tube boilers as the standard for the Navy's high-speed requirements.

Subsequently a somewhat diverse range of these ships was laid down between July 1892 and completed as late as July 1901 and

HMS *Charger* in the all-black colour scheme so favoured at the time. (en.wikipedia.org)

their average cost was £35,780. While known as Twenty-six and Twenty-seven Knotters they were grouped together in August 1912 as the 'A' class – although at that time of the forty-two (including the first six mentioned, above), twenty-seven had been scrapped. My drawing of HMS *Charger* is typical of the period.

These were the last ships to have the bow-mounted torpedo. Although a lighter 14in diameter torpedo had been designed, there were three inherent problems with the bow-mounted torpedo: first, the bulge occasioned by the tube's door, no matter how it was faired into the stem, created unacceptable amounts of spray to an already exposed gun and bridge position; second, the weight right forward was detrimental to good seakeeping, causing the bow to dig in and, third, it was difficult to reload. Until the advent of gyroscopes to steer torpedoes, the ship had to be aimed at the target first having allowed for deflection occasioned by the target's perceived course and speed: not an easy task given the poor conning position and being open to the elements and subject to spray, even in calm conditions.

Refer to Appendix A for class details.

THE THIRTY-KNOTTERS

The speed ante was upped in the 1894–5 Estimates when 30 knots was required of new designs. Armament requirements remained largely as before although quicker-firing Maxims were found preferable to the 6-pounders – a requirement that was later

HMS *CHARGER* 1896

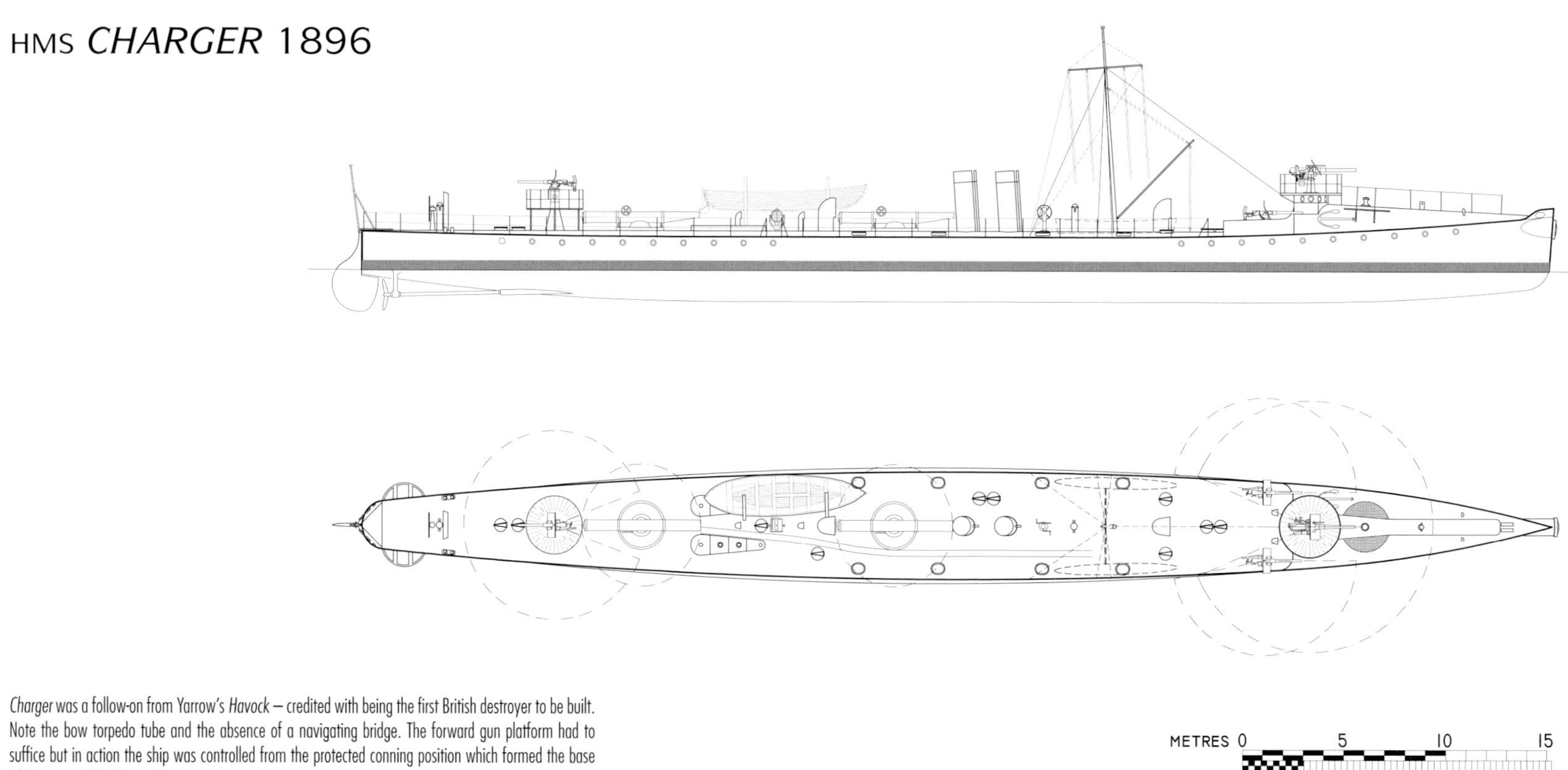

Charger was a follow-on from Yarrow's *Havock* – credited with being the first British destroyer to be built. Note the bow torpedo tube and the absence of a navigating bridge. The forward gun platform had to suffice but in action the ship was controlled from the protected conning position which formed the base of the gun, a QF 12-pounder.

reversed. Again, bunker capacity and expected crew numbers were defined but the anticipated displacement had risen to 280–300 tons in trial conditions – that is, not fully loaded – a reflection on the fact that more speed meant bigger engines and so forth, the design conundrum described earlier.

Yarrow, Thornycroft and Laird were the preferred tenders for three, three, and one ship respectively but this was changed so that each builder could submit two or three. A total of eight were approved in the Estimates. The builders' responses to what was essentially a performance specification varied considerably:

Yarrow	200ft LOA, with 5,700 IHP, using special steel and expected to stay within the 300-ton limit.
Thornycroft	210ft LOA with 5,400 IHP, using high-strength steel and displacing 260 tons.
Laird	207ft, 6,000 IHP and 6,000 IHP displacing the full 300 tons.[6]

Despite all three designs being approved in April 1895, Yarrow's – often in conflict with the Admiralty over various issues, principally intellectual property – fell out over price and each of the two remaining builders were awarded contract for four ships. Freidman states that 'Sir Alfred Yarrow [he was not actually knighted until 1916] circulated the claim that he had invented the destroyer' as part of Yarrow's bid to win Admiralty contracts after having been excluded in 1895.[7] Yarrow went on to export their design and others to Russia (*Sokol,* the first vessel ever to attain 30 knots),[8] Argentina (the *Corrientes* class), Sweden (*Mode*) and Portugal built *Tejo* to a Yarrow design. In 1899 Japan ordered eight destroyers (the *Sazanami* class) and ten torpedo boats.[9]

In 1975 I was a guest at a luncheon at the Royal Thames Yacht Club and was seated next to Sir Eric Yarrow, then Chairman of Yarrow & Co Ltd. My interest in matters naval was such that I asked him about the 'Yarrow stern' which I had heard about as it had applied to their destroyers. Unfortunately, and somewhat unexpectedly I thought, he was unable to enlighten me. He had never heard of it. Yarrow's were taken over less than two years later by the British Shipbuilders Corporation. It was only when I read Friedman's excellent book that I discovered that it consisted of a broader stern, angled outwards from the deck and was flatter underneath. It reduced weight and was credited with a knot to a knot-and-a-half extra speed compared with conventional sterns.[10] Also having interests in motor racing, I liken Yarrow's to Colin Chapman of Lotus whose philosophy was to 'simplify, then add lightness'. The Yarrow designed-and-built destroyers were always of a lighter displacement than their contemporaries due to the application of a philosophy in much the same vein, starting with their own boilers which were lighter and, it is said, more efficient than their competitors. LOTUS is often derogatively said to be an acronym for 'Lots Of Trouble Usually Serious' and, in that, if true, there is a common thread with Yarrow's in that the American First World War-built 'flush-decker' destroyers with Yarrow boilers were the first to be scrapped due to their unreliability.[11]

In common with what later became the 'A' class, these latest designs were not a homogeneous group but represented very many interpretations of the Admiralty's requirements. Despite this, they were lumped together and the twenty-four destroyers entered service with the Royal Navy between 1897 and 1898. Their average cost was £60,000.[12] One constant aspect was the relative consistency of their armament: a QF 12-pounder 12 cwt and five QF 6-pounders plus two 18in torpedoes on revolving mounts on the centreline.

HMS *Surly* was fitted with Holden and Rusden & Eeles oil-fired boilers in order to compare performance measured against their coal-fired sister-ships. They apparently produced a lot of smoke and were adjudged to be only 82 per cent as efficient as coal but when reboilered in 1901 with Kermode and Orde systems, the former proved 14 per cent better than coal.[13]

They were classified as the 'B' class on 30 August 1912. Despite the lack of uniformity, the one distinguishing feature of this class was that they all had four funnels, although differently spaced according to their particular boiler and engine arrangement. The most common appears to have been boilers opposite each other with the engine between pairs of boilers to distribute weight appropriately.

Unlike the 'A' class which saw only a few ships served in the First World War, all but two ships served in that conflict; one foundered in 1901 and the other was wrecked in 1904. Of the twenty-two that served, by July 1918 two had been lost; one wrecked in December 1914 and the other mined in March 1917.

Refer to Appendix A for class details.

THE BUILDERS' 'SPECIALS'

Builders designing and building ships 'on spec' – on the speculation that they would be taken up by the Admiralty – was a fairly common, albeit expensive, practice which resulted in some innovation and some incremental evolution but also more of simply slightly different repeats of what had been done before. The most notable, insofar as they progressed the genre in some form or other were as follows, in chronological order:

Triple-Expansion Reciprocating Engine-powered:
The entrepreneurially-minded Thornycroft's designed and built *Albatross*, laid down in November 1896. Unlike Thornycroft's later and more innovative designs, she had a conventional

HMS *EXPRESS* 1902

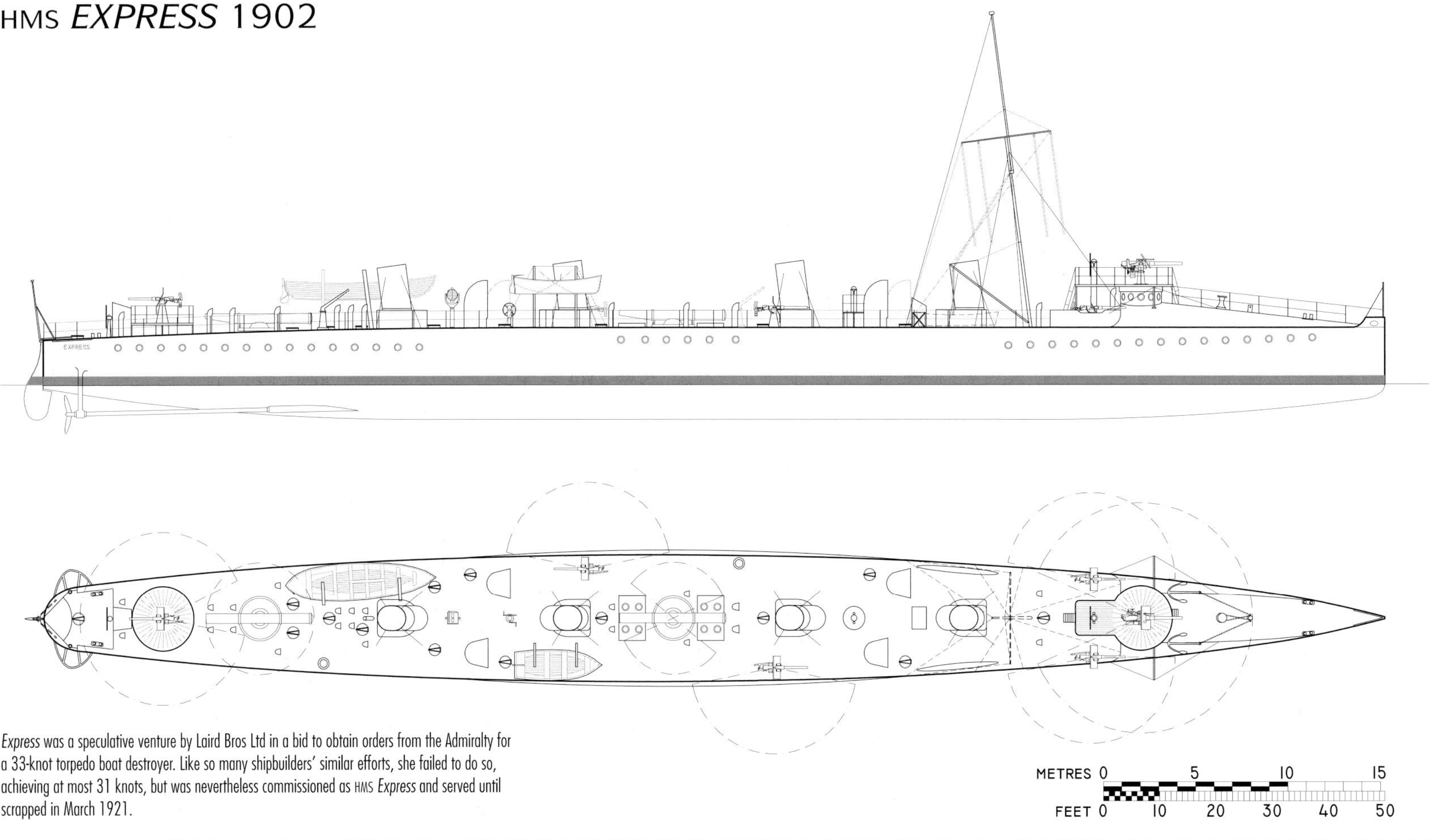

Express was a speculative venture by Laird Bros Ltd in a bid to obtain orders from the Admiralty for a 33-knot torpedo boat destroyer. Like so many shipbuilders' similar efforts, she failed to do so, achieving at most 31 knots, but was nevertheless commissioned as HMS *Express* and served until scrapped in March 1921.

underbody with stern-hung rudder and two shafts. She made in excess of 32 knots on trials.

Laird Bros Ltd laid down *Express* late in December 1896. Despite boosting the two engines to deliver just over 10,000 IHP from her vertical triple-expansion (VTE) reciprocating engines – which was in excess of the designed power – plus some experimenting with different propellers, she failed to make more than 31 knots.

John Brown & Co's first speculative venture involved two ships, *Thorn* and *Tiger*, both laid down in 1899 (no date available). *Thorn* was launched on 17 March 1900 and was commissioned into the RN in June 1901. *Tiger* was launched on 19 May 1900 and was also commissioned in June 1901. Little is known about these two ships. Records indicate that they were only the second and third warships built by Brown's.

J & G Thomson Ltd's contribution, *Arab*, was laid down in March 1900 and went into RN service in 1902 having failed to make her promised 32 knots by more than 1 knot. High speeds on the drawing board were one thing, reality quite another.

Turbine-powered:
The turbine designer and builder, Parsons Marine Turbine Company, entered a speculative venture in that their contract had to guarantee 31 knots. The hull was subcontracted to R & W Hawthorn Leslie and Company Limited and the result was *Viper*, laid down in 1898. She featured a four-shaft design with tandem propellers to absorb the energy and the high-speed revolutions (just under 1,000 RPM) from high and low-pressure turbines. The inner shafts had astern turbines for limited manoeuvring. Later trials delivered a little short of 37 knots making her the fastest warship in the world, albeit at a level of coal consumption that put huge demands on the stokers and trimmers. *Viper* was wrecked in August 1901, almost exactly one year after her trials began.

Sir W G Armstrong Whitworth & Co. Ltd, Newcastle upon Tyne, contributed a turbine destroyer which was laid down in 1899, bought by the Admiralty and renamed HMS *Cobra* in 1900. She had three tandem propellers on each of her four shafts and recorded a top speed on trials averaging 31-plus knots with 40 tons of coal aboard. *Cobra* had a short life, foundering in September

HMS *Viper* at speed. The 'black gang' must be hard at work judging by the bow wake and the amount of smoke she's making! (*Grace's Guide to British Industrial History*)

HMS *Bonetta.* Note the combination of the higher bow, turtleback, and the breakwater forming the base of an enlarged gun platform-cum-navigation bridge.

1901 but provided the Admiralty with the sort of turbine test experience it was seeking.

R & W Hawthorn Leslie and Company Limited were relative newcomers having only been founded at Tyneside in 1886. Their speculative venture teamed with Parsons to produce *Python* in 1902 which became HMS *Velox* in 1904. The two outer shafts were powered by high-pressure turbines and the two inner shafts had a low pressure and reversing turbine on each shaft coupled to a VTE cruising engine. Trials delivered slightly in excess of 33 knots but with a token coal load aboard. Despite a forward-mounted retractable rudder she was difficult to manoeuvre using engines because the astern engines were close together on the inner shafts

Palmers' contribution was two thirty-knotters, *Albacore* and *Bonetta* (laid down in May and September 1905 respectively) with turbines on three-shafts. They were higher in the bow with a less-pronounced turtleback and with a solid breakwater supporting the gun platform with the rudimentary conning position set a little further aft than had been the custom behind it. Neither ship ever achieved 30 knots because the trial conditions had changed and ships were supposed to demonstrate their speed prowess with bunkers almost full rather than with the token loads that had been the custom.

THE GERMAN SCHICHAU-WERKE DESTROYERS

While not seen at the time as potential enemies, concern was expressed at the widely believed rumour that German destroyers were capable of speeds in excess of 30 knots – even 35.2 knots was mentioned. The proof of the proverbial pudding's falsehood was established when four Schichau-designed and built destroyers for the Chinese navy were captured during the Boxer Rebellion. The one that fell into British hands – *Hai Lung* – was renamed HMS *Taku* and was found to be of lighter and weaker construction and tank tests of her hull form indicated she was not as well adapted to high speed as a commensurate RN destroyer.[14] Nonetheless, she served until October 1916 when she was scrapped. It is interesting to note that John I Thornycroft had an input insofar as the first German destroyers were concerned and was responsible for offering their design HO 6918 A

HMS *TAKU* 1900

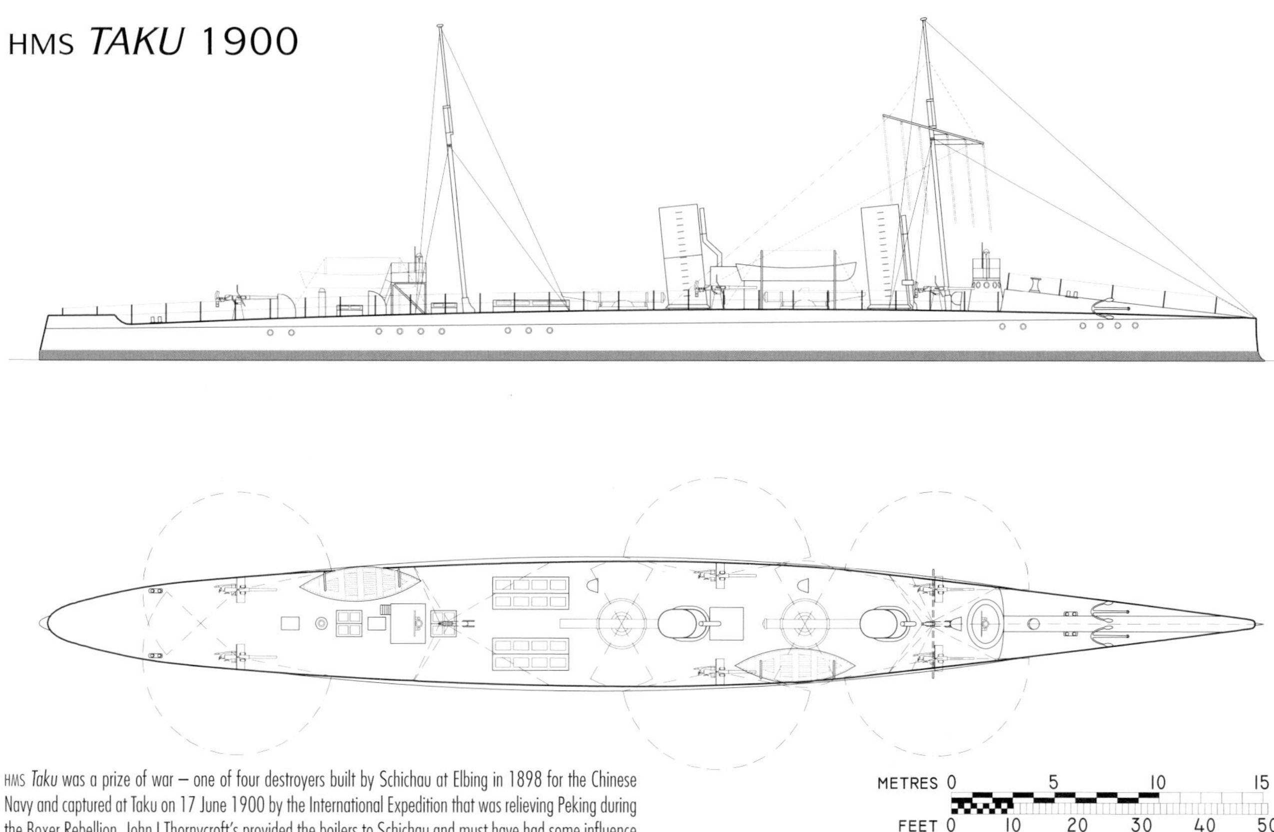

HMS *Taku* was a prize of war – one of four destroyers built by Schichau at Elbing in 1898 for the Chinese Navy and captured at Taku on 17 June 1900 by the International Expedition that was relieving Peking during the Boxer Rebellion. John I Thornycroft's provided the boilers to Schichau and must have had some influence in the design as the flat-sided funnels of equal height are their very early trademark. Previously named *Hai Lung*, HMS *Taku* proved to be frail and remained in the Far East and was scrapped in Hong Kong in 1916

and B to Germany in 1895 as a 'division boat' and this subsequently became Yard No. 322 and *D 10* for the German Navy and was, broadly, a duplicate of the 30-knotters.[15] The subsequently Schichau-built destroyers that followed had Thornycroft boilers, apparently, and although drawings of these are vague (coming mainly from Russian 1:350 scale modelmakers' instructions of the *Lieutenant Burakov* version of one of the four Chinese destroyers captured and re-distributed), the very characteristic Thornycroft flat-sided funnels of equal height are easy to distinguish as trademarks of this shipbuilder.

Refer to Appendix A for class details.

3: THE NEW CENTURY: EVOLUTION NOT REVOLUTION

THE 'RIVER' CLASS – 1901–04 PROGRAMMES

Just as the 'River' class frigates of the Second World War were a significant landmark in the evolution of anti-submarine vessels, the 'River' class destroyers were a similar and significant step in the evolution of the destroyer. Prior to this design it is fair to say that the 'A' to 'D' classes (117 built) could more properly be described with the suffix of 'boat' – as indeed they were so-named – but the 'River' class properly deserved the prefix of 'ship' or, simply, destroyer.

The basic design originated in the DNC as distinct from the entrepreneurial shipbuilders, as had tended to be the case. According to Friedman, the main instigator for an improvement in what had become more-or-less accepted as the standard specification for a torpedo boat destroyer (240–350 tons, 185–215ft LOA, two torpedo tubes, one 12-pounder, five–six 6-pounders, coal-fired with range limited by the amount of coal carried and the crew necessary to tend the boilers and the weapons) was Commander J M de Robeck, then the senior destroyer officer (captain of HMS *Angler* ['D' class] then HMS *Mermaid* ['C' class]) and elevated to captain in January 1902.[1]

De Robeck wrote to the Admiralty at the end of 1900. He was not a voice crying in the wilderness. His views were identical to the influential Admiral 'Jacky' Fisher and, later, Admiral C F Hotham – Commander-in-Chief at the Nore. Fisher, apparently, had noted the improvements effected in the German navy's equivalent ships

The German approach to destroyer design was entirely different. Note the position of the forward torpedo tubes behind a raised forecastle and an enclosed navigation position.

GROßE TORPEDOBOOTE S 90 1899 – 1907

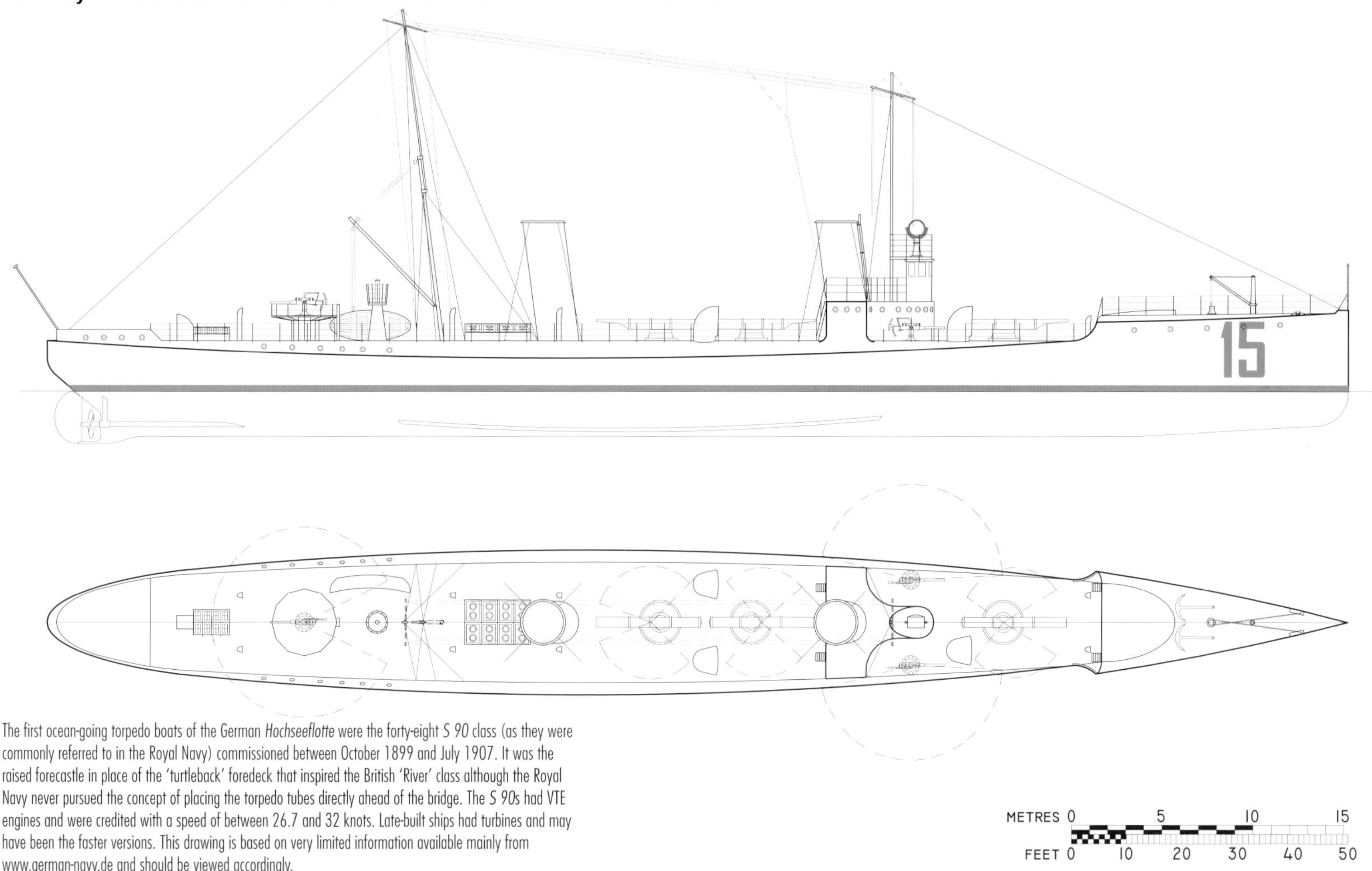

The first ocean-going torpedo boats of the German *Hochseeflotte* were the forty-eight *S 90* class (as they were commonly referred to in the Royal Navy) commissioned between October 1899 and July 1907. It was the raised forecastle in place of the 'turtleback' foredeck that inspired the British 'River' class although the Royal Navy never pursued the concept of placing the torpedo tubes directly ahead of the bridge. The *S 90*s had VTE engines and were credited with a speed of between 26.7 and 32 knots. Late-built ships had turbines and may have been the faster versions. This drawing is based on very limited information available mainly from www.german-navy.de and should be viewed accordingly.

(*S 90* class) which had raised forecastles, such as the *Große* or *Hochsee Torpedoboote* (large or high sea torpedo boat) of 1898. That is, instead of the flush deck with raised turtleback, the German ships had two decks forward with considerably more freeboard. Somewhat unconventionally, they mounted single torpedo tubes in the space between the forecastle and the bridge which was, as a result, further aft and not subject to the sort of spray and worse that plagued the RN – and French – torpedo boat destroyers. Furthermore, they mounted two torpedo tubes between the funnels and had reloads.

HMS *Waveney* at speed. Note the QF 6-pounder gun position abreast the bridge which was later removed. (en.wikipedia.org)

HMS *Teviot* was another interpretation of the 'River' class with paired funnels. (en.wikipedia.org)

Operating in the English Channel, close to their bases, suited existing RN designs. However, the North Sea and Western Approaches to the British Isles, together with the long distances between defended Mediterranean ports accessible to the RN, such as Gibraltar, Malta and Alexandria, required bigger, more substantial destroyers with greater range and the ability to function effectively in adverse weather. If it wasn't just de Robeck who perceived this need, it was he who, with Fisher's imprimatur, gave it voice. De Robeck wanted the destroyer speeds thought necessary to be more realistically achieved – not theoretical speeds when lightly loaded but realistic and achievable speeds when fully loaded. He also had views on raising the forecastle, giving it more flare, providing a separate navigating bridge and separating it from the forward gun and searchlight position. These were not revolutionary ideas but they had been rejected in the past.[2]

The DNC responded, somewhat reluctantly because the wish-list would involve bigger, heavier and consequently more expensive ships. After several sketch plans with variations, Rear Admiral W H May, Third Sea Lord and Controller of the Navy, approved the design in October 1901 but wanted greater strength, at the expense of speed – 25.5 knots – and ten such ships were included as part of the 1901–02 Programme, two of which would be equipped with turbines (direct drive). However, as had generally been the case, the shipbuilders interpreted the orders in their own ways: Palmer and Yarrow-built ships were 225ft LBP (but with different LOAs of 233ft 6in and 231ft 4in respectively) and had the four funnels grouped in two pairs while the Laird and Hawthorn Leslie interpretation was for 220ft LBP (again with different LOAs of 226ft 6in and 221ft 3in respectively) with the funnels trunked together. Despite these differences, and slight differences in beam and draft, standard displacements only varied between 533.6 and 550 tons.[3] Further variations resulting from shipbuilder interpretations came in the following year when further orders were placed: Thornycroft's being 225ft 9in LOA and White's 224ft 6in LOA. The thirty-six that were built were all named after rivers in the British Isles – the first destroyer class to be systematically named – but they were designated the 'E' class in October 1913.

The armament was a duplicate of the previous classes: a QF 12-pounder 12 cwt on a P.I mounting (range 9,500 yards), five QF 6-pounders on Mark I* recoil mountings (range 4,000 yards) and two single 18in torpedo tubes on the centreline. The 6-pounders were initially on the iron deck at the break of the forecastle with sponsons but were relocated on the foredeck beside the charthouse.

The armament was revised in 1906 after examining the results of the Russo-Japanese War (1904–05) so the three 6-pounders by then located on the iron deck only were replaced by a slightly lighter QF 12-pounder 8 cwt on a converted high-angle (HA) mounting for greater firepower. Similarly, in 1907 the 18in torpedoes were standardised on the 'A' to 'River' classes as the Mk VI SR (short range). In 1909 fixed loading trays for 18in torpedoes for deck storage of a spare torpedo per tube in time of war were considered and a 21in torpedo was trialled in HMS *Waveney*. In 1907, the ships began to be equipped with Fore Bridge Firing Gear and in 1909 the heater-type torpedoes, Mark VII, Mark VII* or Weymouth Mark Is.[4]

The year 1907 also saw the 'River' class begin to be fitted with radio equipment. This required taller masts (60ft) and the aerials stretched down to the aft awning station. Strangely, only one telegraphist was provided per ship. The office with the transmitting and receiving equipment varied in location between being on the bridge as part of an extended charthouse or on the upper (iron) deck between the mast and fore funnel.[5]

The three turbine-engined 'River' class were HMS *Eden*, *Stour* and *Test* – the last two being the last of the Class built, being completed in 1909, some three-and-a-half years after the last of the VTE-engined sister-ships. These were not Admiralty-ordered but built 'on spec'. However, the Admiralty cancelled orders for further 'Rivers' until *Gala* and *Blackwater* were lost (in collisions in April 1908 and April 1909 respectively) and then after satisfactory trials in October 1909 *Stour* and *Test* were bought two months later for bargain-basement prices of £50,000 each as compared with costs of £67,000–£87,000. They were coal-fired like the others of the 'River' class and, in that, were still a major step away from what could be considered the ultimate – an oil-fired destroyer. With oil-fired boilers came increased size, range, speed and armament. Britain had to import all its oil but had coal aplenty.

The 'River' class were not, as undoubtedly the Admiralty always hoped, a homogeneous class. Apart from lengths varying from between 225ft to 233ft 7in and beams varying from 23ft 6in to 23ft 11in, there were two basic differences, appearance-wise: while

HMS *Boyne* in dry dock. Note the fine lines forward, the deep forefoot and high freeboard. Also, the armoured conning tower that forms the base of the QF 12-pounder gun. The bridge is still basic with the chart table covered by a canvas hood. (en.wikipedia.org)

'RIVER' CLASS DESTROYER 1904

The 'River' class destroyers – a disparate mix and not one homogeneous class in fact – can justifiably lay claim to be the first true destroyers as distinct from the torpedo boat destroyers with the emphasis on the word 'boat'. Despite shortcomings that would be ironed out over successive designs, these were the first such ships with true ocean-going potential that could accompany the Fleet. They introduced the raised forecastl and a charthouse with a proper navigation bridge above, no matter how basic. This drawing is of an early version which had the QF 6-pounder guns in sponsons at the break of the foredeck. These were later removed and the guns placed a deck higher abeam the charthouse.

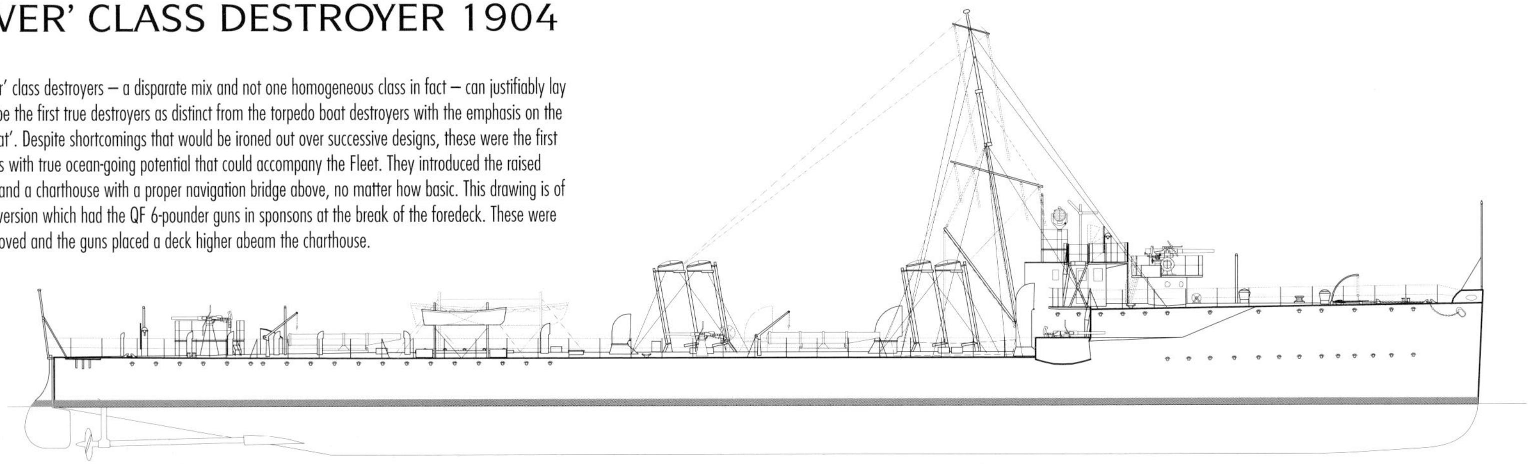

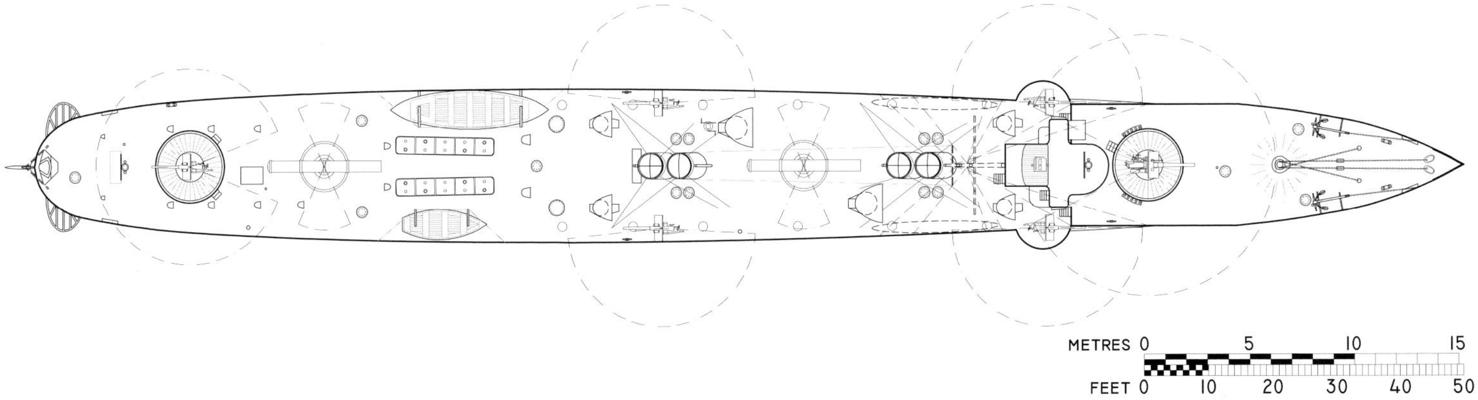

METRES 0 5 10 15

FEET 0 10 20 30 40 50

essentially two-funnelled due to their boiler arrangement, some builders such as Palmers chose to group the funnels as two pairs with no appreciable gap between them. Also, when first built, the 6-pounders mounted at the break of the forecastle were on sponsons projecting over the sides and with the foredeck cut away to allow both guns to have a limited forward-firing capability. The low placement of these guns and the projection of the sponson was soon found to be counter-productive and in 1902–3 the guns were moved to the foredeck, abreast of the charthouse and the ships' side built back out to the maximum beam allowable. These too were removed in 1906 as mentioned earlier. The accommodation was revised and in general the new layout was followed for the next 30 years.[6]

One of the reasons advanced for the alleged superior performance of the German equivalents of the British destroyer was the design of the stern, being wider and flatter. In 1902 Alfred Yarrow suggested that this should be tried and in later years Yarrow-designed and built destroyers had this distinguishing feature. A photograph in Norman Friedman's book shows a Yarrow-built destroyer with this caption:

> Yarrow designs could often be distinguished by their characteristic broad sterns, their sides angled inwards to reduce hull weight for a given waterline length. . . . These sterns were flat underneath . . . the firm credited its special stern with a knot and a half advantage over a conventional V-shaped stern.[7]

These sterns were so readily identifiable as to be worthy of inclusion by way of a sketch drawing (along with other types of sterns; cruiser, counter, transom etc.) on page 30 of a publication by the US Navy Department as late as 9 December 1942 titled, *Ship Shapes: Anatomy & Types of Naval Vessels*, designed as a warship identification and recognition aid.

'RIVER' CLASS SPECIFICATIONS[8]

Displacement (designed)	540–555 tons (standard), 545–590 tons (on trials)
LOA	231ft 3in – 233ft 6in[9]
LBP	220ft–230ft 0in*
Beam	23ft 6in–23ft 11in
Draft	7ft 1in–8ft 0in (standard)
Propulsion	4 boilers, coal-fired, 2 shafts, 4-cylinder VTE except Hawthorn Leslie and Laird-built with 3-cylinder VTE and two with turbines
SHP (designed)	Not stated (6,957 – 8,024 on trial)
Speed (designed)	Not stated (25.255 – 26.24 knots on trials)
Guns	1 x QF 12-pounder 12 cwt on P.I mountings, 5 x QF 6-pounders on recoil mountings**
TT	2 x 18in

Notes

*March only provides LBP data in this instance.

**Replaced by 3 x 12-pounders in 1906.

Refer to Appendix B for class details.

It would take the following batch of twelve destroyers – the 'Tribal' class of 1905–08 – to make the breakthrough to oil-fired boilers driving turbines.

HMS *Eden*, a turbine-engined 'River' class. (en.wikipedia.org)

THE 'TRIBAL' CLASS – 1905–08 PROGRAMMES

Even while the 'River' class were building, instead of simply increasing their numbers in successive years' programmes, a new design was evolved – not by the Admiralty but, again, by the entrepreneurial shipbuilders responding to a brief that was not particularly specific: able to steam at full power, 33 knots, for eight hours (quite what was to happen to the destroyer after that was not spelt out), oil fuel only, provisions for four days, armament to be generally as per the 'River' class (but this was changed to three 12-pounders). Beyond that, the seven candidate builders had a free hand to interpret the brief which may have been deliberately vague to try and flush out some innovations. It did not. In fact, the opposite was the case. The tenders that closed on 1 December 1904 (after only 11 days, apparently!) revealed a return to the principles of the old designs in order to achieve the sort of weight reductions necessary to achieve the speed (33 knots) and endurance. Turbines were backed up by VTE engines for cruising. Armaments varied in type and disposition.[10]

HMS *Affridi* from Armstrong Whitworth. Nominally rated at 14,250 SHP, she had to produce 21,000 SHP to achieve her contract speed of 33 knots. (en.wikipedia.org)

As a result, a more substantial brief was issued: turbine power only, sufficient oil for the greater of 1,500 miles cruising or 8 hours full speed, trials to be run fully loaded, 15ft 9in freeboard at the bow, shaft-and-gear steering to replace chains, and the armament arrangement to be what had become standard practice. The delayed timing of the requirements meant that the fourteen destroyers expected to be part of the 1904–05 Programme were dropped and five more were shuttled to the 1906–06 Programme: *Afridi* (Armstrong), *Cossack* (Cammell Laird), *Ghurka* (Hawthorn Leslie), *Mohawk* (White's) and *Tartar* (Thornycroft).[11] As might be expected, there were again considerable variations between ships in what was expected to be a homogeneous 'Tribal' class. *Mohawk*, for instance, had a turtleback, thereby omitting the specified forecastle and had to be so modified. Next year's Programme added only two more: *Amazon* (Thornycroft) and *Saracen* (White's) and the 1907–08 Programme added *Crusader* (White's), *Maori* (Denny), *Nubian* (Thornycroft), *Viking* (Palmers) and *Zulu* (Hawthorn Leslie). I am not quite sure how *Crusader* and *Viking* qualified as 'tribes'.

Performances were as varied as appearances. *Cossack* reached the required 33 knots over a six-hour trial but at enormous fuel consumption. She had three funnels. *Viking* had no less than six funnels, four of which were paired together. *Afridi* – three low funnels – and *Amazon* – four funnels – each used 9.5 tons of fuel for 6 miles Harwich to Felixstowe and return! *Tartar*, *Saracen*, *Nubian*, *Zulu*, *Crusader* and *Maori* had four funnels, the foremost of which had to be raised to keep smoke clear of the bridge. Some had the somewhat antiquated stern-hung rudders and other – like Palmer's *Viking* – went to the opposite extreme with an extremely raked cruiser-type stern and a

HMS *Cossack*. Note the side-by-side 12-pounder guns on the longer-than-usual foredeck. (en.wikipedia.org)

streamlined, balanced spade-type rudder tucked away underneath: quite a contrast to her six funnels! To give some idea of the variations: displacements varied between 865 and 1,026 tons standard, LOA between 260ft 6in and 290ft 3in and beams between 24ft 6$\frac{13}{16}$in and 27ft 1in and they had five or six boilers.[12]

As March so rightly says, 'all the twelve were built to different designs which varied as much as the characters of the tribes whose names they bore'.[13]

The Thornycroft-built HMS *Nubian* was torpedoed on 27 October 1916 and the Hawthorn Leslie-built HMS *Zulu* was mined on 8 November 1916, losing their bow and stern respectively. To make somewhat of a mockery of the disparity between the various builders and the lack of uniformity, the bow of *Zulu* was joined to the midsection and stern of *Nubian* to form HMS *Zubian*.

The 'Tribal' class of twelve destroyers – designated the 'F' class in October 1913 – were as flawed and unsuccessful as the 'Tribal' class of 1936 were brilliant in all respects other than their anti-aircraft defences, a problem not solely theirs.

'TRIBAL' CLASS SPECIFICATIONS[14]

Displacement (designed)	855–1,090 tons (standard), 845–1,072 tons (on trials)
LOA	260ft 6in–290ft 3in[15]
LBP	250ft 0in–280ft 3⅞in*
Beam	24ft 6$\frac{13}{16}$in–27ft 1in
Draft	9ft 9½in–10ft 3in (deep)
Propulsion	5 or 6 boilers, oil-fired, 3 shafts, direct drive turbines
SHP (designed)	Not stated (21.320–27.717 knots on trials)
Speed (designed)	Not stated (33.168–35.36 knots on trials)
Guns	3 x QF 12-pounder 12 cwt on P.I mountings (increased to 5 in 1909)
TT	2 x 18in
Notes	

*March only provides LBP data in this instance.

Refer to Appendix C for class details.

HMS *Nubian*. Note the mainmast to accommodate additional wireless aerials. After she was torpedoed on 27 October 1916, her aft section was joined to the bow section of the mined HMS *Zulu* to become HMS *Zubian*. (historail.com)

THE *BEAGLE* CLASS – 1908–09 PROGRAMME

Somewhat strangely, having proved the viability of and the improvements to oil-fired boilers, the *Beagle* class of the 1908–09 Programme reverted to coal-burning, a decision not related to performance or crewing numbers but purely as a money-saving exercise – the only way to provide sufficient numbers at a lower unit cost. These were, in effect, 'Tribal' class ships but up-gunned, with the forward and aft 12-pounders replaced with a 4in BL Mark VIII gun on a P.III or V mounting. This set the trend for many RN destroyers to come. The bow mount was higher on a large, raised platform (as had been the case in some 'Tribals') which acted, in part, as a breakwater. Some of the 'Tribal' class were retrofitted with this gun. The aftmost torpedo tube was positioned as in the *Parramatta* class but was frequently unusable right over the antiquated stern-hung rudder. Another major upgrade in armament was the new RGF Mk VIII 21in torpedo with the

***BEAGLE* CLASS SPECIFICATIONS**[16]

Displacement (designed)	897–976 tons (standard), 912–992 tons (on trials)
LOA	278ft 9in[17]
LBP	263ft 11¼in–275ft 0in*
Beam	26ft 10in–28ft 7in
Draft	9ft 5½in
Propulsion	5 boilers, coal-fired, 3 shafts, direct drive turbines
SHP (designed)	14,300 (14,144–16,337 on trials)
Speed (designed)	27 knots (26.791–27.984 knots on trials)
Guns	1 x BL 4in LV Mk VIII on P.III mountings, 3 x QF 12-pounder 12 cwt
TT	2 x 21in
Notes	

*March only provides LBP data in this instance.

Hardcastle heater that was adopted in this class. It ran at 50 knots for 984yds or 11.920yds at 30kts.

While the policy of placing design and construction in the hands of shipbuilders had the hoped-for result of forcing down prices, it also involved the DNC's staff in considerable work analysing the bids and attempting to satisfy themselves not just as to basic suitability but more comprehensively as to structural integrity, an area the shipbuilders were generally found wanting in the quest for speed. It was only a matter of time before the Admiralty would take over responsibility for design and documentation and then be able to assess the shipbuilders' bids based on common ground. These were the last destroyers not to be built to Admiralty requirements and specifications from which no deviation was permitted except for the individual shipbuilder 'specials'.[18] Reclassified as the 'G' class in October 1913.

Refer to Appendix D for class details.

THE *ACORN* CLASS – 1909–10 PROGRAMME

The Admiralty finally learnt the lesson that leaving the design and construction of their destroyers to free enterprise might deliver cheaper ships but it did not deliver better ships or ones properly suited to its requirements. The 1909–10 Programme was placed back in the hands of the DNC for a standard design and, after many changes, this was finally approved in May 1909. The *Acorns* were, at last, to be only oil-fired, turbine-driven and 4in gunned, albeit breech-loaders and not, as yet, quick-firers. No more coal, VTE engines and 12-pounders as the main gun so, in that respect, they were a milestone in British destroyer development. Speed-wise, at a designed speed of 27 knots (13,500 SHP) they were, however, a backward step. Nonetheless,

HMS *Basilisk*, a *Beagle* class which reverted to coal-burning. (wikivisually.com)

HMS *Redpole*. The *Acorn* class reverted to oil-firing. (en.wikipedia.org)

twenty were successfully tendered for and built, all with three shafts and Parsons turbines except *Brisk* which, for some unaccountable reason was differently engined with Brown-Curtis turbines with two shafts, albeit at extra cost. The two 4in guns were BL Mark VIIIs on P.III mountings with 120 rounds per gun and could elevate to 20° and depress to 10°. The two QF 12-pounder 12 cwt guns with 100 rounds per gun were mounted on the port and starboard beams but opposite each other and not *en echelon* as had been the case in previous destroyers. The *Acorn* class introduced the tower-mounted searchlight – presumably the 20in model – on the engine casing between the two 21in torpedo tubes, a feature that was to continue in British destroyers for the next 25 years.

Somewhat unusually, despite the twenty ships having been built to the same set of documents, there were slight differences in dimensions and displacements. Turning circles varied considerably and some turned better to port, others to starboard. Fuel consumption and therefore endurance varied too.[19] When I wrote *Town Class Destroyers: A Critical Assessment*, I found it difficult to accept that identical designs (the American *Wickes* and *Caldwell* classes) from different shipbuilders could have vastly different performance figures. Having found the same sort of thing happened to the *Acorn* class, seven years earlier, made this easier to accept that it happened but no less difficult to understand in principle.

***ACORN* CLASS SPECIFICATIONS**[20]

Displacement (designed)	772 tons (standard), 738–790 tons (on trials)
LOA	246ft 0in
Beam	25ft 3in–25ft 5½in
Draft	8ft 6in load, 7ft 4½in–8ft 1in[21]
Propulsion	4 boilers, oil-fired, 3 shafts (except *Brisk*), direct drive turbines
SHP (designed)	13,500 (13,726–16,730 on trials)
Speed (designed)	27 knots (27.05–29.381 knots on trials)
Guns	2 x BL 4in Mk VIII on P.III mountings, 2 x QF 12-pounder 12 cwt on PV mounting
TT	2 x 21in

Reclassified as the 'H' class in October 1913.

Refer to Appendix E for class details.

THE *ACHERON* CLASS – 1910–11 PROGRAMME

In some respects, the Admiralty could be said to have thrown the baby out with the bathwater in that the 1910–11 Programme was to have been repeats of the *Acorn* class. However, and perhaps reflecting the speed deficit referred to above, instead of undertaking the necessary design to achieve its ends, the Admiralty reverted to its old practice and ordered six 'specials' before the repeat *Acorns*.

The decidedly handsome HMS *Firedrake* at speed. She formed the baseline for the *Acasta* class. (en.wikipedia.org)

The three chosen shipbuilders, Denny, Thornycroft and Yarrow, were again given a free hand to increase length and power (up 2,000 SHP) – both necessary ingredients in the search for speed brought about, apparently, by the usual German-inspired scare.

The final mix was fourteen Admiralty Repeat *Acorn*/*Acheron* class, two Denny specials with Parsons semi-geared turbines, two Thornycroft specials and five Yarrow specials made up of the original two plus three more, faster, 'specials' (*Firedrakes*, 33.17 knots with nominal 20,000 SHP).

While not a homogeneous class, they did, at least, look more so than the preceding ones, with two level-topped funnels. Sizes varied less (LOA between 246ft 0in and 251ft 0in – but *Firedrake* was 261ft 7in). Five had Brown-Curtis turbines to two shafts, three had Parsons turbines to two shafts, two had Parsons semi-geared turbines to two-shafts, and the remainder Parsons turbines to three shafts. SHP varied between 14,161 and 21,747 and speeds between 26.942 knots and 35.345 knots.

To further complicate the issue of homogeneity, a version of the *Acheron* class was redesigned by Sir John Harvard Biles for the soon-to-be-created Royal Australian Navy (10 July 1911) and was termed the 'River' or *Parramatta* class.

***ACHERON* CLASS SPECIFICATIONS**[22]

Displacement	745–810 tons (on trials)
LOA	246ft 0in–261ft 7in
Beam	25ft 8in–26ft 5¼in
Draft	8ft 9in (standard)
Propulsion	3 boilers, oil-fired, 2 and 3 shafts, direct drive and semi-geared turbines
SHP	14,161–21,747 (on trials)
Speed	26.942–35.345 knots (on trials)
Guns	2 x BL 4in Mk VIII on P.III mountings, 2 x QF 12-pounder 12 cwt on P.VI mounting
TT	2 x 21in

Reclassified as the 'I' class in October 1913.

Refer to Appendix F for class details.

THE *PARRAMATTA* CLASS

Three 'River' class destroyers were ordered by the Australian Government in 1909; two to be built in Britain and one to be built in sections and shipped out for local re-assembly. Three more would be built locally with the experience gained from the assembly of the third. These were to be the first units of a fleet to consist of one battlecruiser (ultimately of the *Indefatigable* class), three light cruisers (ultimately *Chatham* class), three submarines (ultimately 'A' class) and auxiliaries like depot and store ships.[23]

Coming at the tail-end of the 'River' class these destroyers were, in effect, a modified version and benefited from lessons learnt. They were oil-fired with three turbines and mounted a BL 4in Mark VIII gun in place of the forward QF 12-pounder 12 cwt but replaced

PARRAMATTA CLASS DESTROYER 1910

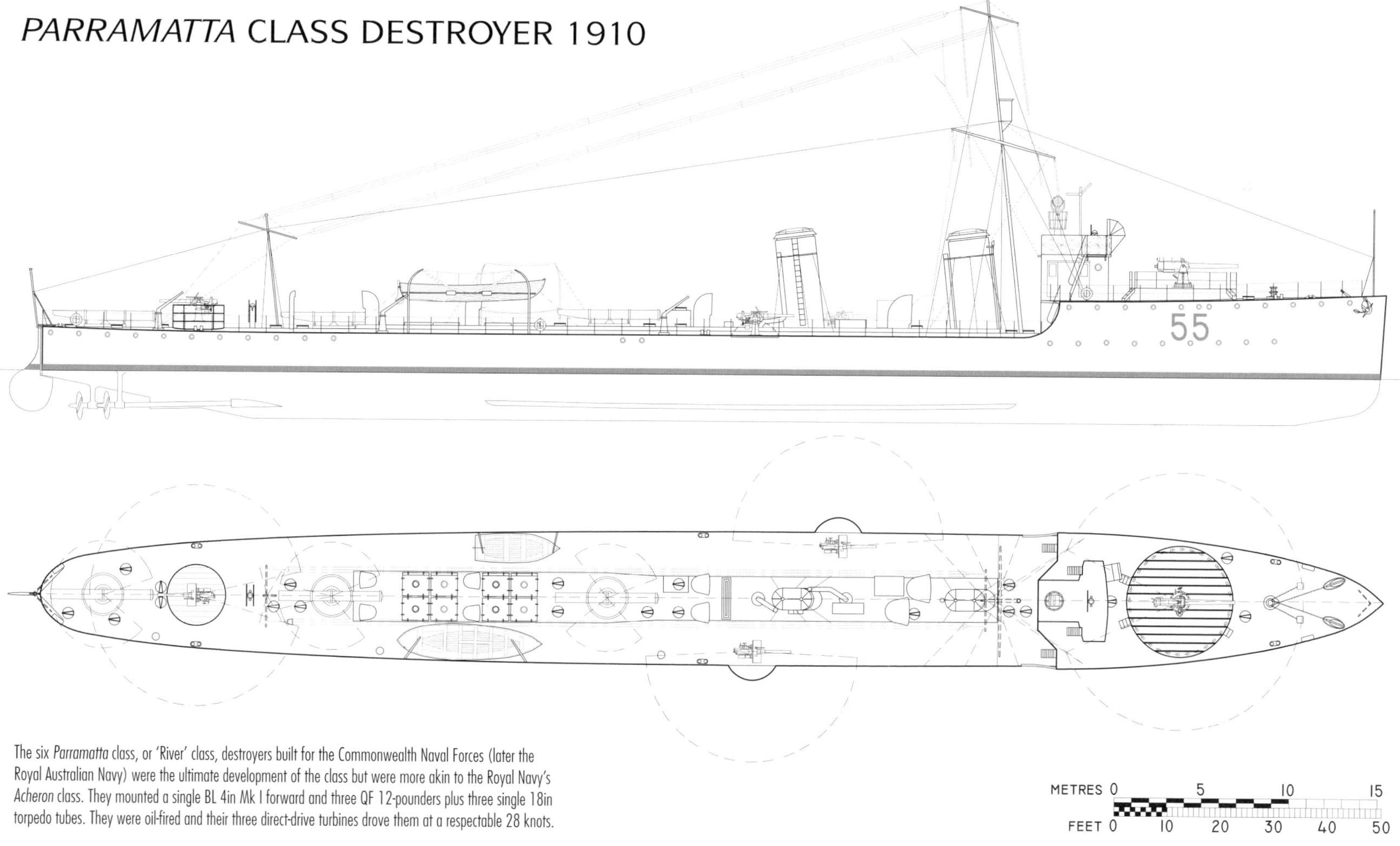

The six *Parramatta* class, or 'River' class, destroyers built for the Commonwealth Naval Forces (later the Royal Australian Navy) were the ultimate development of the class but were more akin to the Royal Navy's *Acheron* class. They mounted a single BL 4in Mk I forward and three QF 12-pounders plus three single 18in torpedo tubes. They were oil-fired and their three direct-drive turbines drove them at a respectable 28 knots.

HMAS *Huon*. Commissioned at the end of 1915 and scrapped in 1928, she was in many respects a 'River' class in name only. (navy.gov.au)

the QF 6-pounders with 12-pounders – the precise model is unknown but it may have been the 12 cwt. There was an additional 18in torpedo tube located right astern where it had the widest training arc.

***PARRAMATTA* CLASS SPECIFICATIONS**[24]

Displacement	700 tons (standard)
LOA	250ft 0in
Beam	24ft 6in
Draft	9ft 0in (standard)
Propulsion	3 boilers, oil-fired, 3 shafts, direct drive turbines
SHP	10,000
Speed	26–28 knots
Guns	1 x BL 4in Mk VIII, 2 x QF 12-pounder 12 cwt
TT	3 x 18in

Reclassified as the 'J' class in October 1913.

Refer to Appendix F for class details.

THE *ACASTA* CLASS – 1911–12 PROGRAMME

The 1911–12 Programme resulted in yet another Admiralty–private enterprise mix, this time in a 12:8 ratio. Yarrow's *Firedrake* became the baseline.[25] The firepower of the 4in gun – its hitting power and firing rate as compared with the lighter but faster-firing 12-pounder – again raised armament issues but a quick-firing equivalent was yet to be developed when the *Acasta* class were on the drawing board. Similarly, the placement of the three gun mounts on the centreline was debated, there being a reluctance to adopt a practice which later became common of placing the centre mount supported on either a dividing bulkhead between boiler rooms or on a column, in both cases between the funnels albeit with limited firing arcs but offering good broadside fire. In the end an aft location was opted for – a bad choice due to the blast effect on adjoining gun crews and the possibility of a direct hit knocking out both mounts. They were the first Royal Navy destroyers to drop the 12-pounder gun and use only 4in guns, increasing to three such weapons from two, although the third only had 35° of firing arc on each beam. The last seven of the *Acasta*s to be completed were fitted with the new QF 4in Mk IV on P.IX mountings. The two 21in torpedo tubes were D.R. Mark I with 50° arcs on each beam.

The basic design was approved in April 1911 and more formally in June. The bidders for the eight private orders offered a mixed bag. While there was commonality in that all were two-shaft designs, at one stage all-diesel propulsion was considered and mixed steam and diesel (for cruising) was considered to the point where Thornycroft's *Hardy* was so ordered but not completed in this form due to the inability to supply the necessary engines. Had this happened the Royal Navy would have had a destroyer with exceptional range, suitable for overseas deployment away from established bases. Denny bucked tradition and after considerable research embarked on longitudinal framing – as compared with the traditional transverse framing – something that was to become the norm in later years since it produced greater strength and lighter weight. Parson's semi-geared turbines appeared in Cammell Laird's *Garland* and Fairfield produced a bow shape with more flare. Instead of the usual plumb stem, a handsome raked, clipper-type bow in their *Fortune* which also had the middle 4in mount raised on a bandstand between the second and third funnels. So, while in some respects there were negative aspects to the involvement of private enterprise in the design and construction of the Admiralty's destroyers, insofar as trying to achieve standardisation of the best vessel possible to serve its needs, the ones that offered the best blend of performance over cost – the old value-for-money equation – the entrepreneurial shipbuilders could be innovative. Sometimes it was just necessary to simply gather the best of these innovations together into one package. That time had still to come.

However, the *Acasta*s were not a great success. To begin with they steered badly and had very large turning circles. These were compared with the far superior *Firedrake* with the Yarrow stern, referred to earlier and were cured, to some extent, after experimentation. Rebuilding the stern to the Yarrow style was considered but rejected.

ACASTA CLASS SPECIFICATIONS[26]

Displacement (designed)	1,072 tons (standard), 903–1,121 tons (on trials)
LOA	267ft 6in Admiralty, 265ft 0in Thornycroft
Beam	27ft 0in Admiralty, 26ft 6 ¾in–27ft 8¼in Thornycroft and Parsons
Draft	9ft 3in (deep)
Propulsion	4 boilers, oil-fired, 2 shafts, Parsons Impulse Reaction turbines except one with semi-geared turbines and three with Brown-Curtis turbines
SHP (designed)	24,500 (23,364 – 27,897 on trials)
Speed (designed)	29 knots (29.503 – 33.174 knots on trials)
Guns	3 x BL 4in Mk VIII on P.VII mountings
TT	2 x 21in

Reclassified as the 'K' class in October 1913.

Refer to Appendix G for class details.

THE *LAFOREY* OR 'L' CLASS – 1912–13 PROGRAMME

The 1912–13 Programme sought a cheaper destroyer than the *Acorn* class. But, again, perceived German intentions – if not what they had actually done – seemed to be the determining factor in the Admiralty's attitude to destroyer design. Instead of being proactive, everything the Admiralty seems to be doing at this time is entirely reactive – looking across the North Sea, making assessments and trying to counteract a trend rather than getting a jump ahead. This despite the fact that British shipyards were designing and building what might be termed super-destroyers for foreign powers – as was Germany – which were much more heavily armed in both torpedoes and guns by comparison with current British destroyers. Accordingly, in January 1912 the Controller issued a fresh Staff Requirement for a twin-screw destroyer with 24,500 SHP, three 4in guns, two twin torpedo tubes and three boilers, length not to exceed 260ft. A later requirement may have been to be able to stow four Vickers Elia Mk IV mines. None of these specifications were revolutionary – even the increasing of the torpedoes to two double tubes, since German equivalents had mounted three singles with reloads for some time.

HMS *Fortune* of the 'Builders' Specials'. Note the clipper bow from Fairfield. (naval-history.net)

While the QF 4in was a better weapon than the German 88mm SK L/35, having a similar muzzle velocity and range but twice as heavy a projectile, destroyers were so lively in a seaway it was frequently impossible to make use of that superior firepower. A more stable base was needed. Such stability could be improved by deeper and longer bilge keels but these reduced speed and manoeuvrability, so the use of Frahm anti-rolling tanks was considered and approved but only fitted to the White and Yarrow-built ships. Whether they were fitted to all twenty-two destroyers is unknown but there is some record of them being used for extra oil fuel. *Leonidas* and *Lucifer* had all-geared turbines rather than the less efficient direct drive.

Commonality was limited to being the first class with consistency of naming. They originally had Shakespearean and Sir Walter Scott's Waverley novels' names but the change to names beginning with 'L' was by order of the Admiralty of 30 September 1913 following the previous decisions to allocate alphabetical letters to all previous classes, the *Acasta*s being the 'K' class in 1913. Six had three boilers instead of four. The White and Yarrow-built ships had two funnels but all others had three funnels.

Again, there were considerable differences in performance which was not unexpected given the lack of uniformity. For instance; the two-funnel design had three boilers – either White-Forster of Yarrow while the three-funnel design had four Yarrow boilers. Eight ships had Brown-Curtis turbines, two had geared Parson turbines the rest having Parsons Impulse Reaction direct drive turbines.

***LAFOREY* CLASS SPECIFICATIONS**[27]

Displacement (designed)	1,112.5 tons (standard), 940–1,141 tons (on trials)
LOA	268ft 10in
Beam	27ft 8in
Draft	8ft 6½in (standard)
Propulsion	3 or 4 boilers, oil-fired, 2 shafts, 2 geared turbines, 8 Brown Curtis, remainder Parsons Impulse Reaction turbines
SHP (designed)	24,500 (23,135–27,342 on trials)
Speed (designed)	29 knots (29.168–32.562 knots on trials
Guns	3 x QF 4in Mk IV on P.IX mountings
TT	4 x 21in (2 x 2)

Refer to Appendix H for class details.

THE ADMIRALTY 'M' CLASS – 1913–14 PROGRAMME

The 1913–14 Programme had the impetus of impending war and the First Lord of the Admiralty, Winston Churchill. Speed became the dogma: six knots more boat speed (that is, 36 knots maximum) and speed of delivery.

The ever-innovative and equally entrepreneurial Thornycroft's led the charge for orders closely followed by White's and Yarrow's accepting two orders each before contracts were signed. In March 1913 when the Controller issued the official invitations to tender, three Thornycroft ships, two each at Hawthorn Leslie and Yarrow's were purchased by the Admiralty just as though they had been built 'on spec' by the shipbuilders. Hawthorn Leslie had taken White's role and Thornycroft had picked up one more. Thus, seven orders were underway ahead of what might be regarded as the normal schedule and, in that, the Admiralty was being progressive. Where it could not yet be progressive was in making the necessary determinations as to the acceptability or otherwise of such items as the geared turbines or the longitudinal framing because the ships so affected had not completed their trials for assessment.

The year's order was topped up by a further six so there wasn't a twenty-strong flotilla, money being diverted to the *Arethusa* class light cruisers. They were similar to the *Laforey*s in appearance except that the midships gun was not raised on a bandstand (it was believed its elevated position meant it would be blanketed by funnel smoke). Yarrow-built versions had two funnels and the bridge set well back on the forecastle. In this respect they resembled the 'R' class which followed. Thornycroft-built versions had their trademark flat-sided funnels, of which there were three tall ones, contrasting with the Admiralty's short funnels, and had more freeboard. They were generally the more handsome ships, as was the usual uncanny yet very deliberate Thornycroft practice. Hawthorn's version was four-funnelled. The very basic drawings referred to as 'Plan 18/A and B' on pages 144–5 of March's book and traced by him from Admiralty sketch designs show raked stems whereas the photographs and the drawing of HMS *Mandate* ('Repeat M' class) on pages 172–3 quite clearly have plumb stems. It seems strange, however, that despite the variations in

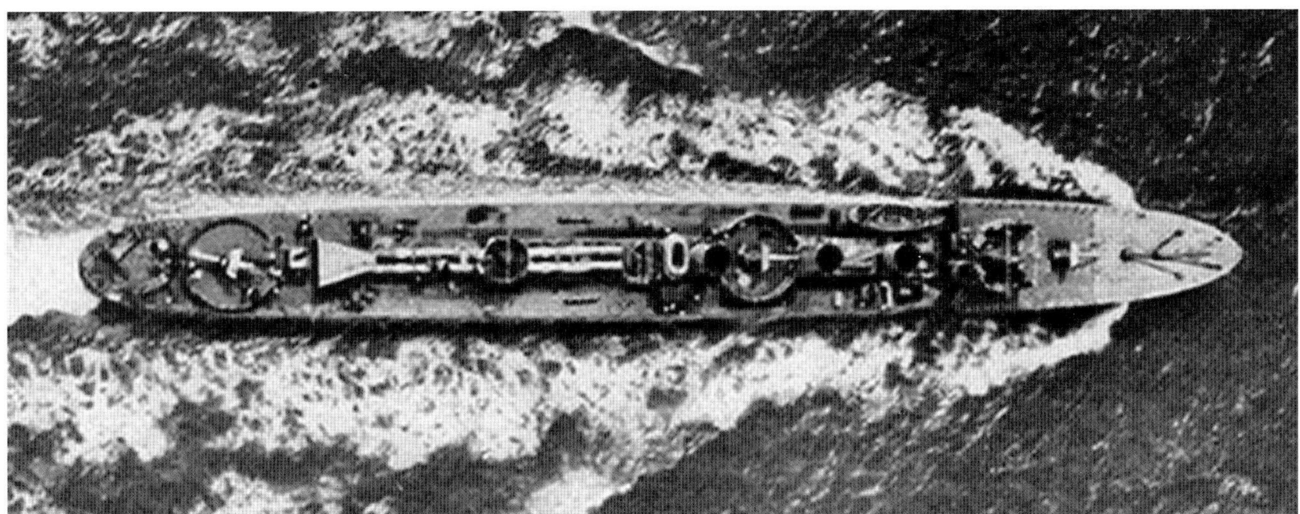

A rare aerial photograph of an 'M' class destroyer. (Public domain)

HMS *Mary Rose*, sunk on 17 October 1917 in a one-sided fight against two German light cruisers. (dreadnoughtproject.org)

appearances, these destroyers should be given the nomenclature of Admiralty 'M' class as if they were one homogenous group. The six Admiralty destroyers were three-shaft but three Parsons Impulse Reaction and three had Brown Curtis turbines with geared cruising turbines. The seven 'specials' were almost similarly split. Note the considerable differences in the specifications table below.

The visual differences in the three major variations of the 'M' class are shown in my drawings below. The Admiralty version is based on the drawing in March's book (above). I was unable to locate any drawings of the Thornycroft and Yarrow versions so had to rely on photographs of actual ships and of models held by museums.

I have seen references to the Admiralty 'M' class as being 'fleet destroyers'[28] but have been unable to determine just how and when this sort of nomenclature was established and precisely to which classes it applied. For instance, was there a cut-off point as to

'M' CLASS DESTROYERS 1913

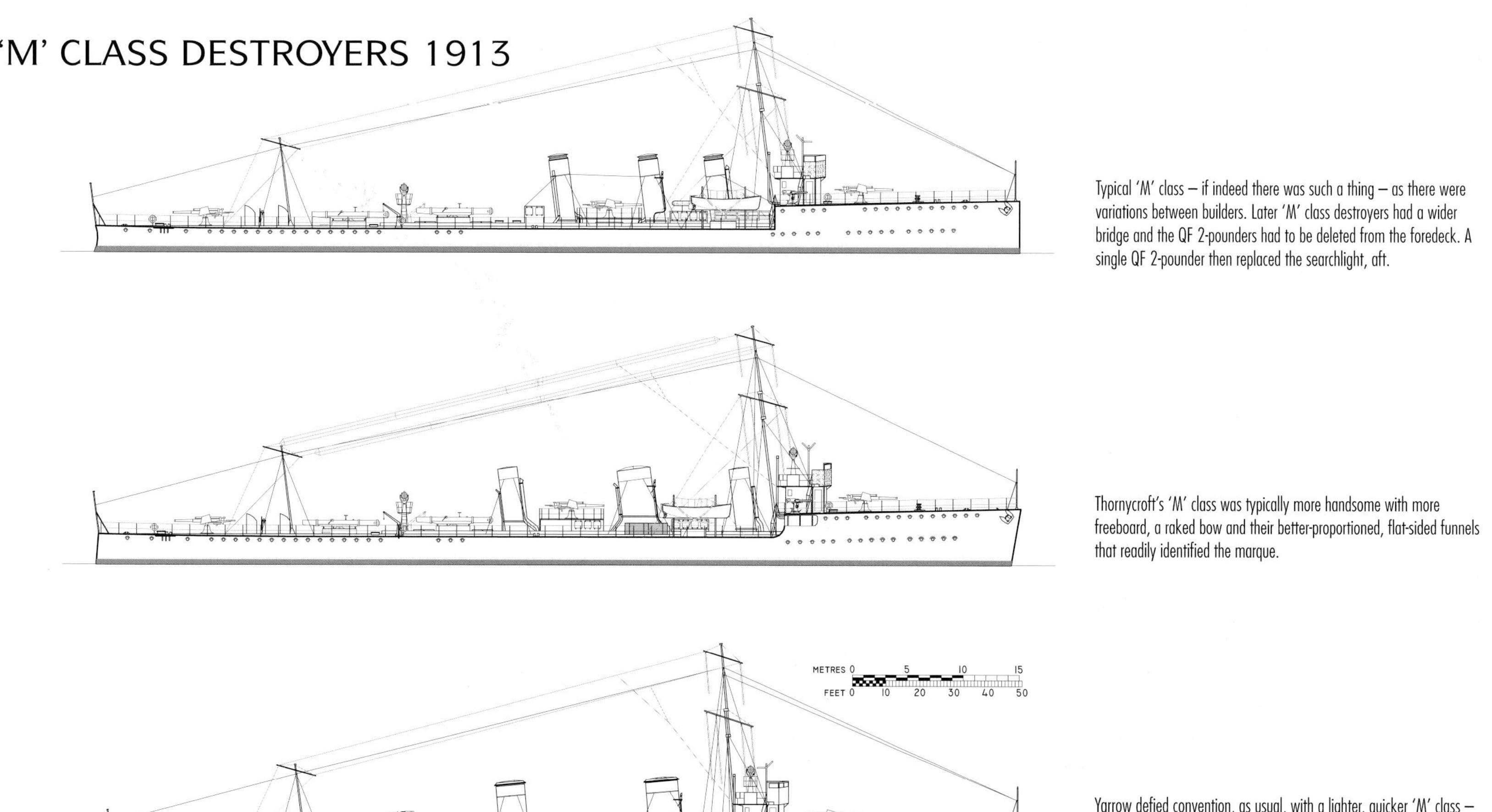

Typical 'M' class – if indeed there was such a thing – as there were variations between builders. Later 'M' class destroyers had a wider bridge and the QF 2-pounders had to be deleted from the foredeck. A single QF 2-pounder then replaced the searchlight, aft.

Thornycroft's 'M' class was typically more handsome with more freeboard, a raked bow and their better-proportioned, flat-sided funnels that readily identified the marque.

Yarrow defied convention, as usual, with a lighter, quicker 'M' class – this time with two funnels by trunking boiler uptakes together. It allowed the bridge to be set further back and presaged the 'Modified R' class.

HMS *Patrician*, later HMCS *Patrician*, was Thornycroft's response and six ships were to this distinct and pleasant-looking design. (photoship co.uk)

tonnage, armament, endurance or some other criteria that determined this?

ADMIRALTY 'M' CLASS SPECIFICATIONS[29]

Displacement (designed)	900 tons Admiralty, 1,055 tons Hawthorn Leslie, 980 tons Thornycroft, 883 tons Yarrow (standard), 817–1,126 tons (on trials)
LOA	273ft 4in Admiralty, 271ft 6in Hawthorn Leslie, 274ft 3in Thornycroft, 269ft 6in Yarrow
Beam	26ft 8in Admiralty, 27ft 0in Hawthorn Leslie, 27ft 3in Thornycroft, 25ft 7½in Yarrow
Draft	9ft 0in designed, 9ft 7in (deep) Admiralty
Propulsion	3 or 4 boilers, oil-fired, 3 shafts in Admiralty, 2 shafts in others, Brown-Curtis turbines in 6 ships, Parsons Impulse Reaction turbines in remainder.
SHP (designed)	25,000 Admiralty, 27,000 Hawthorn Leslie, 26,500 Thornycroft, 23,000 Yarrow (23,120 – 28,255 on trials)
Speed (designed)	Admiralty 34 knots, others 35 knots (30.589–37.165 knots on trials)
Guns	3 x QF 4in Mk IV on 20° elevation P.IX mountings
TT	4 x 21in (2 x 2)

Refer to Appendix I for class details.

THE ADMIRALTY 'REPEAT M' CLASS – EMERGENCY WAR PROGRAMME

A further ninety were built under the War Emergency Programme (as it was also termed) for a total of 103 making it, to date, the largest single class. Of these, seventy-nine were the Admiralty design vessels and twenty-four were builders' specials: twelve Thornycroft, ten Yarrow and two Hawthorn Leslie.

They appeared in the following Programmes:

First War Programme, September 1914
20 ships – 16 Admiralty, 4 Yarrow Specials (all 'M' names)
Second War Programme, November 1914
10 ships – 9 Admiralty, 1 Yarrow Special ('M' and 'N' names)
Third War Programme, November 1914
22 ships – all Admiralty ('N' and 'O' names)
Fourth War Programme, February 1915
18 ships – 16 Admiralty, 2 Thornycroft specials ('N','O' and 'P' names)
Fifth War Programme, May 1915
20 ships – 16 Admiralty, 2 Thornycroft, 2 Yarrow Specials ('M' and 'P' names)

The Admiralty design displaced 1,025 tons, Thornycroft's 985 tons and, typically, Yarrow with their lighter and stronger philosophy

HMS *Oracle*, 'Repeat M' class, Third War Programme. (Public domain)

895 tons. Yarrow's *Mounsey* was the fastest at 39.01 knots, three knots faster than the requirement. Fairfield's *Mandate* could only manage 32.06 knots displacing 980 tons.

While the armament was the same as the 'M' class, single 14in torpedo tubes for short-range cold torpedoes were retrofitted on each beam to some destroyers. Similarly, the searchlight between the twin torpedo tubes was replaced by a QF 2-pounder Mk II in some as was minesweeping equipment fitted in some. In some, the length was increased by 3–4in and beam up to 2in.[30]

Refer to Appendix I for class details.

THE ADMIRALTY 'R' CLASS – EMERGENCY WAR PROGRAMME 1915

By July 1915 the Admiralty had, thankfully, learnt sufficient from the trials of its geared-turbined destroyers, *Leonidas* and *Lucifer*, to determine that all future designs should be so specified and preferably with the Brown-Curtis variety – apparently due to the fact that their direct drive turbines offered better fuel economy – which much have come as a blow to the pace-setting Parsons. Comparative trials run between *Romola* (the lead ship of what became the Admiralty 'R' class) and *Norman* (Admiralty 'M' class) showed that the Admiralty 'R' class used 15 per cent less fuel at 18 knots and 28 per cent less at 25 knots, resulting in an increase of 17.8 per cent more range and 40 per cent more range at those speeds respectively. *Romola* also maintained the required 36 knots for four hours in light condition and 32.5 knots in deep load condition on her designed 27,000 SHP.

The Admiralty 'R' class had more flare and a foot more freeboard forward than the 'M' class that it in many ways duplicated. The aft 4in gun was elevated on a bandstand as was the midships 4in, contrary to its previous positioning, as it was

ADMIRALTY 'R' CLASS SPECIFICATIONS[31]

Displacement (designed)	1,172.9 tons (standard), 776–1,186 tons (on trials)
LOA	276ft 0in Admiralty, 274ft 3in Thornycroft, 273ft 6in Yarrow
Beam	26ft 8in Admiralty, 27ft–27ft 3in Thornycroft, 25ft 7½in Yarrow
Draft	8ft 10½in (standard)
Propulsion	3 boilers, oil-fired, 2 shafts, single-reduction geared turbines
SHP (designed)	27,000
Speed (designed)	36 knots (31.38–40.44 knots on trials)
Guns	3 x QF 4in Mk IV on 20° elevation P.IX mountings, 1 x QF 2-pounder Mk II
TT	4 x 21in (2 x 2)

HMS *Taurus*, Thornycroft's design and sister-ship to *Taurus*, the fastest of the twelve 'Builders' Specials'. (Public domain)

felt safer and be more on a par with the forward mount. The bridge was made wide, by some 9ft thus denying space for the two QF 2-pounder Mk IIs mounted port and starboard at the break of the forecastle. A single 2-pounder thereby replaced the 21in searchlight on its platform between the two twin 21in torpedo tubes.

Fifty-one ships were built, as follows:

Sixth War Programme, May–July 1915
26 ships – 19 Admiralty, 3 Thornycroft and 4 Yarrow Specials ('R' and 'S' names)
Seventh War Programme, December 1915
10 ships – 8 Admiralty, 2 Thornycroft Specials ('S' and 'T' names)
Eighth War Programme, March 1916
15 ships – 12 Admiralty, 3 Yarrow Specials ('T' names and one 'U')

Twelve were builders' 'specials': five Thornycroft and seven Yarrow. This time Thornycroft's had the fastest performer, *Teazer* clocking 40.44 knots displacing 939 tons as compared with the slowest, Beardmore's *Tancred* at 31.48 knots displacing 1,172 tons.

Refer to Appendix J for class details.

THE ADMIRALTY 'MODIFIED R' CLASS – EMERGENCY WAR PROGRAMME 1916

In the middle of 1916, a proposal by the DNC to reverse the boiler rooms in all destroyers ordered from December 1915 onwards was accepted with the bridges to be moved aft and forecastles extended, the middle gun to be now atop the fan intake for No 2 boiler, two funnels instead of three. They were all to be called the Admiralty 'Modified R' class.

The transposition of No 1 and No 2 boiler-rooms in order to enable the trunking to be combined into one fatter funnel permitted the forward 4in gun and the bridge to be moved further aft improving the serviceability of both. The gun was now the QF 4in Mk V on a CP.III mounting capable of 30° elevation which increased range by 20 per cent. Some had a single 18in torpedo tube port and starboard on the iron deck at the break of the forecastle for 'browning shots' – snap shots against enemy ships.

Eighth War Programme, March 1916
11 ships – ('T' and 'U' names)[32]

Refer to Appendix K for class details.

THE ADMIRALTY 'S' CLASS

With these modification to the Admiralty 'Modified R' class any potential for further significant improvement of these 975-ton, 276ft destroyers had been exhausted. While they continued to be built as the near-identical Admiralty 'S' class – of which sixty-seven were completed between April 1918 and December 1919 (apart from *Shikari* and *Thracian*) – they failed to meet fleet demands. A new destroyer design was clearly needed.

However, by continuing the 'Modified R' class with certain improvements incorporated from war experience and feedback from destroyer captains, the Controller believed it would be more expedient to maintain what was already being done – in effect the basic tenet of the iron law of mobilisation; that something in production when war starts should remain in production as long as it is useful.

For marginally better seakeeping, a type of turtleback was reintroduced to the forecastle which had a slightly higher prow. The side-mounted 18in torpedoes were made trainable but this was counter-productive as cutting away the forecastle sides to allow the tubes to train made the decks wet and caused spray to be thrown up to the bridge. Ever the innovator, Yarrow's placed their 18in torpedoes in such a way that they could be trained to 90° to the centreline. Thornycroft's answer was fixed athwartships tubes which avoided the weatherliness problem and their raised mounting for the forward 4in was an improvement in this regard also. Ultimately, the 18in torpedoes were removed as either ineffective and not worth the weight penalty they involved.

HMS *TRIBUNE*: 'S' CLASS 1918

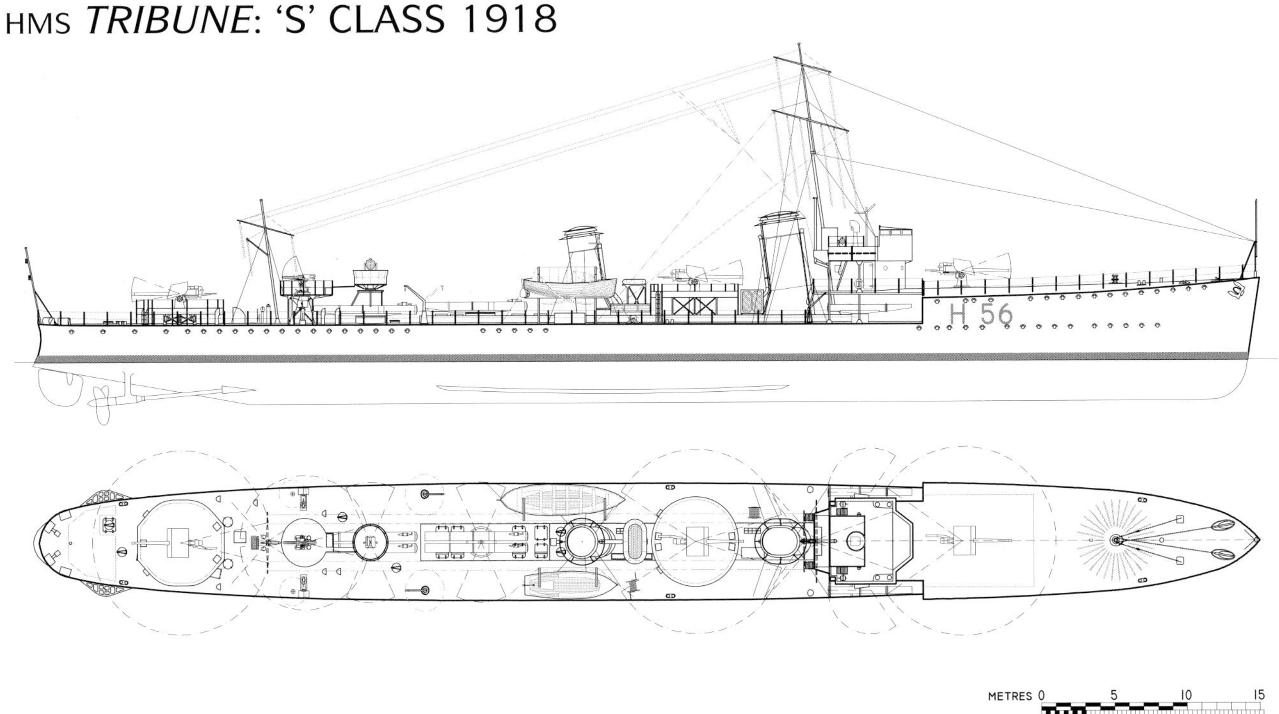

The 'S' class destroyers were the most numerous class of British destroyers, although only eleven were finished by the end of the war. These were smaller, quicker destroyers favoured by the command charged with defending the English Channel where endurance and sea-keeping were less of importance than for those larger destroyers operating with the Grand Fleet in the North Sea. They were an improvement on the earlier 'R' class and several soldiered on to serve in the Second World War. HMS *Tribune* shown here had the unusual funnel caps that mark her as being a White-built ship.

ADMIRALTY 'S' CLASS SPECIFICATIONS[33]

Displacement (designed)	1,075 tons (standard), 846–1,210 tons (on trials)
LOA	276ft 0in Admiralty, n/a Thornycroft, 273ft 6in Yarrow
Beam	26ft 8in Admiralty, 27ft 4in Thornycroft, 25ft 7½in Yarrow
Draft	9ft 10in (deep)
Propulsion	3 boilers, oil-fired, 2 shafts, Parsons Impulse Reaction in 7 ships, Brown Curtis single reduction turbines in all others but direct drive turbines in Yarrow ships
SHP (designed)	27,000 (25,707–34,262 on trials)
Speed (designed)	36 knots (32.02–39.401 knots on trials)
Guns	3 x QF 4in Mk IV on CP.III mountings, 1 x QF 2-pounder Mk II on an HA II mounting
TT	4 x 21in (2 x 2), 2 x 18in (2 x 1)

HMAS *Tasmania*, an 'S' class commissioned as HMS *Tasmania* on 20 January 1920 and gifted to the Royal Australian Navy seven days later – one of five 'S' class together with the leader, HMS *Anzac*. She had two stints in reserve and served in eastern and southern Australian waters before decommissioning on 9 January 1928 where she languished until sold on 4 June 1937 for scrapping – prematurely given the war which followed two years later. (navy-gov.au)

HMS *Tenedos*, one of the sixty-seven Admiralty 'S' class destroyers which had names commencing with 'S' or 'T'. She served until being sunk by Japanese bombers in Colombo harbour while under repair on 5 April 1942

To make up for the lack of the previously aft-mounted searchlight which had been replaced by the single QF 2-pounder, a rather strange arrangement was effected whereby the searchlight was reinstated in a tower that revolved with the aft torpedo tube mounting and the 2-pounder was mounted immediately aft of that.

Refer to Appendix K for class details.

4: Foreign developments

As previously indicated, British shipbuilders had responded to foreign orders for destroyers of a bigger, more powerfully-armed nature than they were accustomed to providing the Admiralty with.

In 1910 Argentina placed orders with Britain, France and Germany each for four destroyers:

Britain	Cammell Laird – *San Luis* class.
France	Ateliers et Chantiers de Bretagne – *Mendoza* class.
	Dyle and Bacalan – *Mendoza* class.
Germany	Krupp-Germaniawerft – *G 101* or *Catamarca* class.
	Schichau – *La Plata* class.

While there were three different designs, they were all of very similar dimensions, varying between 289ft 0in and 295ft 3in LOA and 1,175 and 1,368 tons displacement. They were all fired by a mixture of coal and oil, had turbines and speeds ranged between 27 and 32 knots. The armament was standardised at four 4in and four 21in torpedoes and in both respects they were more heavily armed than their British-designed and operated equivalents. The British-built ships were sold to Greece in October 1912. The French-built ships were taken over by France at the outbreak of war. The German-built ships were delivered to Argentina.

Cammell Laird's *San Luis* class for the Argentinian Navy.

Of greater significance were the four large destroyers ordered for Turkey. These – designed by Armstrong Whitworth but contracted to Hawthorn Leslie – were taken over by the Admiralty before building even commenced and became the *Talisman* class. They were impressive ships, bigger and more heavily armed than any destroyer yet designed and built for the Royal Navy, with three sets of twin torpedo tubes and five 4in guns. At almost 1,100 tons standard displacement and 309ft 0in LOA, these destroyers were larger than anything in the Royal Navy other than the white elephant HMS *Swift*.

There is an alternative history according to navypedia.com which is worth quoting verbatim, as follows:

> Although all sources, including Admiralty records, state that four destroyers were on order for Turkey in August 1914 modern historians claim that no trace of such an order exists in Turkish records (nor for the two 'E' class submarines). This prompts the question of where these four destroyers originated. There are only two valid explanations: that Hawthorn Leslie had ordered material for four 'M' class hulls on speculation; or that some secret deal was still under negotiation between the British and the Turks, possibly under the aegis of the international arms dealer Sir Basil Zaharoff. However attractive this latter explanation might sound, it clashes with the known facts that the Young Turks were already heavily under German influence, and there is also the indisputable fact that no written evidence for these contracts has turned up, neither in Turkish nor British archives.

Irrespective of this, the *Talisman* class were minnows compared with the six Chilean-ordered *Almirante Lynch* class with six 4in guns (four of which could technically fire forwards) and four single or two twin 21in torpedo tubes. Two were delivered to Chile on completion (*Almirante Lynch* in 1913 and *Almirante Condell* in 1914) and the other four taken over by the Royal Navy which became the *Faulknor* class. My drawing which appears on page 44 is based on a structural drawing, Plate X that appeared in the September 1913 edition of the *Engineer* magazine and is of *Almirante Lynch* in her 'as-designed' state. I mention this specifically because of discrepancies in both descriptions and photographs that may appear. For instance, *Almirante Lynch* is credited variously with three single torpedo tubes or two twins or three twins. If the latter, this would have been a most impressive torpedo armament for the time for a British-designed destroyer but it should be remembered she was significantly larger than usual. Also, photographs of the four *Faulknor* class destroyers clearly show the 'midships'-mounted 4in guns on what appears to be an extended forecastle rather than on a special platform with hinged sides immediately abreast the foremost funnel – which was extended in the *Faulknor* class but may not necessarily have been done so in the Chilean destroyers, at least at the time of delivery. These were well-equipped ships. They had searchlights and rangefinders (possibly a 7ft type) fore and aft to make the best use of their powerful armament. On the debit side, while there was some perceived advantage in having two side-by-side guns on the foredeck for essentially ahead fire – shades of the long-barrelled Nelsonian bow-chasers – their arcs were limited by the presence of the adjoining gun crews and blast effects as indeed would have been the limited forward fire from the midships guns even when elevated to the foredeck. Also, the available firing arcs for the torpedoes were limited by what seems a rather poor location of ships' boats and the inevitable torpedo-handling davits. When coming into action, I could not help wondering what happened to the many ventilators that had to be dismantled to clear room for the torpedo tubes to swing and, in rough weather, what prevented the ingress of water the ventilators were meant to keep out. Why weren't the torpedo mountings elevated so that they cleared mushroom-type ventilators and the life rails? While they certainly had their disadvantages, the American emergency-build First World War four-stackers/flush-deckers (*Caldwell*, *Wickes* and *Clemson* classes) had their four triple torpedo tubes en echelon, off-centre on the deck edge meaning they could be brought into action without any dismantling of equipment.

HMS *Botha* was a flotilla leader of the *Faulknor* class for the Chilean Navy and two, *Almirante Condell* and *Almirante Lynch*, had been delivered by the outbreak of the First World War. (Public domain)

ALMIRANTE LYNCH **CLASS SPECIFICATIONS**

Displacement	1,453 tons (standard)
LOA	331ft 4in
Beam	32ft 6in
Draft	11ft 0in (standard)
Propulsion	6 boilers, coal and oil-fired, 3 shafts, direct turbines
SHP	30,000
Speed	31 knots
Guns	6 x QF 4in Mk VI (as built)
TT	3 x 21in (3 x 1) (see text)

Novik 1911 Russia and *Almirante Lynch* 1912 Chile

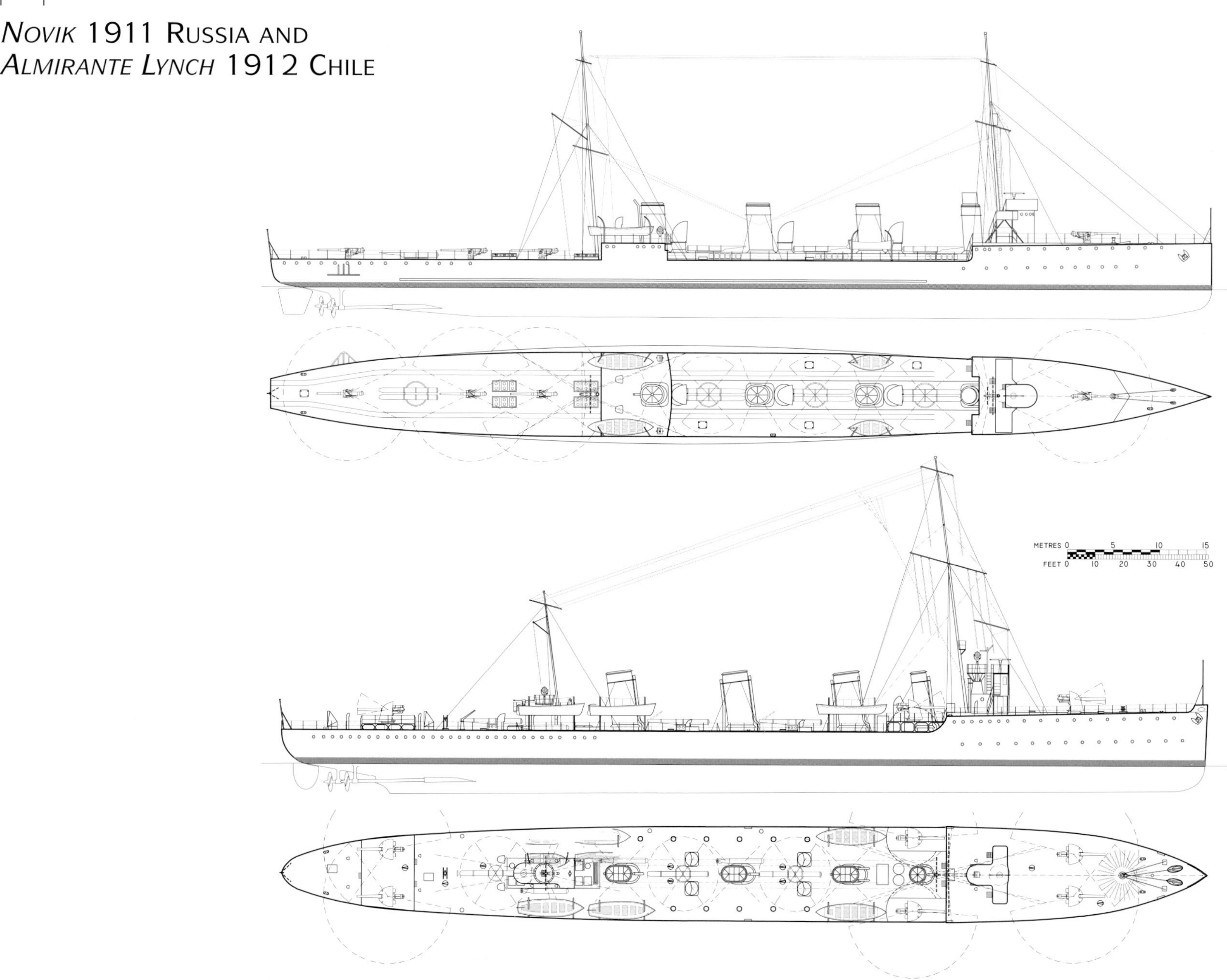

The Russian Navy's *Novik*. (en.wikipedia.org)

NOVIK CLASS SPECIFICATIONS

Displacement	1,250 tons (standard)
LOA	335ft 11in
Beam	31ft 2in
Draft	7ft 2in (standard)
Propulsion	6 boilers, oil-fired, 3 shafts, turbines
SHP	39,000
Speed	37.3 knots
Guns	4 x 4in Pattern 60
TT	8 x 18in or 500mm (4 x 2) (depending on sources, some drawings show triple torpedo tubes giving a total of 12)
Mines	80

The Russian *Novik* class was about the same sort of dimensions as *Almirante Lynch* but was, on paper at least, an even more powerful warship, if not in gun power, certainly in speed and torpedo power albeit the smaller equivalent of the 18in type. Of similar length, the *Novik*s had less beam, less draft and, consequently, less displacement than the Chilean destroyers and almost 25 per cent more shaft horsepower which accounted for their superior speed. According to some sources, *Novik* was the fastest warship in the world when commissioned in 1913. While built in St Petersburg, *Novik* was not Russian-designed. Indeed, it is not known just what input the Russian Navy had into the design process. The Imperial Russian Navy learnt bitter lessons as a result of the Russo-Japanese War and decided that a faster and more powerful type of destroyer was required, what they referred to as a 'Universal Destroyer' and what would have been a 'super destroyer' had that term been in vogue in those times. Various shipbuilding companies apparently submitted proposals but it was the German AG Vulkan Stettin that was successful and which also provided the boilers and the turbines via AEG Vulkan.

Her basic concept was repeated in four succeeding classes that totalled forty-three ships (some sources state fifty-one but I cannot substantiate these) as follows:

Derzy class	9 ships launched 1913–14.
Orfey class	22 ships launched 1914–16.
Izyaslav class	5 ships launched 1915.
Fidonisy class	8 ships launched 1916–24.

A feature of all of these destroyers was the number of torpedo tubes carried, varying from five twins to three and four triple tubes, numbers never equalled in any destroyer built for the Royal Navy. The drawing on page 44 is based on drawings relating to resin kits which show some quite contradictory detail which may relate to *Novik* at different times of her career. Note that while there are four twin torpedo tubes (and one drawing shows four triple tubes), the four 4in guns are mounted rather inefficiently with only one able to fire forward and the three mounted on the quarterdeck having very limited firing arcs.

The German influence in the design of the Russian *Novik* saw a similar reiteration in the *B 97* class of *Torpedobootzerstörer* of 1915. The *raison d'etre* for these ships was apparently not so much as requirement of the German Navy but more a result of the fact that Blohm & Voss was building a shipyard for the Tsarist government in St Petersburg and when war broke out four destroyers to their design (*Orfey* class, above) were under construction (*Leytenant Ilyin*, *Kapitan Konon Zotov*, *Gavriil* and *Mikhail*). Accordingly, the 40,000 SHP AEG Vulkan turbines then in Germany became available without hulls to accommodate them. Apparently, Grand Admiral Tirpitz pushed through a proposal to have *Zerstörers* designed around them and the class was subsequently enlarged to eight (two of which were built by AG Vulkan Stettin).

These took the basic design concept of the smaller, torpedo-oriented torpedo boat to a true destroyer with four guns – albeit the 88mm L/35 to begin with – but with six 500mm torpedo tubes arranged as to two trainable singles to port and starboard in the well created by the break in the high protective forecastle and the equally high and well-designed bridge plus two twin mountings in that peculiarly German arrangement of one tube aligned along but off the centreline and the other at 15° to it. It is of interest that the arcs over which the torpedoes could be fired were considerably greater than that which pertained in British-designed destroyers due to more thought being given to the location of equipment that would otherwise impede this efficiency. For instance, there were no torpedo-loading davits in the way and the placement of ventilators and ships' boats seemed far better integrated into the overall design than the somewhat random distribution as seen on British designs of the time. The same efficiency can be seen in the firing arcs of the four centreline-mounted guns. There were rangefinders (absent in British destroyers) and searchlights fore and aft and twenty-four mines could be carried. Rails on the starboard side may have been used in part for this, but certainly for torpedo reloads and to move spare torpedoes forward or aft.

My drawing opposite is based on a rather basic drawing found online that relates to the instructions for a Czech-manufactured 1:700 scale resin kit and as such lacks a lot of the sort of detail I would have liked to include. It serves, however, as a means for comparing one ship with another as to the basic design approach and, particularly, how very different this was to the British answer

A *B 97 Klasse* probably photographed on trials, not yet fitted with torpedo tubes. (commons.wikemedia.org)

B 97 KLASSE 1915 GERMANY AND *CLEMSON* CLASS 1916 USA

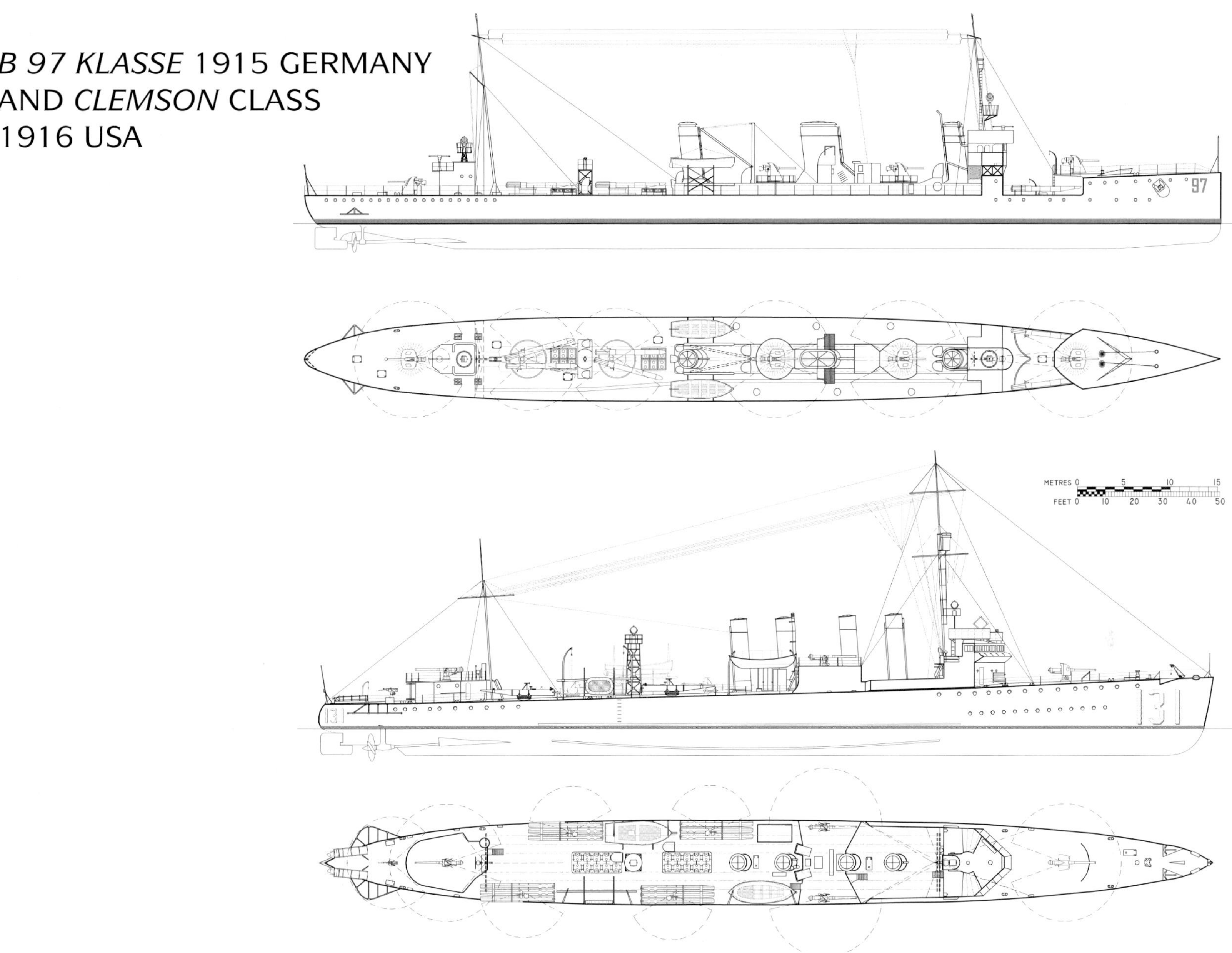

to the perceived problem. If one compares the decks plans the immediate difference that is obvious is the hull shape. The German entry and resultant deck width above is much finer whereas the British designs always favour flare to the bows to give reserve buoyancy and to reduce spray. Note that the Germans seem to eschew the use of davits of any type to launch and recover their ships' boats, using a derrick instead. This would seem quite impractical in the event of a disaster but would minimise obstructing firing arcs – something that seems often overlooked around this time in British destroyers where the many ships' boats seem to be distributed without a lot of thought. However, instead of using tubular vents with round cowls – which must be slow and expensive to make – their boiler room vents are just big rectangular affairs like one sees on industrial and office buildings: entirely practical. Note also the recessed anchors, a very modern touch for 1915 but how necessary?

B 97 KLASSE SPECIFICATIONS

Displacement	1,374 tons (standard)
LOA	321ft 6in
Beam	30ft 8in
Draft	11ft 1in (standard)
Propulsion	4 boilers, oil-fired, 2 shafts, turbines (it is not known whether these were direct or geared)
SHP	40,000
Speed	37.4 knots
Guns	4 x 88mm SK L/35
TT	6 x 19.7in (500mm) (2 x 1, 2 x 2)
Mines	24

Across the Atlantic the United States Navy was able to place no less than three twin 18in torpedo tubes on their 293ft LOA *Paulding* class destroyers of 1909–11. Their five 3in/50 cal guns were roughly the equivalent of the then-being-discarded QF 12-pounder 12 cwt both in range and rate of fire but lacked the hitting power with a much lighter projectile. Nevertheless, the deck plan found room for five of these mounts. At a mere 754 tons standard displacement and 12,000 SHP to direct drive turbines on three shafts, the *Paulding*s managed almost 30 knots. The *Paulding*s were by no measure to be held up as paragons of destroyer development. Indeed, together with the *Smith* class they were derided as 'flivvers', the name borrowed from Henry Ford's T-Model Ford, so-called because of its light weight. Contrast the *Paulding*s with the *Acorn* class of the same period: 730–780 tons standard displacement, 246ft 6in LOA, 13,500 SHP, 27 knots, two 4in and two 12-pounders and two single 21in torpedo tubes.

The *Paulding*s grew to a succession of similar, only larger 'thousand-tonners' until the exigencies of the First World War saw the emergency programme to build the 273 destroyers of the *Caldwell*, *Wickes* and *Clemson* classes – the 'flush-deckers/four-

USS *Mayrant* DD-31, a modified *Paulding* class.

pipers/four-stackers' as they became widely known. These featured no less than four triple 21in torpedo tubes which could be fired simultaneously using gyro angling whereby torpedoes could be set to alter course once they had entered the water.

***CLEMSON* CLASS SPECIFICATIONS**

Displacement	1,154 tons (standard)
LOA	314ft 4½in
Beam	30ft 11¼in
Draft	9ft 0in (standard)
Propulsion	4 boilers, oil-fired, 2 shafts, geared turbines
SHP	24,610
Speed	35 knots
Guns	4 x 4in/50 cal, 2 x 3in/32 cal
TT	12 x 21in (4 x 3)

In retrospect, it seems like the Admiralty – unlike foreign navies – had adopted a quantity rather than quality approach at this time, figuring that in the event of defending the fleet or attacking the enemy fleet, that – like the Soviet T-34 tanks of the Second World War – the sheer weight of numbers of ships would be paramount. In the case of the destroyers, the ability to mass-launch torpedoes from the maximum number of ships was more important than the maximum number of torpedoes from the minimum number of ships and would persuade the enemy fleet to break formation and turn away. Even so, why did it take the Admiralty so long to go from single torpedo tubes to double and, indeed, not to squeeze as many torpedo tubes on to the decks as possible? If the private designer-builders were able to do it for foreign customers and foreign navies could do that for their own ships, what was holding back the Royal Navy from adopting that protocol itself?

While the Royal Navy was the biggest and most powerful in the world and its Dreadnought battleships of 1912 were to become the cutting edge of naval warfare, I think it is a reasonable judgement to make that its destroyers of this time were not necessarily any better than any other navy's, or perhaps not even as good as the best. But that was to change. It was just going to take a couple of small, incremental steps. They were on the horizon.

This photograph of USS *Pruitt* illustrates the vastly different approach to destroyer design adopted by the United States Navy as compared with the 'V & W' destroyers of the Royal Navy. The low freeboard limited the forward 4in gun's effectiveness in a seaway and the beam-mounted torpedo tubes which had to be extended over the ships' sides to be fired. *Pruitt* was the last of the *Clemson* class to be completed, on 9 June 1920. She was converted to a minelayer in 1937, was decommissioned on 5 December 1945 and scrapped the following year. (navsource.org)

5: THE FLOTILLA LEADERS

WAR'S COMPETING AND COMMON REQUIREMENTS

The role of what were now self-contained fighting ships, teamed into flotillas and now termed destroyers, had become scouting ahead of the fleet, warding off attacks from flotillas of other destroyers and attacking the enemy fleet. Other roles would eventually follow such as minesweeping ahead of the fleet, strategic minelaying and anti-submarine operations. In 1910, destroyers became organised more formally into flotillas led by a light cruiser heading two squadrons led by smaller cruisers each containing two divisions made up of three sub-divisions of two destroyers; twenty-four destroyers in total.[1]

The outbreak of war in 1914 saw the Royal Navy with basically two fleets; the Grand Fleet and the Channel Fleet. The former was based in Scotland's Scapa Flow and subject to the rough northern weather and was torpedo-centric whereas the latter was based in the south and operated in generally more benign conditions and was gunnery-centric in its requirements but with short-range torpedoes (even the small 14in type) as an option. Clearly a destroyer design specifically for one fleet would be unsuited to the other.

Competing requirements aside, the common fleet requirement was for higher freeboard, bridges to be moved further aft so they weren't subject to breaking waves at worst or spray at best, and better ahead fire than just the one gun on the centreline on the forecastle or two side-by-side with their own inherent limited arcs of fire and associated manning issues.

Freeboard at the stem was set at around 15ft. A naval architect's rule of thumb is that minimum freeboard forward should be the square root of LOA multiplied by 1.1. Also, it seemed to be a basic tenet that the lower of the two decks created should not be below water level. Increasing height added weight. Weight affected speed. Giving more flare to the bows reduced spray but increased strains when punching into a head sea requiring more stiffening adding more weight. There was always a trade-off.

If one looks at the inboard profile of any steam-driven destroyer – as compared with the modern gas-turbine and gas-diesel hybrids – the very large amount of space taken up by boiler rooms and engine rooms is immediately obvious. It was normal practice in the Royal Navy for destroyers to have three boilers so that if any one boiler was down for maintenance the other two could still deliver a reasonable speed. It was also normal practice for the boiler rooms to be split up so that the larger one with two boilers was foremost and the smaller one adjoined the engine room. This was partly due to the necessity to provide support for the midships gun (between the funnels) and as a damage-control measure to reduce the risk of losing the ship if the bulkhead between the large boiler room and an adjacent engine room was breached. This determined where the foremost boiler uptake (funnel) was located and, therefore, the bridge.

THE *MARKSMAN* CLASS (SOMETIMES REFERRED TO AS THE *LIGHTFOOT* CLASS OR *KEMPENFELT* CLASS)

The period 1903–13 saw two each of the *Adventure*, *Forward*, *Pathfinder*, *Sentinel*, *Blonde* and *Boadicea* classes, and three *Active* class scout cruisers to serve as flotilla leaders for destroyer-type vessels built for the Royal Navy. When their maximum speeds peaked at 25 knots and destroyers were exceeding this it was clear that it was necessary to have a flotilla leader of an appropriate speed that was properly equipped with all the necessary staff, and, particularly the communication equipment, to lead a flotilla into battle and direct it through the conflict. The one-off leader HMS *Swift* had been Admiral 'Jacky' Fisher's inspiration and, while the idea was sound enough, the hurried execution left a lot to be desired. The result was a 'jack-of-all-trades-master-of-none' sort of result. Basically, HMS *Swift* under-delivered on all counts except style, for she was a handsomely-proportioned warship, and it was probably fortunate that further orders were not placed. Even the largest navy in the world cannot afford functional lemons like the *Swift*. Something more specifically and purpose-designed was needed to perform the role of destroyer alongside its sister-ships but be big enough also to accommodate the Captain (D) plus ten staff. Also, the ship itself would need a bridge capable of bearing the appropriate signalling equipment and masts suitable for the spread of extra wireless aerials and flag hoists.

In August 1913 the Controller instructed the DNC to prepare a design: 1,800 tons maximum, 33 knots minimum but 34 knots preferred, four 4in guns, two pom-poms (type not specified), endurance at 15 knots better than current destroyers, and signalling equal to the latest cruisers. The design with four funnels with No 2 gun between the first and second funnel and No 3 gun between the third and fourth funnel was approved in December.[2]

The final design for the *Marksman/Lightfoot/Kempenfelt* class was a standard displacement of 1,607 tons (sometime reported as 1,700 tons), 324ft 10in LOA with a beam of 31ft 9in and powered by 36,000 SHP to give a respectable 34 knots. They had a distinctive appearance with four slim raked funnels to serve their four boilers. The funnels were, somewhat unusually, broader athwartships and narrower fore and aft. The foremost funnel was appreciably taller to keep smoke clear of the bridge with its vital signalling operations. The guns were all on the centreline, being one on the foredeck, one between the first and second funnel, one between the third and fourth funnel and the fourth on the quarterdeck. The two twin 21in torpedo tubes were conventionally located on the engine casing and aft of it but the aft searchlight was aft of the mainmast. Strangely, considering their intended and very specific use as flotilla leaders, *Abdiel* was converted as a minelayer to handle eighty mines, sacrificing torpedo tubes and her two aftmost guns to do so.

Two ships were ordered in the 1913–14 Programme, two in the 1914–15 Programme and three in the War Emergency Programme of November 1914. However, six flotilla leaders were not enough. Indeed, it seems to have been a common feeling in the Grand Fleet that this size and type of destroyer with the general seaworthiness, endurance and armament balance they possessed was what was required as a fleet destroyer and not just as a flotilla leader of destroyers of lesser capabilities.[3]

HMS *Ithuriel*, a *Marksman/Lightfoot/Kempenfelt* class. (Public Domain)

THE *PARKER* CLASS

One cannot say that the success of the *Marksman/Lightfoot/Kempenfelt* class led to the *Parker* class simply because, like every one of the preceding classes, each year's programme simply cannot be based on the results of the previous year's programme. Those ships would not have been completed – indeed, may not even have been launched. Such are the problems of placing orders for warships each year when the preceding 'improvements' that have hopefully been encapsulated in the preceding orders have not as yet proven to be justified. Nevertheless, the *Parker* class was a repeat in that it shared the same hull design and dimensions but incorporated improvements resulting from the feedback that it would appear Royal Navy officers were not shy in making known. Seakeeping seems to have been highest on their wish-list of improvements. This resulted in two changes to the previous design. The 'M' class destroyer HMS *Napier* had been given a raked bow as an experiment and this had proved beneficial so the design principle was adopted in HMS *Anzac*'s hull which, like her sister-ship HMS *Saumarez,* was also given another foot of freeboard

HMS *Anzac*, a *Parker* class destroyer and the first to introduce the superfiring guns. (awm.gov.au)

forward.[4] There was always pressure to move the bridge further aft, to get it as far away from the inevitable spray and seas that broke over the foredeck. The determining factor was the funnel to the first boiler. If this could be moved aft, then so could the bridge. Trunking the No 1 and 2 uptakes together into a thicker funnel by changing the boiler arrangement around so that the three boilers were in two rather than three boiler rooms allowed the bridge to move 13ft aft.[5] But, doing so lost the space allocated to No 2 gun, between the first and second funnels which now had to move somewhere else and this is where the incremental changes referred to previously begin to accumulate to great effect.

The breakthrough was to relocate No 2 gun forward of the bridge, superfiring behind No 1 gun in a battleship/cruiser 'A' gun, 'B' gun arrangement on a shelter deck/deckhouse, which had two benefits: extra accommodation and it raised the bridge an extra level. If there could be considered another breakthrough moment in destroyer design, this was it. In one simple move – combining the trunking for the first two boilers and moving the most forward of the funnels aft by a mere 13ft – a British destroyer leader had two superfiring forward guns that could be operated in all weathers, overviewed by a bridge one level higher than before with all the benefits that offered and the extra accommodation needed for the task it was intended for. The concept of a gun mount superfiring over another in warships was not radical. Admittedly the precedents were in much larger ships – but, then, they were much larger guns too. The first instance of superfiring, and not a very successful one at that because the blast from the upper (smaller-calibre) gun interfered with the lower (large- calibre) gun, was the French pre-Dreadnought battleship *Henry IV* of 1899. The USS *South Carolina* introduced the concept of the main armament

HMS *ANZAC*: *PARKER* CLASS LEADER 1918

HMS *Anzac* was untypical of the last six ships of the *Parker* class leaders – often referred to as repeat *Kempenfelt* class. She was completed with additional freeboard and a raked bow reflecting experience gained in other ships such as HMS *Napier*. Note the searchlights in the bridge wings, the considerably larger bridge and the extra yardarms for visual and wireless signalling required to fulfil the role of flotilla leader.

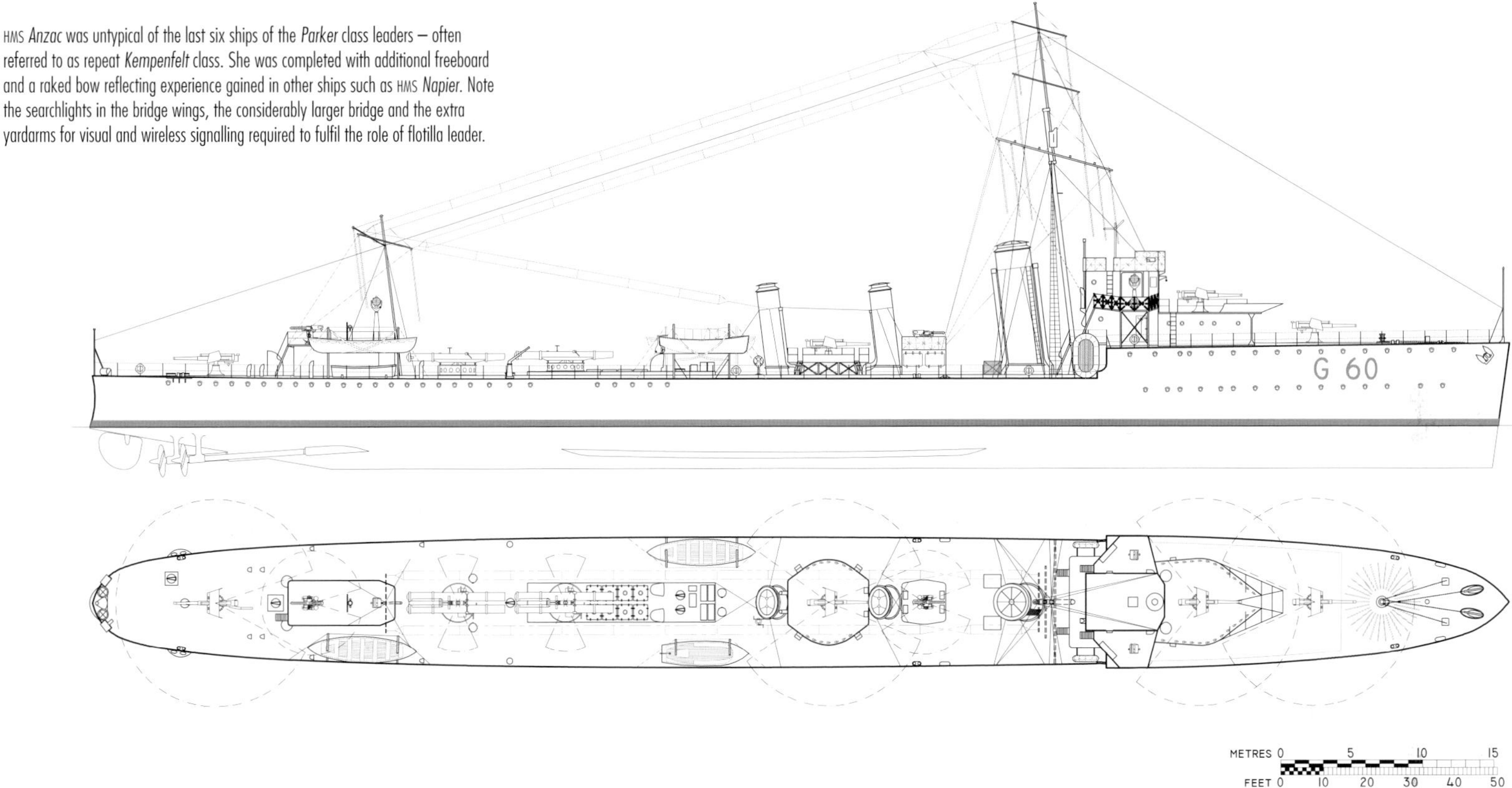

superfiring in 1906. So, one would have to ask, why wasn't this fundamental principle applied earlier to destroyers? Clearly the added topweight of an additional gun mount one deck higher affected the metacentric height, but this was easily overcome in any new design by a combination of added draft, beam or compensating ballast. Making that sort of addition to an existing design means that the basic *Parker* class must have had some of that combination to accept the extra topweight.

To take advantage of the higher bridge and more efficient gunnery system, the class introduced a new director-firing system whereby instead of individual gun crews being responsible for laying their own fire independently, the director on the bridge indicated the training (direction) and elevation and a gyroscopic device fired the guns on the ship's roll simultaneously. Insofar as roll-rate was concerned, the preceding *Marksman*/*Lightfoot*/*Kempenfelt* class had a rapid roll rate – they were very 'stiff', to use the less technical term, meaning they were too heavy below their centre of gravity and too light above it – bottom-heavy. Hence the fact that *Anzac* and *Saumarez* were easily able to take the weight of the extra freeboard and the higher 'B' mount and the shelter deck and the higher bridge and not be the opposite to 'stiff', that is 'tender' or top-heavy.

The armament was completed with the third 4in gun mounted between the second and third funnels and the fourth on the quarterdeck. A fifth 4in mount could not be fitted superfiring aft because the necessary support for it, being on the centreline, would have interfered with the centre propeller shafting so a 2-pounder was fitted in its place on the aft deckhouse with a good firing arc. Two twin 21in torpedo tubes were fitted. Some sources refer to two depth-charge throwers and two depth-charge chutes but it is not known if these were fitted at the time they were commissioned.

When I came to draw HMS *Anzac*, shown on page 53, I could not help thinking how much more progressive the design was over the three 'M' class variants I had drawn immediately before. Apart from the better armament disposition, the bridge, with its large wings each containing a searchlight, seemed almost cruiser-like compared with those that had come before it. Of course, the increase in length of over 50ft (18 per cent) with a proportionate increase in beam makes these sorts of things more easily attainable but, on the other hand, there still seemed to be something strangely Nelsonic in the foredeck-mounted capstan for raising the anchors of a warship with four boilers and three propeller shafts.

HMAS *Anzac* in 1929. (navy.gov.au)

***PARKER* CLASS SPECIFICATIONS**

LOA	325ft 0in (*Anzac* 327ft 7in due to the raked bow)
Beam	31ft 10in
Draft	12ft 1½in (standard)
Displacement	1,660 tons (standard)
Propulsion	4 boilers, oil-fired, 3 shafts, geared turbines
SHP	36,000
Speed	34.0 knots
Guns	4 x QF 4in Mk IV, 2 x QF 2-pounder Mk II
TT	4 x 21in (2 x 2)

Time was to prove these to be very successful warships. But that knowledge was not available of course when the process was put in place to take the design principles that so easily seemed to have fallen into serendipitous place to the next logical step.

As mentioned earlier, there seemed to be a requirement for two types of destroyers: one to be based in the south with an emphasis on guns to counter German torpedo boats and the other with better seakeeping, better endurance, speed and the ability to work with the Grand Fleet, based in the north. Admiral Jellicoe favoured this approach but the Controller, the Third Sea Lord, was opposed. Why not have a destroyer that could fulfil both roles? Unfortunately, no such destroyer existed.

THE 300FT LEADER

There are various slightly contradictory versions as to how the next step in the destroyer design process was initiated and when. What was clear, however, was that the 276ft 'R' class destroyers – and the follow-on 'S' class – were going to need flotilla leaders to spearhead them in order to be effective. Further, as always, reports of German advances in up-gunning their torpedo-carrying forces from the 88mm SK L/35 or L/45 to the 105mm SK L/45 produced the usual reactive response. A better-armed flotilla leader would help redress this balance.

According to Norman Friedman, the Controller asked DNC to design such a leader using the same power plant as the 'R' class[6] and two alternative designs were available by 27 March or 1 April according to Raven and Roberts,[7] but submitted to the Board on 7 April.[8] One was a three-funnel design with five 4in guns and the other a two-funnel design with four 4in guns – both designs duplicating the superfiring concept fore and aft from the *Parker* class. Endurance offered was 3,500 miles at 15 knots and 35 knots speed at 75 tons oil of the 320 tons capacity. Cost was expected to be 20 per cent less than the *Parker* class leaders at £200,000.[9]

I have seen the reference in Wikipedia that suggests that the four *Talisman* class destroyers designed by Armstrong Whitworth for the Ottoman Navy (see above) had a 'hull form [that] was considered particularly successful and was adopted for the V and W class of 1917'. There is no citation but the one that appears in the sentence immediately before it is in *Conway's All The World's Fighting Ships 1906–1921*. The *Talisman* class had very similar dimensions to the 'V & Ws': 1,098 tons and 309ft 0in LOA, 28ft 7in beam but had direct-drive three-shaft turbines developing 25,000 SHP achieving 32 knots. It is an interesting concept and may not be that far-fetched. The fact that the design appeared so promptly adds some weight to the theory.

The three-funnel design was refined into a two-funnel design by trunking the aft uptakes from the No 1 boiler with the forward uptake from the No 2 boiler into one broader funnel and deleting the midships gun that had been between the second and third funnels. This allowed the bridge to be moved further aft. The pom-pom was moved aft of the fatter second funnel but was replaced by a QF 3in 20 cwt HA Mk III. This was a Vickers'-designed and built weapon and the Mk I was the first specifically designed anti-aircraft weapon of its type. The Mk III was an emergency wartime design with a parallel screw breech block and a two-motion breech mechanism. Nonetheless, the Mk IV remained in service until 1939.

On 28 April approval was given to upgrade the 4in guns to the new, high-velocity Mk V 45-calibre models. Various alterations pushed the displacement up by 28 tons and the speed down to 34 knots according to Raven and Roberts[10] but 48 tons and a loss of a quarter-knot according to March and an increase in cruising range of 15 per cent.[11] Whatever the loss of speed, this seems to be an accepted fact as a trade-off for using the already-in-production 27,000 SHP power plant of the 'R' class and the saving in time that would result. Moving the bridge aft and with it the two forward guns altered the distribution of weight and reduced the vertical acceleration (when pitching) and this added to their reputation as good sea boats.[12]

THE 'V' CLASS LEADERS
(FIVE SHIPS)

Two orders were placed in April 1916 and three more in July and a fifth in October, as follows. Following normal naming protocols, the new class would have been 'V' but the first three names allocated when the first were ordered in July 1916 were for some strange reason *Malcolm, Montrose* and *Wallace* – later *Valkyrie, Valorous* and *Vampire*.[13]

Valkyrie laid down at William Denny 25 May 1916, launched 13 Mar 1917, completed 16 Jun 1917.
Valorous laid down at William Denny 25 May 1916, launched 8 May 1917, completed 21 Aug 1917.
Valentine laid down at Cammell Laird 18 Jul 1916*, launched 24 Mar 1917, completed 27 Jun 1917.
Valhalla laid down at Cammell Laird 8 Aug 1916, launched 22 May 1917, completed 31 Jul 1917.
Vampire laid down at J S White 10 Oct 1916, launched 21 May 1917, completed 22 Sep 1917.

*Records of this date vary.

It is interesting to note that the last ten of the twenty-four contemporary 'C' class light cruisers (six *Caroline* class, two *Calliope* class, four *Cambrian* class, two *Caledon* class, five *Ceres* class and five *Carlisle* class) mounted superfiring 6in guns fore and

HMS *VAMPIRE*: 'V' LEADER 1918

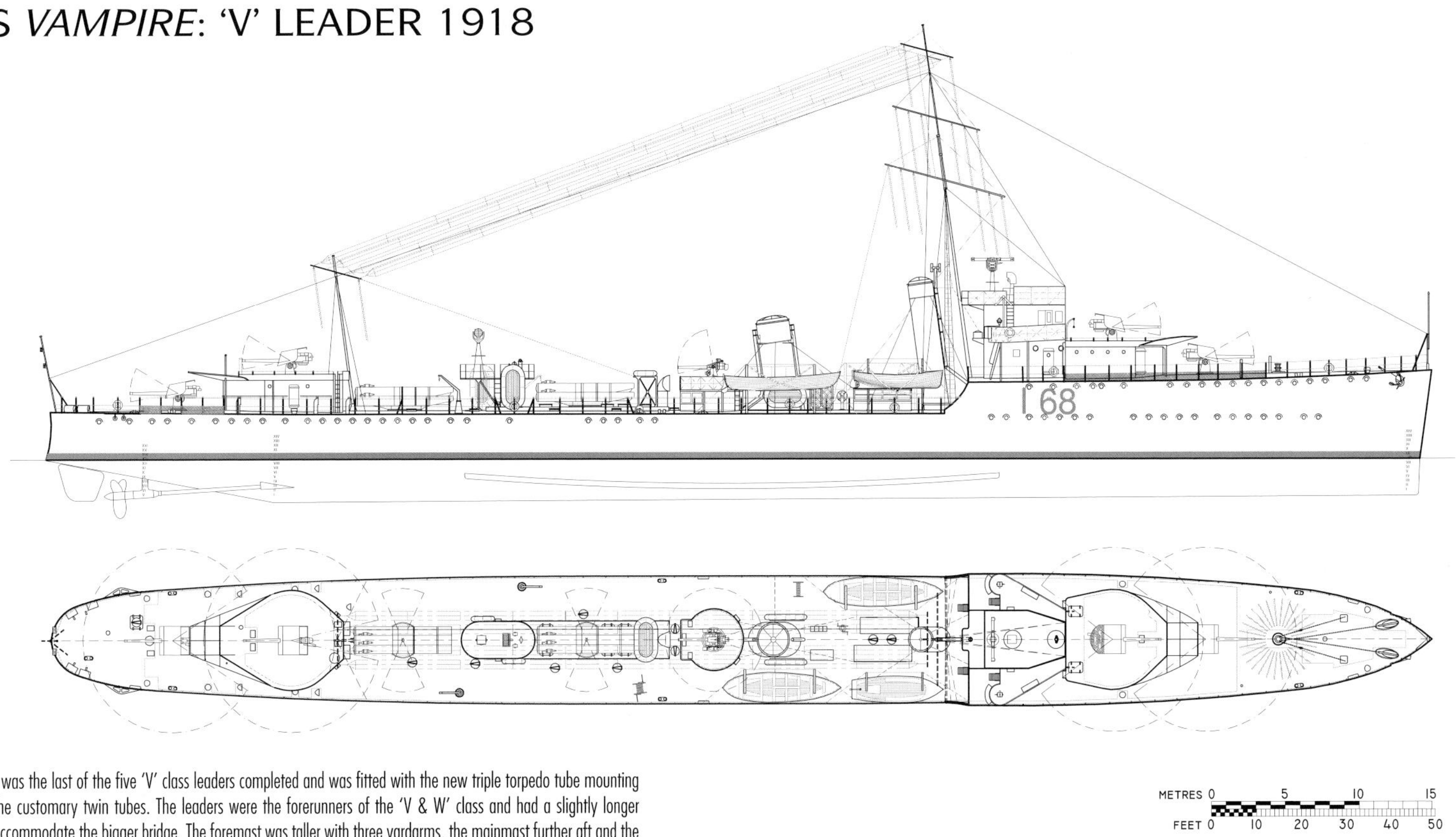

HMS *Vampire* was the last of the five 'V' class leaders completed and was fitted with the new triple torpedo tube mounting in place of the customary twin tubes. The leaders were the forerunners of the 'V & W' class and had a slightly longer foredeck to accommodate the bigger bridge. The foremast was taller with three yardarms, the mainmast further aft and the emergency steering position was forward of the searchlight.

aft so the concept was being introduced into light cruisers (6in guns), heavy cruisers (*Hawkins* class 7.5in guns) and destroyer leaders at the same time. It is also of some interest that the first of the 'C' class to have the superfiring arrangement, HMS *Ceres*, was laid down on 11 July 1916 – almost seven weeks later than *Valkyrie* – yet was commissioned over two weeks earlier; a shorter time to build a light cruiser than a destroyer leader.

Vampire trialled a new triple torpedo mounting that weighed less than the twin mounting. The third tube was superimposed above the two tubes and not in the later and favoured a side-by-side arrangement. This became common in later versions.

The class were officially designated 'half-leaders' although their accommodation (nine cabins on the lower deck, aft, one in the deckhouse, two at the break of the forecastle and a sick bay, dining, sleeping and sea cabin for the captain) was up to the standard of the *Parker*s and their sister-ships. The foremasts were taller than subsequent derivatives and had three yardarms for the increased amount of visual signalling and wireless aerials and the mainmast was hard up against the aft deckhouse with the emergency steering position between it and the aft set of torpedo tubes. There's a contradiction here in that the drawing of HMS *Valhalla* on page 170 of Friedman's book quite clearly shows the aft bank of torpedo tubes hard up against the mainmast and the emergency steering position in the forward section of an elongated searchlight position between the two torpedo-tube mountings. It was quite common for the shipbuilders to 'do their own thing' when it came to minor details like searchlight towers, funnel caps and bridgework and this Cammell Laird-built ship may just reflect such a choice. However, what that particular drawing does show, or rather does not show, is the extra ships' boat/s abreast the after funnel that the 'V'-Leaders were supposed to have carried, presumably as a reflection of the extra crew carried and the necessity to move between the flotilla when at anchor. The director-firing system introduced in the *Parker* class was retained.

The operational concept was that these destroyers would head up flotillas or divisions of the numerous but disparate smaller destroyers, such as:

- 36 'River' class dating from 1904–05 (less 2 lost pre-war) (redesignated 'E' class), coal-fired VTE but 3 with turbines.
- 12 'Tribal' class (redesignated 'F' class) dating from 1905–08, oil-fired, turbines.
- 16 *Beagle* class (redesignated 'G' class) dating from 1908–10, coal-fired, turbines.
- 20 *Acorn* class (redesignated 'H' class in 1913) dating from 1910–11, oil-fired, turbines.
- 23 *Acheron* class (redesignated 'I' class in 1913) dating from 1911–12, oil-fired, turbines.
- 20 *Acasta* class (redesignated 'K' class in 1913) dating from 1912–13, oil-fired, direct-turbines, but one semi-geared.
- 22 *Laforey* class (redesignated 'L' class in 1913) dating from 1913–14, oil-fired, turbines (2 geared).
- 85 Admiralty 'M'class dating from 1914–16, oil-fired, direct-drive turbines.
- 62 Admiralty 'R' class dating from 1916–17, oil-fired, geared turbines.
- 11 Admiralty 'Modified R' class dating from 1916–17, oil-fired, geared turbines.
- 67 Admiralty 'S' class dating from 1917–19, oil-fired, geared turbines.

374 TOTAL*

*Note: this total does not reflect war losses up to the time the first 'V' class leader was completed.

'V' CLASS LEADERS SPECIFICATIONS

Displacement	1,188 tons (standard), 1,473 tons (full load)
LOA	312ft 0in
Beam	29ft 6in
Draft	10ft 8in (standard), 11ft 7½in (max. load)
Propulsion	3 boilers, oil-fired, 2 shafts, geared turbines
SHP	27,000
Speed	34 knots
Guns	4 x QF 4in Mk IV on CP.II mountings, 1 x QF 3in 20 cwt HA Mk III
TT	4 x 21in (2 x 2)*
Notes	

* Except *Vampire* 2 x 3 21in TT

HMAS *Vampire*. Note the extra ship's boat aft of the Montagu whaler. (State Library of Victoria)

6: The Benchmarkers

At the risk of being repetitive, I think it is important to restate the fact that as each new order was placed, as each new design's requirements were thrashed out, documented, the designs evaluated, calculations made and requests for tenders finally issued, the process which culminated in orders being placed was still a leap of faith insofar as the improvements that were hopefully embodied in the newest class of destroyer would be based on the preceding class from the previous batch of orders which would still be on the slipways – indeed, may even be based on the batch of orders before that and which, because of the huge lead time, might not have even been launched. For instance, construction times varied between 15 and 18 months although there were cases of some taking just under 12 months, but these were exceptional. Under ideal circumstances, ships would be launched, fitted out, commissioned, trialled, and after experiencing a wide range of conditions which would preferably include the rigours of combat, feedback would lead to improvements being incorporated in the next class of ships. Wartime did not allow such luxuries. Hence the leaps of faith. Lessons learnt, experiences gained, needed to be evaluated and decisions made on the run, so to speak, as to how best to prioritise and accommodate the requirements in the next design on the drawing board – given, of course, the ever-present constraints of what was practical and what was affordable. In this respect, I am reminded of the saying 'getting the most bang for your buck'. While I am sure this term was not current in 1916, if ever it was applicable then it truly was to the destroyers that followed on from the 'V' class leaders.

The Admiralty 'V' Class
(23 Ships)

The 140 destroyers that made up the Admiralty 'R' and 'Modified R' class and Admiralty 'S' class were completed between August 1916 and as late as April 1920. They represented the ultimate expression, the very peak to which a destroyer design of around 1,000 tons and 276ft LOA could be pushed. There was no room left for development. Everything that could be done, had been done to make that design as efficient, as seaworthy, as battleworthy as possible. They could not be made to go faster, to carry more weapons or to have greater endurance. They had reached the very limits of their potential. Something better was needed to replace them, especially in the light of the possibility that German destroyers were being up-gunned with four 105mm SK L/45 guns.

The Battle of Jutland had been fought in May 1916 and lessons learned. The Royal Navy wanted to improve its destroyers' gunnery and torpedo armament, to give them more firepower with longer-range guns and more torpedoes, but the 276ft destroyer could not accommodate these upgrades.[1] Even replacing the QF 4in Mk IV with the harder-hitting Mk V was a problem because the increased weight of the mounting and the room necessary to adequately man it meant they were not simply interchangeable. Similarly, a suggestion that the QF 2-pounder Mk II should be replaced as the anti-aircraft weapon by one of the 4in guns being converted to a HA weapon or that a 3in HA/LA gun simply replace or it or the 2-pounder lent weight to the argument that a larger destroyer was needed. But a larger destroyer would need a larger power plant – say 30,000 SHP to attain the believed-to-be-required speed of 37 knots and this meant designing and building new plant with all the attendant delays that this would incur.

Friedman states that Sir Eustace d'Eyncourt (DNC) suggested on 1 June 1916 the 300ft leader as the solution to the ongoing dispute between the two schools of thought as to the right type of destroyer: the fleet destroyer and the destroyer of German torpedo boat types for southern waters. A version of the 300ft leader would mount the necessary gun armament to satisfy the latter requirement and provide the extra range for the former.[2] On 5 July the Board of the Admiralty decided that the Ninth War Programme would be entirely the new destroyers of the 300ft leader type.[3]

March deals with the process by which what became the 'V' class was created in a very offhand manner considering its importance in the hierarchy of destroyer design. He simply states that Treasury approved thirty-one destroyers (presumably the Ninth Order of which he only gives details of twenty-five),[4] that orders had been placed for the five 'V' leaders when the Board considered the design of the remaining twenty-six boats and on 30 June 1916 it was decided to place provisional orders for twenty-one destroyers and in order to save time the design and armament should, in general, be that of the 300ft leaders with modifications to accommodation and bridge, Type IV wireless and high-speed sweep.[5] While March's book is a valuable reference, it is also a frustration. He frequently minimises or even neglects to mention items of importance yet includes a *potpourri* of items that are, in my opinion, absolutely trivial and of no consequence whatsoever.

While dimensionally the same as the 'V' leaders, the armament specification was to have replaced the twin torpedo tubes with a new, compact triple tube thus increasing in one stroke their torpedo armament by 50 per cent. However, these were not available (except for *Voyager*) when completed and were only retrofitted after the war ended. The torpedo tube positions were, however, strengthened to provide for these.[6] The accommodation layout was different, reflecting the fact that they were not required as flotilla leaders, and visually the main difference was the shorter foremast and the emergency steering position now between the aft deckhouse and the mainmast. As usual, the builders placed their individual stamps on their ships, particularly as to searchlight towers and funnel caps. Hawthorn Leslie-built ships had prominent funnel caps whereas the Thorneycroft flat-sided funnels were minimalistic by comparison and I'll deal with their contribution separately, later. White's funnels were apparently cut flush, parallel with the waterline although I am yet to see a photograph that absolutely confirms this. This may have only applied to the tall fore-funnels which are often difficult to distinguish in photographs.

The forecastle was marginally shorter than the 'V' leaders, the bridge front being 86ft 6in from the stem[7] and the bridge structure was shorter, fore and aft, as a result. David Brown gives some interesting comparisons of the distances of bridges and positions of 'A' gun and freeboard forward of the earlier 'M' and the 'V & W' classes, as follows:[8]

'M' class	LOA 267ft	Bridge 23 per cent of LOA from bow 'A' gun 18 per cent of LOA from bow 17ft freeboard forward
'V & W' class	LOA 320ft	Bridge 29 per cent of LOA from bow 'A' gun 15 per cent of LOA from bow 18.8ft freeboard forward

One advantage of moving the bridge aft is that vertical acceleration is reduced – a major cause of seasickness.

The QF 4in Mk V had a 30° elevation (instead of the Mk IV's 25°) and with a muzzle velocity of 2,600ft/sec gave an increased range of 900 yards.[9] In September, well after the orders had been placed, and probably as the first were about to be laid (*Vanoc,* 20 September) a major design change was approved to mount a QF 3in 20 cwt HA Mk III immediately abaft the second funnel. One advantage over this weapon *vis-à-vis* the 2-pounder was that it could fire starshell, useful in night engagements. Other changes, undated, that were made were Barr & Stroud receivers and director firing for the 4in guns, bridge firing gear for the torpedoes, gear necessary for streaming paravanes and the combined sweep – all of which added weight which had to be compensated for in some way. These involved many items including deleting an upper bridge in favour of increasing the size of the bridge wings but one which was reversed was that steel plates to the bridge were retained in place of the proposed canvas screens. A 9ft rangefinder and two hydraulic releases for depth charges (for chutes either side at the stern) were added.[10] Whereas the 'V' leaders had Type II and ZA wireless for ship-to-ship and long-range communication respectively, the 'V' class only had the Type IV ship-to-ship.[11]

It is not clear what the final all-up additional weight added by the variations to the original design amounted to. The Legend was 1,160 tons.[12] Additions increased the Legend displacement to 1,188 tons and a decrease in speed to 34 knots.[13] This amounts to only 28 tons which is quoted elsewhere but March and Friedman refer to 68½ tons additional weight.[14] However, they were built of HT (high tensile) steel, riveted and with transverse frames – a structural system that was cheap and easy to build and inherently light in weight.

On trials, the best information is sketchy and provided by March to the effect that *Vivien*, a Yarrow-built ship and thus lighter than typical, did 36.79 knots on the shallow Skelmorlie measured mile – hardly disappointing.[15] The fact remains, however, that while weight was always uppermost in the designers' and builders' minds, its effects on performance and stability was such that successive changes to the design were permissible without detriment, a testament to the basic soundness of the 'V & W' design.

Changing operational requirements resulted in the First Sea Lord requesting in January 1917 if four 'V' class destroyers could be completed to carry sixty Type H mines providing the necessary conversion did not delay completion. While this was agreed to (*Vanoc*, *Vanquisher*, *Vehement* and *Venturous*), the concept was extended by a further eight (*Vancouver* – renamed *Vimy* – *Velox*, *Venetia*, *Versatile*, *Vesper*, *Vimiera*, *Vittoria* and *Vortigern*). Since each mine and its sinker weighed 1,840lbs, No 4 gun, or 'Y' gun as it became known, was removed as were the aft torpedo tubes and two torpedoes. However, these could be re-instated within 24 hours to restore the ships to normal destroyer capability, albeit with the minelaying tracks presumably still in position. One change that could not be so readily altered was to the propellers. For minelaying purposes, the propellers were 8ft 9in diameter instead of the usual 9ft 6in in order to 'give the best results on the out journey with ½ oil and all mines on board', the load being about 50 tons heavier

HMS *VENTUROUS*: ADMIRALTY 'V' CLASS, MINELAYER 1918

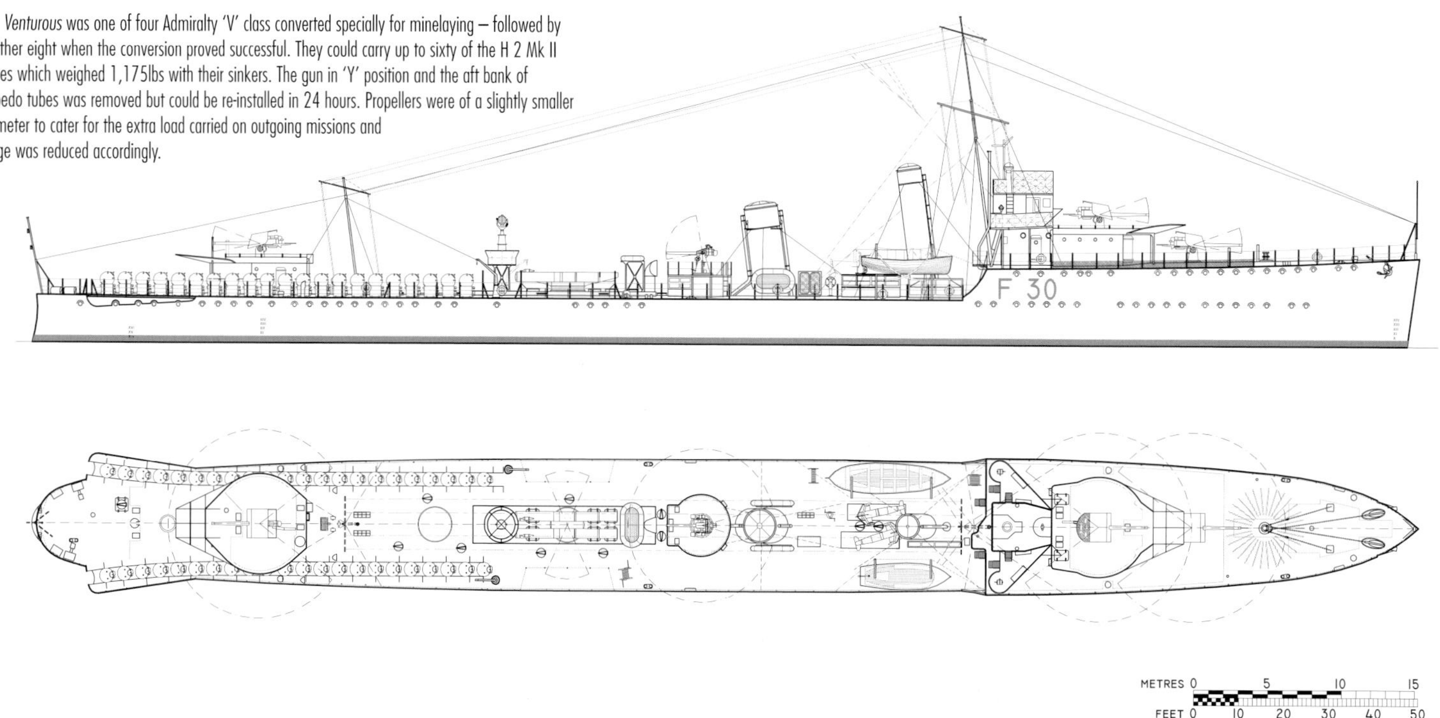

HMS *Venturous* was one of four Admiralty 'V' class converted specially for minelaying – followed by another eight when the conversion proved successful. They could carry up to sixty of the H 2 Mk II mines which weighed 1,175lbs with their sinkers. The gun in 'Y' position and the aft bank of torpedo tubes was removed but could be re-installed in 24 hours. Propellers were of a slightly smaller diameter to cater for the extra load carried on outgoing missions and range was reduced accordingly.

despite less oil and reduced radius of action. As with the conversions of HMS *Abdiel* and HMS *Gabriel* of the *Marksman* class leaders, canvas screens were suspended with silhouettes of the normal gun and torpedo dispositions painted on them to cover the rows of mines that extended from close to the stern forward to the searchlight tower. The only photographs I was able to find were of HMS *Venturous* and while not particularly good, one doubts that they would actually fool anyone except from a great distance – but perhaps that was all that was intended.

HMS *Venturous*, the minelayer version of the Admiralty 'V' class. Note the screens aft with painted silhouette of the missing 4in gun.

ADMIRALTY 'V' CLASS SPECIFICATIONS

Displacement	1,090 tons (standard)
LOA	312ft 0in
Beam	29ft 6in
Draft	10ft 9in (load) 11ft 7½in (deep)
Propulsion	3 boilers, oil-fired, 2 shafts, geared turbines
SHP	27,000
Speed	34 knots
Guns	4 x QF 4in Mk IV on CP.II mountings, 1 x QF 3in 20 cwt HA Mk III
TT	4 x 21in (2 x 2)

THE THORNYCROFT 'V' CLASS
(2 SHIPS)

If Edgar J. March was offhand about the V class's origins, he was positively taciturn about Thornycroft's contribution, limiting it to two sentences which give no satisfactory explanation of an important aspect of the overall story.[16]

The twenty-one orders placed on 30 June 1916 were extended by another four by the end of August, two of which went to Thornycroft's. I will quote directly from Raven and Roberts here because they sum up the situation well lest I be seen to have a bias towards Thornycroft's:

> The firm had a penchant for advancing new designs and ideas, occasionally to the Admiralty's annoyance. However, because of the general excellence of their destroyers, they were sometimes allowed to proceed their own way. The Admiralty considered that the end results were, in the long term, valuable for the overall development of destroyers, and the oft-experienced delays in the production of Thornycroft vessels was 'tolerated'.[17]

Thornycroft's response was typically non-standard: the nominal 30,000 SHP machinery from *Taurus*/*Teazer*-Thornycroft Admiralty 'R' class 'Specials' (which had achieved 40.44 knots – see Chapter 3) and boilers from their *Shakespeare* class leaders (see below), contained in a hull made necessarily wider – by 1ft 2½in – and with generally fuller lines and characteristically more freeboard. Friedman says they were 9ft deeper but this may refer to the depth (main deck to keel) and hence the freeboard and not the draught as I could find no reference to suggest this was different to the standard 'V' class.[18] The Thornycroft destroyers had two funnels of similar height and width, flat sided as usual with minimalistic caps as distinct from the tall and skinny fore funnel and short squat aft funnel that so readily marked the 'V' class.

In all other respects, the Thornycroft 'V' class were identical except for performance and here is where the extra 3,000 SHP came into play. According to March, *Viscount* achieved 37.9 knots on the shallow St Catherine's course.[19] This is significant that the

HMS *Vancouver* showing the minelaying rails at the stern. (Public domain)

term 'shallow' can results in slower speeds due to the unusual effect of friction generated by the hull passing through the water being transmitted down to the sea bottom and back to the ship. This is not present in deep water.

THORNYCROFT 'V' CLASS SPECIFICATIONS	
Displacement	1,120 tons (standard)
LOA	312ft 0in
Beam	30ft 8½in
Draft	10ft 9in (mean)
Propulsion	3 boilers, oil-fired, 2 shafts, geared turbines
SHP	30,000
Speed	37 knots
Guns	4 x QF 4in Mk IV, 2 x QF 2-pounder Mk II
TT	4 x 21in (2 x 2)

HMS *VISCOUNT*: THORNYCROFT 'V' CLASS 1918

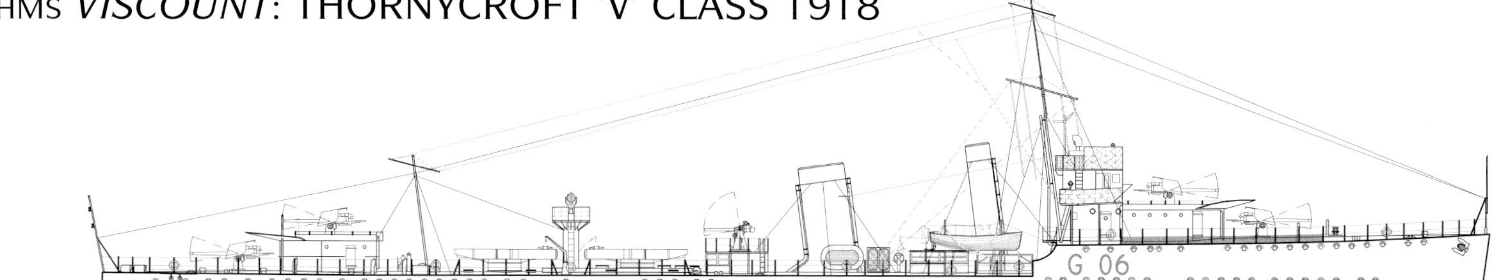

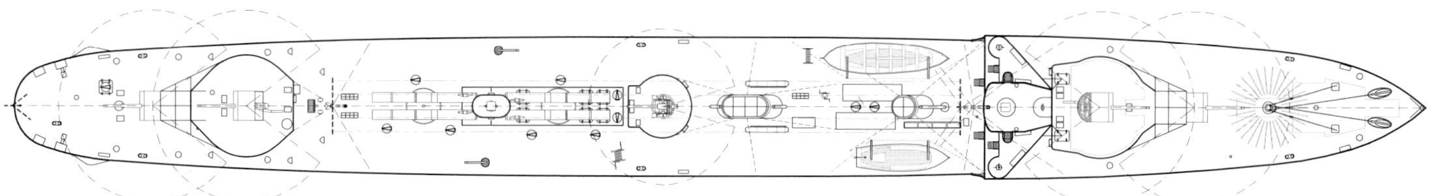

Thornycroft's produced two of their own versions of the 'V' class – HMS *Viceroy* and HMS *Viscount*. As usual, they were quite distinctive in the Thornycroft manner in having more freeboard, wider beam and the trademark flat-sided, taller funnels of equal height. The aft end of the bridge was curved and the QF 3in HA was mounted slightly further aft where it had a better firing arcs.

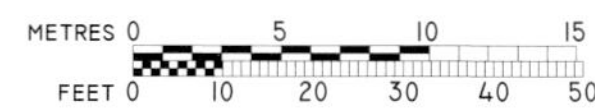

THE ADMIRALTY 'W' CLASS AND 'REPEAT V' CLASS (19 SHIPS)

As I indicated earlier, the production of destroyers takes time and a new design may look good on paper but there's a certain amount of crossing of fingers, hoping that decisions made are the right ones. Sometimes they're not. An instance of this is the Group I 'Hunt' class escort destroyer of 1939 where a serious blunder was made and vital stability calculations were not checked. When the first one was launched she was found to be exceedingly tender. One of her three twin 4in mounts had to be removed plus other modifications were made to all twenty-three of the group. Sister-ships still building were 'kippered' – widened – by 2ft 6in and the original armament – a vital part of their anti-aircraft role – was re-instated. Nevertheless, this sort of potential problem of introducing new untested designs at a time of conflict did not dissuade the First Sea Lord from seeking a faster destroyer design – around 37 knots – armed like the 'V' class but with two triple torpedo tubes. Quite where the pressure for the extra speed was coming from, I was unable to establish. One would have thought that the difference between 34 and 37 knots was not operationally critical considering the measures needed to achieve it. Were three knots of extra speed the difference between destroyers succeeding or failing? At the very least this extra speed would have required 30,000 and possibly 36,000 SHP and turbines to suit and while the DNC shared the same views and produced a design accordingly, it was clear that the delays in producing the propulsive equipment – boilers and turbines – would be unacceptable. An alternative, using the existing

HMS *VOYAGER*: 'REPEAT V' CLASS 1918

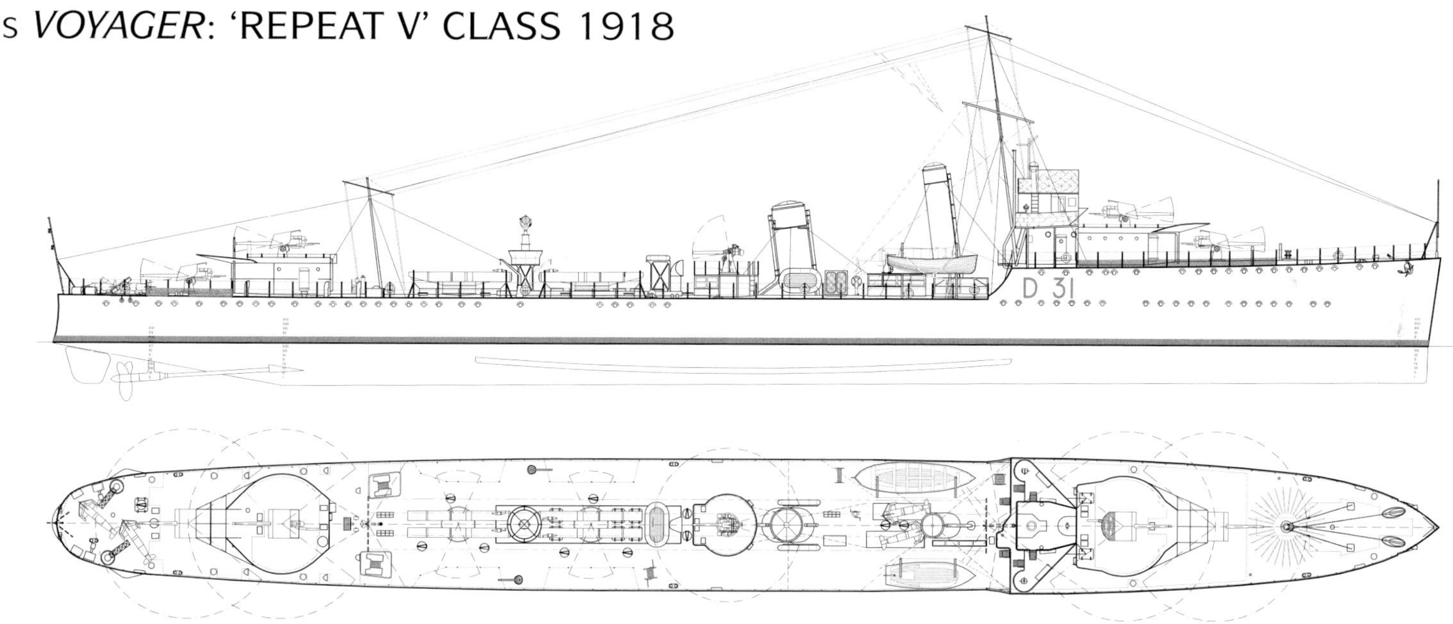

HMS *Voyager* was an Admiralty 'W' or 'Repeat V' class – she was the only one of nineteen beginning with 'V' so always appeared first in any list. She is drawn from the Australian Department of Defence Drawing #a 015521 drawn as late as 28 June 1989. *Voyager* was transferred to the Royal Australian Navy in 1933 and became part of the 'Scrap Iron Flotilla' made famous by Nazi Propaganda Minister Joseph Goebbels for its actions in the Mediterranean in 1940–1. Note that she is shown as commissioned in June 1918 complete with Two Speed Destroyer Sweep (TSDS) equipment including winches abeam the mainmast and special luffing davits with Oropesa floats on the quarterdeck.

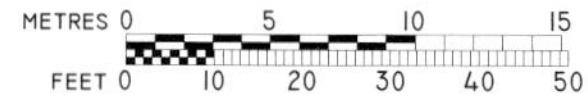

HMAS *Waterhen*, 'The Chook' as she was affectionately known. (State Library of Victoria)

27,000 SHP equipment in production but in the smaller 275ft hull fitted with one twin 4in gun forward and three single mountings – including one on a bridge over the aftmost torpedo tubes – had been proposed by the ever-progressive Thornycroft's. However, development of the new gun would also result in delays.

This conundrum was solved, logically it would seem, in two ways. When the next batch of orders for twenty-one destroyers was approved as the Tenth Order on 9 December 1916, nineteen of these were to be repeat 'V' class and two were to be Thornycrofts, which were to be Thornycroft 'Repeat V' class – see below. Curiously, they were all given names beginning with 'W' – except *Voyager* – hence the start of the 'W' in the 'V & W' class.[20] These relatively meagre numbers were topped up by the Eleventh and Twelfth Orders in April 1917 for sixty-nine of the faster, less well-armed but nevertheless capable repeats of the 'R' class – the 'S' class (see Chapter 3).

In February 1917 the Admiralty 'W' and 'Repeat V' class contracts were varied to provide for the fitting of the triple torpedo tubes which had been tested and approved – the third tube being above rather than alongside the other two tubes. Unexpectedly, the whole mounting was lighter than the twin tube mounting it replaced. Quite how the higher centre tube was reloaded is unknown. Also, the mainmast was made taller but by exactly how much or for what reason is also unknown.

Five ships (*Walker*, *Walrus*, *Warwick*, *Watchman* and *Whirlwind*) were selected for the same minelaying role as the eight from the previous class. By converting a total of thirteen destroyers, the Admiralty's foresight played a significant role in combatting the increasing U-boat threat by laying mines in transit areas.[21]

ADMIRALTY 'W' CLASS AND 'REPEAT V' CLASS SPECIFICATIONS

Displacement	1,090 tons (standard)
LOA	312ft 0in
Beam	29ft 6in
Draft	10ft 9in (load), 11ft 7½in (deep)
Propulsion	3 boilers, oil-fired, 2 shafts, geared turbines
SHP	27,000
Speed	34 knots
Guns	4 x QF 4in Mk IV on CP.II mountings, 1 x QF 3in 20 cwt HA Mk III
TT	6 x 21in (2 x 3)

HMS *Woolston*, one of two Thornycroft 'Repeat V' class. (naval-history.net)

THE THORNYCROFT 'REPEAT V' CLASS (2 SHIPS)

The two orders awarded to Thornycroft were repeats of their previous two orders but fitted, as the above nineteen, with triple torpedo tubes.

THORNYCROFT 'REPEAT V' CLASS SPECIFICATIONS	
Displacement	1,120 tons (standard)
LOA	312ft 0in
Beam	30ft 8½in
Draft	10ft 9in (mean)
Propulsion	3 boilers, oil-fired, 2 shafts, geared turbines
SHP	30,000
Speed	37 knots
Guns	4 x QF 4in Mk IV, 2 x QF 2-pounder Mk II

THE ADMIRALTY 'MODIFIED W' CLASS (1st GROUP – 7 SHIPS)

Once again, the 'tail wags dog' situation prevailed and the Admiralty was reacting rather than proactive in responding to perception rather than reality and the next change to the 'V & W' destroyers was a further upgrade in armament to counter a rumoured threat that the German destroyers were again being up-gunned to heavier weapons. The conundrum was basic: was it better to have the existing faster-firing (10–15rpm) but less hard-hitting (31–35lb) QF 4in Mk V guns or opt for a slower-firing (5–6 rpm) but harder-hitting (50lb) breech-loading type gun with its separate charge and projectile? That conundrum was made more difficult to consider given the lively platform offered by a destroyer in a seaway and/or violently manoeuvring in action with a very basic fire-control system anyway, relying principally on the skill of the individual gunlayers and trainers prior to the British Destroyer Director Firing System which was introduced late in 1918 (see Chapter 12). There were two distinct schools of thought, especially since actions rarely took place at the sort of maximum ranges of which the respective guns were theoretically capable – that is, at maximum elevation. The Director of Naval Ordnance was of the school favouring the QF gun and proposed increasing the elevation to 35° to increase range.[22] The alternative, larger gun in question was an adaptation of the Army's proven 4.7in and was already in use in the big *Shakespeare* class leaders (see Chapter 7). They would require more space to man, would require a bigger gun and ammunition-handling crew, they weighed considerably more and required other modifications such as a slightly taller bridge so that the wheelhouse could see over the taller mount – which would also have to be enlarged for the 9ft rangefinder. Could the hull sustain the extra 29 tons?[23]

The Thirteenth Order (First Group) of January 1918 settled the issue with the order of sixteen 'Repeat W' class and in April the Fourteenth Order (Second Group) was for a further thirty-eight. However, the Armistice saw seven of the January order and thirty-one of the April order cancelled resulting in a total of sixteen of which two were Thornycroft-built (see below).

Three modifications to simplify construction were introduced: the concave stern was scrapped in favour of a simplified straight

HMS *Venomous*. (Public domain)

stern and the shape of the rudder was modified.[24] The hull lines were altered slightly, presumably to simplify construction and reduce building time.[25] Funnel caps were heavier, the wheelhouse and bridge higher (as mentioned earlier) but in all other respects they resembled their predecessors. Unusually though, while bearing the 'W' nomenclature, three ships' names stared with 'V'. Seven ships were built and seven orders cancelled between April and September 1919.

There seems to be some ambiguity about the secondary armament in that some sources quote two QF 2-pounders replacing the QF 3in 20 cwt HA/LA and others state some had one or the other.

ADMIRALTY 'MODIFIED W' CLASS (1st GROUP) SPECIFICATIONS

Displacement	1,112 tons (standard), 1,505 tons (deep load)
LOA	312ft 0in
Beam	30ft 8½in
Draft	10ft 9in (mean)
Propulsion	3 boilers, oil-fired, 2 shafts, geared turbines
SHP	27,000
Speed	34 knots
Guns	4 x BL 4in Mk I on CP.VI* mountings, 2 x QF 2-pounder Mk II
TT	6 x 21in (2 x 3)

ADMIRALTY 'MODIFIED W' CLASS 1ST GROUP 1919

The seven destroyers of the 1st group of Admiralty 'Modified W' class introduced the heavier-hitting, but slower-firing BL 4.7in Mk I gun which became the standard destroyer main gun from then on. While visually similar to the previous classes – Thornycroft-built ships excepted – there were subtle differences. It was a testament to the excellence of the basic design that the heavier guns (in weight and the load they imposed when they discharged) could be mounted without any detriment to stability or structure. None saw action in the First World War, the first not being completed until June 1919.

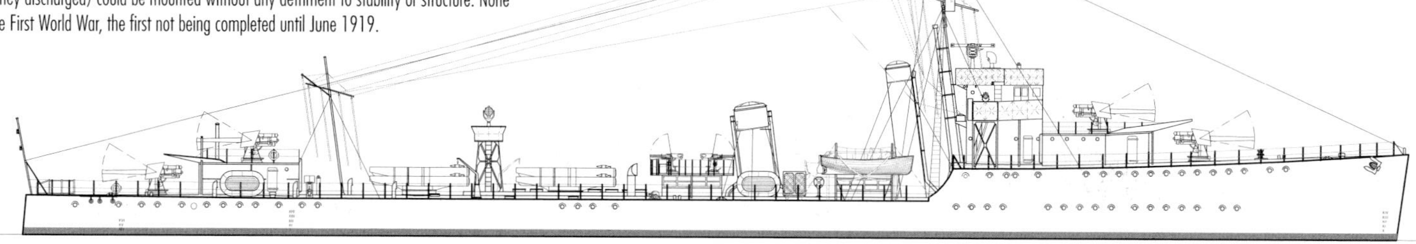

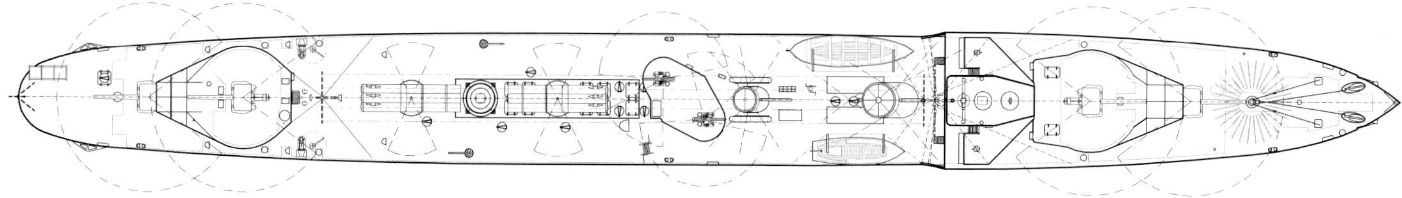

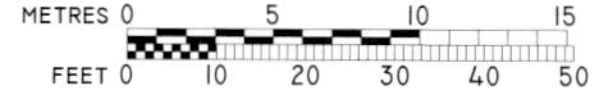

HMS *Veteran* – seemingly a contradiction in having a name starting with 'V', *Veteran* belonged to the 'Modified W' class (2nd Group). Her D 72 pendant number applied from November 1919 to 1940 so it is difficult to date these photographs. However, she appears to be very much as completed. Note the larger fore-funnel due to the different boiler arrangement. (Seaforth)

VETERAN
D72
D72
VETERAN

THE ADMIRALTY 'MODIFIED W' CLASS (2nd GROUP – 7 SHIPS)

A major change was effected in this basic repeat of the previous order in that the position of the boilers was reversed. That is, of the three-boiler arrangement whereby the single boiler was forward and was serviced by the tall and slender fore-funnel and the double boiler room was serviced by the squatter short aft funnel, these were shuffled about. This meant that the long boiler room was now adjacent to the engine room and thereby reduced capability to survive damage amidships.[26] The visual consequences were that the fore-funnel was the taller and thicker of the two but the practical consequences were that 'A' and 'B' guns and the bridge were brought further aft,[27] but by what distance is unknown. Scaling off March's drawings would indicate that 'A' gun was around 10ft further aft and since the frames were 20in apart then it would be logical to move the mounting ten frames. Similarly the bridge. Two QF 2-pounder Mk IIs were mounted *en echelon* between the

'V & W' CLASSES COMPARED

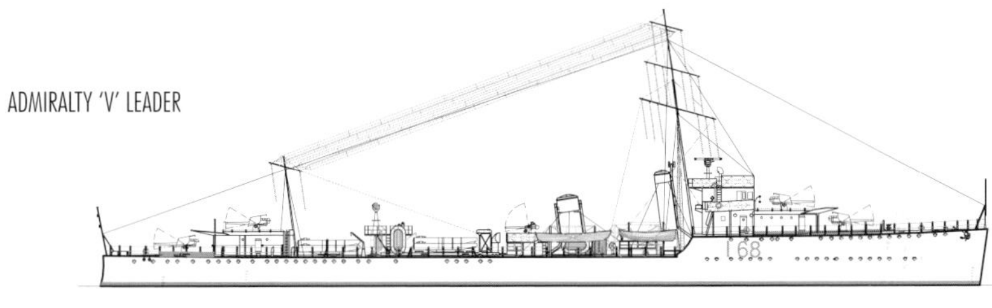

ADMIRALTY 'V' LEADER

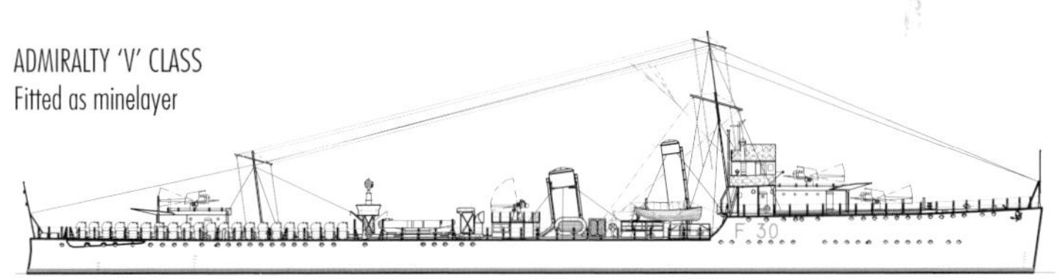

ADMIRALTY 'V' CLASS
Fitted as minelayer

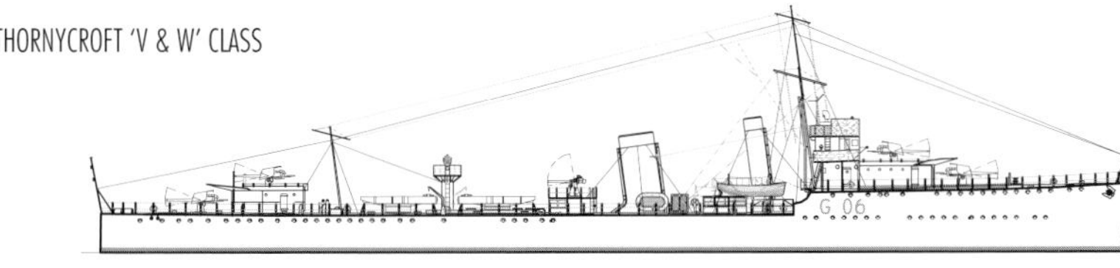

THORNYCROFT 'V & W' CLASS

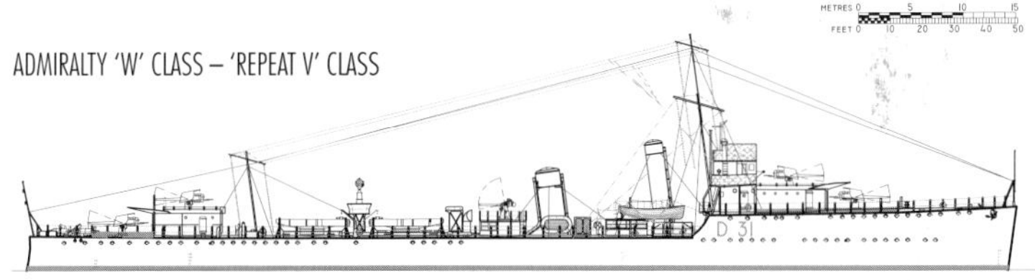

ADMIRALTY 'W' CLASS – 'REPEAT V' CLASS

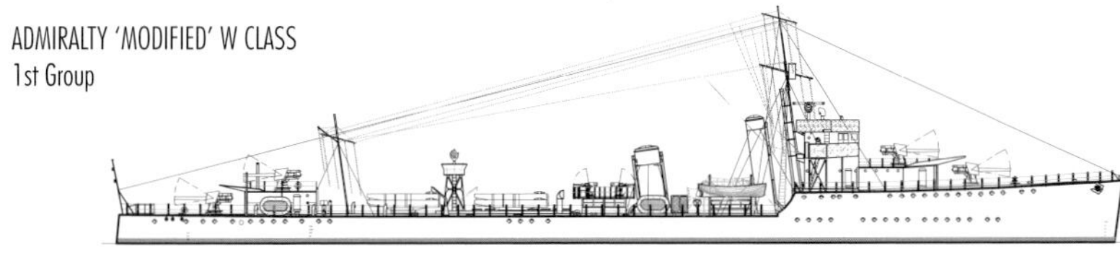
ADMIRALTY 'MODIFIED' W CLASS
1st Group

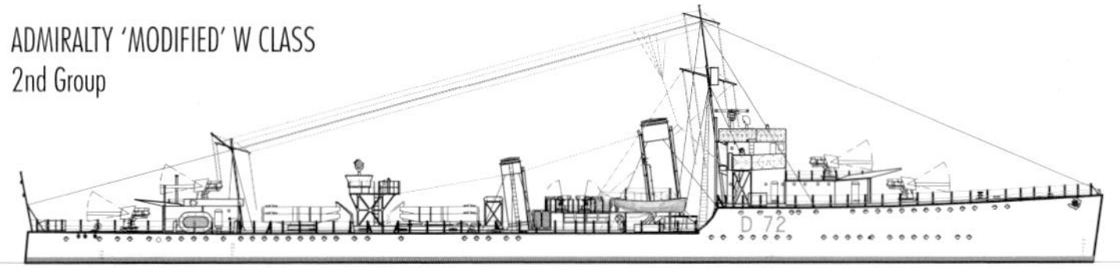

ADMIRALTY 'MODIFIED' W CLASS
2nd Group

HMS *Wishart* at anchor with a steam picket boat preparing a gunnery target. (vandwdestroyerassociation.org.uk)

funnels above the boiler air intakes. Another recognition feature, common to both groups, is the BL 4.7in Mk 1 had no prominent loading tray like the QF 4in Mk V.

The same quirky naming procedure – or rather lack of procedure just to confuse things – pertained with one ship receiving a name starting with 'V'. Seven ships were built and thirty-one orders were cancelled between November 1918 and September 1919.

ADMIRALTY 'MODIFIED W' CLASS (2nd GROUP) SPECIFICATIONS

Displacement	1,120 tons (standard)
LOA	312ft 0in
Beam	30ft 8½in
Draft	10ft 9in (mean)
Propulsion	3 boilers, oil-fired, 2 shafts, geared turbines
SHP	27,000
Speed	34 knots
Guns	4 x BL 4in Mk I on CP.VI* mountings, 2 x QF 2-pounder Mk II
TT	6 x 21in (2 x 3)

THE THORNYCROFT 'MODIFIED W' CLASS (2 SHIPS)

The order for the two Thornycroft ships was part of the Thirteenth Order of January 1918 but is dealt with separately because, as per usual, these were unusual and are, in effect, sub-types.

The Thornycroft boiler arrangement presaged the Group 2 'Modified W' class – basically it was their initiative. They had more freeboard – amount unknown – and retained the taller, flats-sided trademark funnels with no readily apparent funnel caps. As Preston so rightly says: 'they were the best looking of the "V & W" classes'.[28]

THORNYCROFT 'MODIFIED W' CLASS SPECIFICATIONS

Displacement	1,140 tons (standard)
LOA	312ft 0in
Beam	30ft 7in
Draft	10ft 11in (standard)
Propulsion	3 boilers, oil-fired, 2 shafts, geared turbines
SHP	30,000
Speed	35 knots
Guns	4 x BL 4in Mk I on CP.VI* mountings, 2 x QF 2-pounder Mk II
TT	6 x 21in (2 x 3)

7: The big leaders

To purists, it might seem inappropriate to include a chapter on the big leaders – the *Shakespeare* and *Scott* classes – but, like Antony Preston in his book, I feel that the reasoning in his Introduction was correct – that is, to include them because '*Shakespeare* was a Thornycroft design to meet the original 1916 requirement for a destroyer leader, and with the very similar *Scott* type shared a common ancestry with the "V" boats'.[1]

So, perhaps chronologically speaking, these should have been dealt with as Preston dealt with them but, in this respect, I have to disagree. Perhaps he wasn't a Virgo like me. I chose to follow the family tree that led from the 'V' class leader through to the last of the Admiralty 'Modified W' class in the previous chapter rather than be diverted from what were, in effect, two shoots that sprouted next to the same proverbial tree.

HMS *Keppel* of the *Shakespeare* class leaders. Note the extra 4.7in mounting between the funnels which marked the flotilla leaders. Also, the 3in anti-aircraft mounting aft of the second funnel. (Public domain)

THE *SHAKESPEARE* CLASS LEADERS (5 SHIPS)

These were a Thornycroft initiative. You have to hand it to that company; not only did their ships have style but they thought outside the box. Everywhere I researched, I found that the Thornycroft name was at the forefront of innovation, never frightened to try something new, to experiment, to explore new and better ways of doing things. Their Group IV 'Hunt' class escort destroyer of 1940 introduced features that did not initially meet with approval (funny about that) such as a long shelter deck which later became a feature of all frigates, a squarer midships section to reduce rolling, a distinct flare via a very pronounced knuckle in the bow which continued well aft, a pear-shaped funnel with dividing plates to reduce gases, a wooden fender, and a new bridge design to mention a few. Unfortunately, only two were built.

And so it was with the *Shakespeare* class. The Admiralty didn't knock on Thornycroft's doors, Thornycroft knocked on the Admiralty's doors – at an opportune time when the Admiralty was considering a design for a new five-gun leader with 4.7in guns (as distinct from the 'V' leader with four 4in guns). Thornycroft submitted several designs early in 1916. In April 1916 the DNC compared them with the largely *Kempenfelt* class-based Admiralty design, reported on them and rejected all but one and the Board approved a provisional order for two ships for which Thornycroft's had to submit a revised design to comply with the Board's

SCOTT CLASS LEADER, HMAS *STUART* 1939

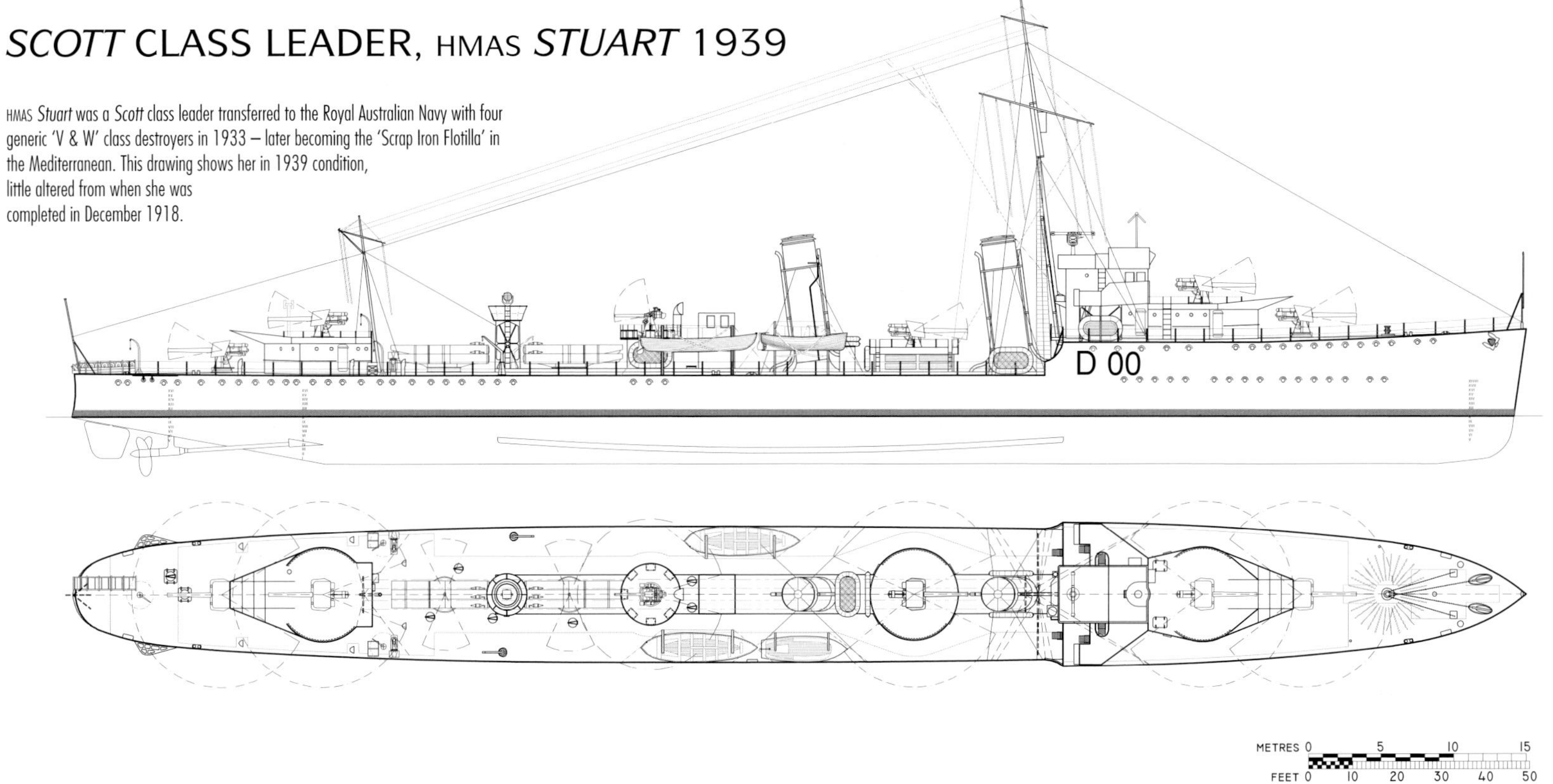

HMAS *Stuart* was a *Scott* class leader transferred to the Royal Australian Navy with four generic 'V & W' class destroyers in 1933 – later becoming the 'Scrap Iron Flotilla' in the Mediterranean. This drawing shows her in 1939 condition, little altered from when she was completed in December 1918.

requirements within the month.[2] Thornycroft's duly complied with a conventional design with two 4.7in guns superfiring forward, two aft and one between the two funnels, eleven cabins, captain's accommodation and the bridge 82ft 0in from the stem.[3] Two propulsion alternatives were submitted: either 40,000 or 44,000 SHP but the former was chosen together with a system of penalties for failing to reach specified speeds, draughts, freeboards or metacentric heights. These were not unusual. As it turned out, orders were completed well ahead of time and no penalties were payable.

Although the first two provisional orders were confirmed in 1916, they were accommodated under the November 1915 and April 1916 Programmes,[4] a third was ordered in April 1917, and four more in March 1918 of which two were cancelled.[5] The two cancelled orders were to have been Thornycroft-designed ships built by Cammell Laird – the first time such an arrangement had ever been considered. However, according to Preston, the contracts were cancelled because it was felt that 'Cammell Laird might not have been able to achieve the spectacular savings in weight which were a feature of all Thornycroft designs, when working with unfamiliar types'.[6] Due to these time delays only the name-ship of the class was completed before the end of the war.

***SHAKESPEARE* CLASS SPECIFICATIONS**

Displacement	1,554 tons (standard)
LOA	329ft 0in
Beam	31ft 6in
Draft	12ft 4in (mean)
Propulsion	4 boilers, oil-fired, 2 shafts, geared turbines
SHP	40,000
Speed	36 knots
Guns	5 x BL 4.7in Mk I on CP.VI mountings, 1 x QF 3in 20 cwt HA Mk III, 2 x QF 2-pounder Mk II*
TT	6 x 21in (2 x 3)

Notes

* The 3in replaced the 2 x 2-pounders but some sources state that the 2-pounders were fitted on the upper deck near the after superstructure.[7]

Refer to Appendix L for class details.

THE ADMIRALTY OR *SCOTT* CLASS LEADERS (8 SHIPS)

Unfortunately, my reliable authority, Norman Friedman, does not have a lot to say about this class so I have to rely on March as my authority and I also found it a difficult to establish many facts here.

Clearly the first *Shakespeare* class – *Shakespeare* and *Spenser* – were laid down (2 October and 9 October 1916 respectively) before any *Scott* class (19 February 1917). Reading March's five small paragraphs on the subject there seems to have been an extraordinary strung-out process of getting the *Scott* class from the point in early 1916 when the Commander-in-Chief asked for a more powerful leader than the *Lightfoot* class to handle severe weather conditions to the point where, in July 1916, Board approval was given to a provisional order (*Scott*) from Cammell Laird based on sketch designs and a legend subject to alterations and the Board approved drawings and repeat orders were placed for *Bruce* and *Douglas* on 12 December 1916.[8]

Four of the eight were completed before the end of the war.

ADMIRALTY – *SCOTT* CLASS SPECIFICATIONS

Displacement	1,530 tons (standard)
LOA	332ft 6in
Beam	31ft 9in
Draft	12ft 0in max
Propulsion	4 boilers, oil-fired, 2 shafts, geared turbines
SHP	40,000
Speed	36.5 knots
Guns	5 x BL 4.7in Mk I on CP.VI mountings, 1 x QF 3in 20 cwt HA Mk III, 2 x QF 2-pounder Mk II*
TT	6 x 21in (2 x 3)

Notes

* The 3in replaced the 2 x 2-pounders but some sources state that the 2-pounders were fitted adjacent to the 3in – at least in *Malcolm*[9] or on the upper deck near the after superstructure.[10]

Refer to Appendix L for class details

8: The First World War and the Baltic Campaign, 1918–1919

There's an old saying that you can't judge a book by its cover and that could apply to the 'V & W' class destroyers. What looked good on paper – that ideal combination of superfiring guns on a seaworthy hull with adequate range and speed – had to prove itself in the rough-and-tumble of the world it was designed for, and even that world had changed in the interim: submarines and mines were now a greater threat than when the draftsmen first put pencil to paper for the 'V' class leaders.

According to Preston, by late summer of 1917 – say end September because *Vampire* was the last completed on the 22nd of that month – all of the five leaders were heading up flotillas.[1] He does not state what class of destroyer they would have been leading or in what locations but most probably 'M' class if based in the North and 'R' class if based in the South. Indeed, he refers to *Valkyrie* operating out of Harwich with 'R' class ships and it was on a mission to escort a 'Beef Run' convoy back from Holland on the night of 22 December 1917 when she and three consorts strayed into a minefield. *Valkyrie* limped home under tow by HMS *Sylph* with considerable damage but was repaired. *Torrent*, *Tornado* and *Surprise* were all lost.

HMS *Warwick* was another mine victim on 10 May 1918 and despite having her back broken was towed back to Dover by her sister-ship *Velox*, repaired and lived to fight another day. Perhaps the damage to *Valkyrie* and *Warwick*, extreme as both were, speaks volumes as to the inherent strength of these ships and the overall soundness of their construction.

The minelaying capabilities of the 'V & Ws' so converted were put to use and the 20th Flotilla operated out of Immingham on the Humber River. Runs were made into German waters at high tide to reduce the risk of both enemy and friendly mines and the mines – both the 'H' type contact mine and the newer magnetic sinker mine – were laid in a herringbone pattern, twenty to a leg at between 15 and 20 knots. As you sow, so shall you reap and *Vehement* was the only 'V & W' lost during the First World War when she struck a German mine on 2 August 1918. Everything forward of the funnels disappeared with the detonation of the forward magazine. The wreck was put under tow, but owas n fire, and as the stern was rising and the wind was freshening the order was given to sink her. As Preston states: 'The toughness of the "Vs" and "Ws" is demonstrated by the fact that the *Telemachus* fired a number of 4in shells at her waterline without any apparent effect: finally the *Vehement* was despatched by a brace of shallow-set depth charges dropped a few feet away.'[2]

While one flotilla, the 13th, was based at Harwich and was an all-'V & W' affair – but with new leaders – the 6th was at Dover and three others (11th, 12th and 14th) were based at Scapa Flow. It was from here that the second use to which the 'V & Ws' were put to a use that was only barely envisaged when their design was being formulated as flotilla leaders: that of anti-submarine patrols.

The U-boat threat had been underestimated by the Admiralty and defensive measures were both primitive and ineffective. Explosive sweeps – essentially cables with explosives attached, towed behind a ship and kept at a required depth by floats or paravanes – were tried but these relied on making contact with a submerged submarine; an unlikely event and more danger to the towing vessel than they were worth. An effective depth charge was not introduced in any numbers until 1917 (the D-type) and a primitive listening device, the hydrophone, followed. These relied on the ship being stationary for best result – a risky procedure. The easiest way to drop a depth charge was to simply roll one off the stern of the ship. Various type of depth-charge throwers were invented including some fearsome but ineffective howitzers. But, it was the ever-inventive Thornycroft that came up with a workable solution that threw a charge 120ft – well clear of the side of the ship – providing the potential for a wider pattern than simply a trail of charges left in the wake of the ship. They delivered the first one in July 1917 and ended up making 3,010 of them. A cartridge from the then-in-use QF 2-pounder Mk II was used to propel the 300lb depth charge which sat on an arbour inside the wide barrel of the thrower.

The supply of depth charges was limited and it may be that even the 'V & Ws' only received four – certainly drawings indicate this. Two could be released hydraulically from the bridge and two had to be released manually. Which of the destroyers received Thornycroft throwers or hydrophones is not known. According to Preston, however, HMS *Vanessa* sank *UB 107* with depth charges on 27 July 1918 off Scarborough, Yorkshire. The submarine had been sighted earlier by the trawler *Calvia* and after it dived was detected by *Vanessa*'s hydrophone and sunk.[3] This is debated by the enthusiasts of uboat.net who have access to German records. According to them:

> **UB 107: 4 Aug 1918** – Sunk by unknown cause one mile north of Flamborough Head at position 54 08N, 00 00W, between July 28 and August 3, 1918. 38 dead (all hands lost). *UB 107* was, however, the only U-boat that could have been responsible for the sinking of the steamers *Chloris* and *John Rettig* two and a half hours later at position 53 52N, 0010E. Divers in recent years discovered the wreck of *UB 107*, which was identified by markings on the propellers, off Flamborough Head together with (under) what remains of the steamer *Malvina*. The *Malvina* was torpedoed and sunk by *UB 104* on August 3, 1918. *UB 107* apparently either suffered an accident of some sort or was lost on a British mine.[4]

No sooner was the Armistice signed on 11 November 1918 and the surrender of the High Seas Fleet accepted than the nine destroyers of the 13th Flotilla were called away to support the newly-independent Estonian, Lithuanian and Latvian governments against the Bolshevik revolutionary forces – Operation 'Red Trek' – following the collapse of the Czarist regime in October-November 1917. The Treaty of Brest-Litovsk of March 1918 had ceded the Baltic States to Germany and with the Armistice the Treaty was effectively terminated and these countries became independent. It was Britain's aim to protect its own interests and this involved the freedom of the seas since Britain had extensive trading routes to and from Baltic ports and because Lenin had declared the Baltic must become a Russian sea. Stopping the rise of the general rise of Bolshevism was also in Britain's interests. It is no exaggeration to say that the 'V & Ws' saw more real action in this conflict than they did in the First World War, as follows.

When the British force entered the Baltic – led by the light cruiser HMS *Cardiff* – they were entering a minefield, both euphemistically and literally. It was shallow, had navigational hazards, was poorly charted in places and was sown with both Russian and German minefields that were poorly recorded. The light cruiser HMS *Cassandra* promptly hit a mine near Osel (now Saaremaa), and her sister-ship *Calypso* hit a submerged wreck of Libau (now Liepaja). Not an auspicious start. Two wickets for no runs. But, that was about to change.

On 26 December, the Soviet destroyer *Spartak* (previously *Kapitan I ranga Miklucha Maklai* and one of the modified versions of the earlier *Novik* class) decided to shell Reval (now Tallinn). In what almost seems like something written in a Boy's Own Annual of the time, HMS *Wakeful* raised steam in only fifteen minutes to give chase to a fleeing *Spartak* that was so inexpertly operated that not only did she run over a shoal at high speed, she opened fire at *Wakeful* using her forward gun trained so far aft that it demolished the charthouse and part of the bridge before running up a white flag, whereupon the boarding crew from HMS *Vendetta* 'liberated' a quantity of jewellery and silverware ultimately landed at Port Edgar. The sinking ship was saved by the simple act of turning off the seacocks and starting the pumps. She was towed to Reval where she was handed over to the Estonians. To add insult to injury, the disposition of Soviet forces was ascertained by documents on board and *Vendetta* and *Vortigern* were able to obtain the surrender of the destroyer *Avtroil*.[5] Scores now even.

In June, *Vivacious* and *Voyager* exchanged fire with two Soviet

HMS *Westminster* alongside the 'C' class light cruiser HMS *Caradoc*.

destroyers without any results and a similar action took place when *Versatile*, *Vivacious* and *Walrus* chased away two destroyers. However, after some run-ins with Soviet submarines – an attack on the RN's *E-40*, a counter-attack by *Watchman*, *Vancouver* and *Valorous* in a similar counter-attack – *Vittoria* succumbed to a torpedo attack by the Soviet *Pantera* off Seskar Island on 31 August 1919, the same submarine believed to have been responsible for the unsuccessful attack on *E.40*. *Verulam* hit a mine, possibly a British one, off Stirs Point off the same Seskar Island on 4 September and suddenly, in the space of less than a week, two 'Vs' were gone. Fortunately, that was the last of their losses but not the last of the action, a lot of it naval gunfire support and counter-battery fire,

9: Their Design Heritage

When the First World War ended the Royal Navy had some 433 flotilla leaders and destroyers in commission.[1] The actual number depends on the sources used and the definition of what was actually in service as compared with what had been decommissioned either temporarily pending repairs or pending assessment as to future use. The definition of destroyer is also a factor as the smaller TBDs are sometimes counted by some sources. Despite contracts having been cancelled for forty-four destroyers and leaders, there were some sixty-three destroyers (and flotilla leaders) in various levels of construction from keels just laid down to almost complete. Again, numbers vary because records of precise dates are often missing or if available can vary between sources but I make these to be eight leaders, fourteen 'Modified W' class and forty-one 'S' class. When completed, this would bring the destroyer and leader fleet up to 496 units – the equivalent of fifty-five nine-ship flotillas – of which many had been built before the war and were, by reason of age and the sheer fact of obsolescence, well past their use-by date. A programme of wholesale scrapping was inevitable.

The first to go were, of course, the oldest or those deemed least useful by reason of general wear and tear or war damage. However, the last to go, strangely, seem to be some of the 'Repeat M' class as late as 1926 although most were scrapped in 1921. The first of the 'R' class were sold for scrapping in 1926 after a ten-year service life and 'S' class scrapping began in 1931.

However, this would not remove the problem of block obsolescence – that is, the simultaneous ageing of large blocks of military equipment in a short period of time requiring their replacement in a similar time frame. The United States Navy faced this problem when the large war-built programme of *Fletcher* and *Gearing* type destroyers would all become due for scrapping at about the same time. They spread this out via a FRAM I and II programme – the Fleet Rehabilitation and Modernisation programmes which saw the destroyers' lives extended and scrapping staggered as new replacements could be provided. What Britain needed was a staged, measured replacement programme to prevent the problems presented by block obsolescence. But that required money – and forethought – and both were lacking immediately after the end of the war.

In 1922 – when most of the pre-war destroyers had gone to the scrapyard – the DNC declared that the lifespan of a destroyer was 12 years and that any war service year would count as two years. If taken as gospel, and not a guideline, that meant that a replacement programme would need to be undertaken so that new destroyers would be coming into service in 10 years at the rate late-war-built destroyers were being scrapped. But, how many destroyers were needed in the future – especially now that the threat from Germany had been extinguished and that the League of Nations held the promise of a world at peace?

The Royal Navy's answer was unequivocal – sixteen flotillas of eight destroyers (two four-ship divisions) each with a flotilla leader; total 144 ships. These were to consist of seven flotillas of fleet destroyers, six of older escort destroyers and three of escort destroyers for coastal waters.[2] The fleet destroyers would be disposed in three flotillas each to the Atlantic and Mediterranean Fleets and one to the China Fleet. While that still left two surplus flotillas as the Royal Navy had 162 destroyers on hand at the time,[3] the problem of block obsolescence meant that a renewal programme was needed.

Accordingly, and despite the financial difficulties of the time – but perhaps spurred on by the decline in shipbuilding activity – the Board of the Admiralty's decision of 21 November 1923 to develop a prototype destroyer was approved by a new government elected in January 1924 and the 1924–5 Programme provided for not one but two new destroyers.

March states that 'five specialist firms, Denny Bros., Hawthorn Leslie, Thornycroft, White and Yarrow were invited to submit designs to fulfil Staff Requirements based on war experience and the progress made in marine engineering . . . the designs of

Thornycroft and Yarrow were accepted'.[4] Friedman says the bids from Denny, Hawthorn Leslie and White were rejected,[5] but others make no reference to any other than Thornycroft and Yarrow being part of the process, generally acknowledging these two shipbuilders as, rightfully, being the specialists in this field. For instance, Lenton and Colledge simply state that 'Wisely, the two foremost destroyer builders were selected – Thornycroft and Yarrow – and were given a free hand within broad Admiralty specifications to evolve a standard type. The Admiralty specified for vessels similar to the most recent design available (Thornycroft's "Modified W" class).'[6]

The November 1923 invitation to bid listed the principal criteria as:

- Length not to exceed 310ft (presumably LBP because both designs came close to this but their LOAs well exceeded it).
- Endurance to be 5,000 nautical miles at economical speed, using 85 per cent of oil capacity.
- No more than 0.75 tons per hour at 1,000 SHP.
- Trial speed should be 34 knots (Lenton says 35 knots[7]).

By way of general direction, the Admiralty supplied a general layout drawing.[8] There was no stipulation as to displacement or propulsion.

HMS *Ambuscade*. While a 'new' design from Yarrow in some ways, the 'V & W' heritage is quite clear in the general layout. (Public domain)

AMBUSCADE AND *AMAZON*

If one looks quickly a drawing of either of the winning bids one sees something very much like a Thornycroft 'Modified W' class of 1918. They both have the same distribution of the fundamental elements, a very similar freeboard, length of foredeck, rake to the masts, funnels – all the distinguishing features. There's nothing new, revolutionary or different. But, why should there be? What happened between 1918 and 1923 to require a change to the successful formula – that combination of ingredients – represented by the 'V & W' class? Indeed, if we look forward to the next sub-heading in this chapter, with the completion of the last of the 'I' class in August 1937, that same basic formula held good until then and it could be argued was only varied slightly in the 'Tribal' class which followed.

My drawing opposite shows the last of the 'V & Ws' – the

HMS *AMBUSCADE'S* SPECIFICATIONS[9]

Displacement	1,173 tons (standard), 1,585 tons deep
LOA	322ft 0in
LBP	307ft 0in
Beam	31ft 0in
Draft	8ft 7½in at half oil and 10ft 0in deep
Propulsion	2 Yarrow 4-drum boilers each supplying 12,000 SHP and one supplying 8,000 SHP, both at 290lbs/in^2, superheat 200° F, oil-fired, 2 shafts, Brown-Curtis single-reduction with Parson geared cruising turbines
SHP	35,500 @ 475 RPM
Speed (6-hour trial)	37.16 knots @ 452.2 RPM @ 1,338 tons displacement
Radius of Action	3,310nm @ 15 knots
Guns	4 x BL 4.7in Mk I on CP.VI mountings, 2 x QF 2-pounder Mk II
TT	6 x 21in (2 x 3)

ADMIRALTY 'MODIFIED W' CLASS 2ND GROUP, HMS *AMBUSCADE*, HMS *AMAZON* – COMPARISON DRAWING

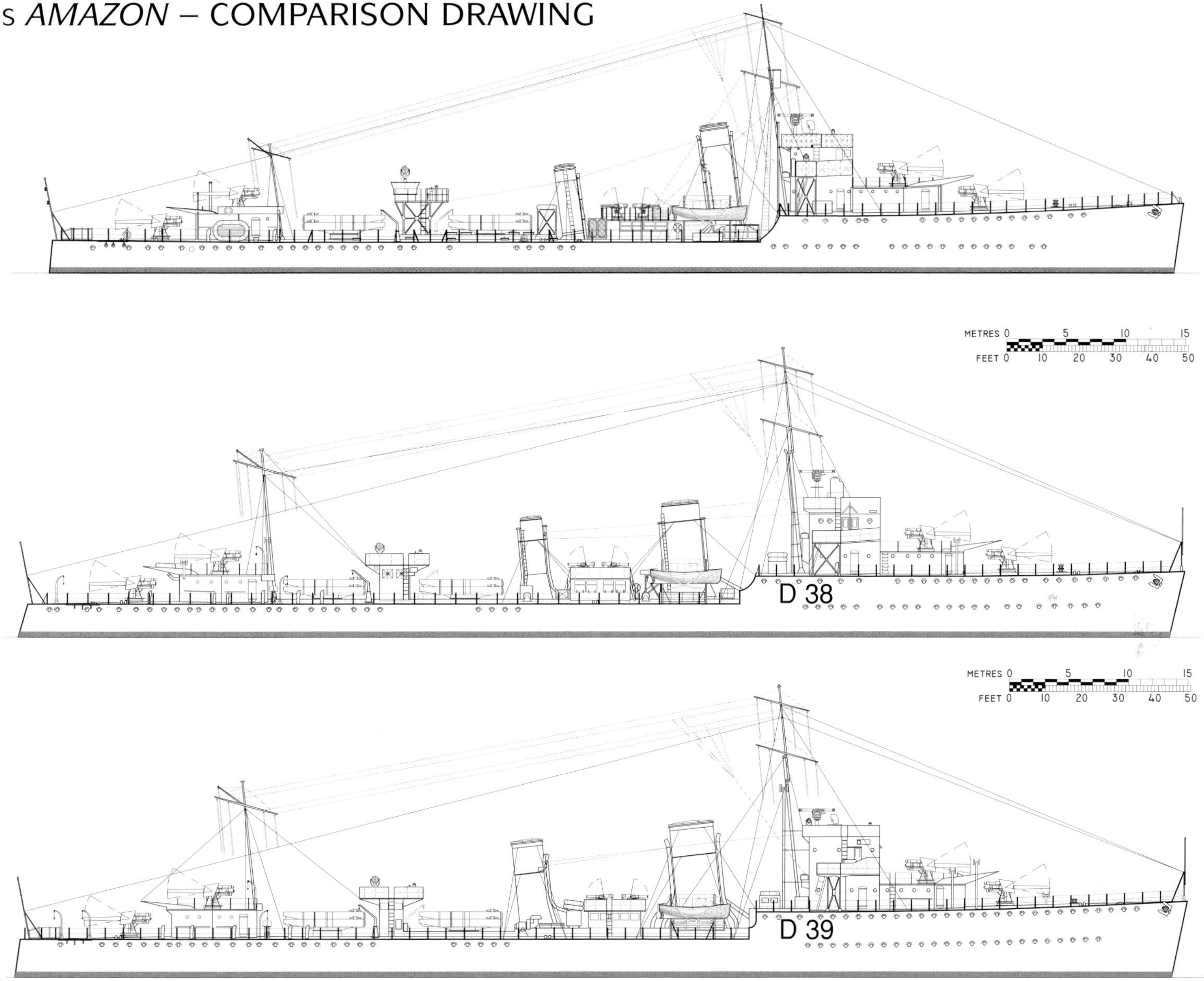

METRES 0 5 10 15
FEET 0 10 20 30 40 50

D 38

METRES 0 5 10 15
FEET 0 10 20 30 40 50

D 39

HMS *Ambuscade* showing the typical Yarrow stern to advantage. (Seaforth)

HMS *AMAZON'S* SPECIFICATIONS[10]

Displacement	1,352 tons (standard), 1,812 tons deep
LOA	323ft 0in
LBP	311ft 9in
Beam	31ft 6in
Draft	9ft 6in (half oil), 11ft 3in (deep)
Propulsion	3 Yarrow 3-drum boilers each supplying 14,000 SHP with two G-type superheaters per boiler all at 260lb/in^2, superheat 150° F, oil-fired, 2 shafts, Brown-Curtis single-reduction with Parson geared cruising turbines
SHP	42,000 @ 430 RPM
Speed (6-hour trial)	37.47 knots @ 445.7 RPM @ 1,519 tons displacement
Radius of Action	3,400nm @ 15 knots
Guns	4 x BL 4.7in Mk I on CP.VI mountings, 2 x QF 2-pounder Mk II
TT	6 x 21in (2 x 3)

Admiralty 'Modified W' class 2nd Group – compared with HMS *Ambuscade* and HMS *Amazon* in profile. Note that 'A' and 'B' mounts and the bridge are slightly further forward on *Ambuscade* and *Amazon* compared with the 'Modified W' class, yet there is a large space aft of their bridges. It was the fact of moving the armament and the bridge aft that was one of the design benefits of the 'V & Ws', yet Yarrow's and Thornycroft's both managed to come up with a design so similar in outward appearance that one could be forgiven for thinking that there was some sort of collusion between the two shipbuilders to produce designs so similar, so conservative, that the Admiralty would be unable to decide between the two and would give each shipbuilders suitable orders.

However, while both destroyers looked similar to each other and to their predecessors, there were some marked differences, particularly to the builders' approaches to the more technical aspects of the designs.

The first thing to note is the apparent discrepancy between the two speeds mentioned above – the 34-knot Admiralty requirement referred to by Friedman and the 35-knot one referred to by Lenton – and those actually achieved. This occurred because Yarrow, the providers of the boilers in both ships, upped the ante by offering the Admiralty 37 knots and Thornycroft had to follow suit, lengthening their design to suit.[11] Not unexpectedly, Yarrow's *Ambuscade* was lighter and shallower as was their wont. Similarly, Thornycroft's *Amazon* was beamier, deeper, heavier and needed more SHP. Nevertheless, *Amazon* was more economical up to 25 knots. *Ambuscade*, with its combination of two large boilers and one small boiler, could make 17 knots on just the small boiler and 22 knots on one large boiler, 27 knots on one of each and 30 knots on two large boilers.[12]

Some other changes or improvements to note were:

- New D steel with an Ultimate Tensile Strength of 37–44 tons/in^2 replaced High Tensile steel for important structural members.
- Deck-to-deck heights were increased and were never less than 8ft 0in.
- *Ambuscade* had electro-hydraulic steering (instead of steam-operated) which saved 1¾ tons and 10 per cent fuel consumption and created less vibration.
- Surgeon's cabin and sick bay provided for the first time.
- Recreation space.
- Bridges were all steel and much larger (too large in some eyes!) to accommodate a new fire-control table, a new type of director and platform for the Control Officer and Rate Keeper.[13]

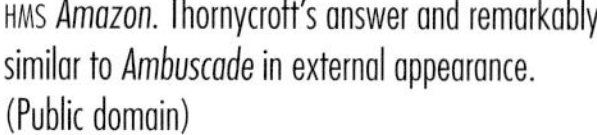
HMS *Amazon*. Thornycroft's answer and remarkably similar to *Ambuscade* in external appearance. (Public domain)

Others not so well received were:

- Heat in the engine room.
- Big, square bridge had adverse effects in head winds.
- No significant improvement in general habitability.

Ambuscade was paid off in 1937 after a succession of problems with her turbine machinery after 10 years' service with the Home Fleet

HMS *Amazon*, port quarter view. (Seaforth)

and in the Mediterranean. The replacement of the propulsion machinery was deferred until 1939 and on completion in 1940 her war service was interrupted by further machinery problems and she was relegated to non-operational use.

Still, they were prototypes, and, while their service in the Second World War was reduced to escort work and by 1943 *Ambuscade* was used only for anti-submarine training and as a test-bed for new ASW devices (see Chapter 11) and *Amazon* had been reduced to becoming an Air Target Vessel for the Fleet Air Arm in November 1943, they had served their purpose and had been instrumental in obtaining orders from foreign navies in the late 1920s and early 1930s.

The Royal Netherlands Navy ordered eight and the Portuguese Navy seven of the Yarrow-type design and the Colombian Navy ordered six of the Thornycroft type.[14]

ACASTAS TO *INTREPIDS*

So, what lessons were learnt and what improvements were passed on from these prototypes into the next batch of destroyers? Well, very little really. Demands were principally that range should be increased – in anticipation of action based from Singapore – requiring an extra 40 tons of oil to be accommodated, that quadruple torpedo tubes replace triple tubes, that the superfiring 'B' gun be capable of HA firing – in this case 60° elevation – that the remaining mounts have 40° elevation, that all guns have full shields, that the bridge be moved further aft and that ASDIC (then reaching development) be provided for, and two depth-charge throwers and four racks[15] plus TSDS (Two Speed Destroyer Sweep) to be fitted. March refers to four chutes for eight depth charges and I believe this to be correct and Lenton mistaken. First, 'rack' is a USN term and no RN destroyer has ever been fitted with four 'rails' – the equivalent of racks.[16] These increased displacement by 200 tons over *Ambuscade*.[17]

The 'A' of *Acasta* class that eventually followed – and not until the 1927 Programme – was the first of an annual replacement of one flotilla of eight destroyers plus one leader. The CP.XIII 60° gun did not materialise for a number of technical reasons. Also, it was found impractical to combine TSDS and anti-submarine activities in the one ship due to congestion on the quarterdeck, so the 'A' class was completed without ASDIC fitted, only three depth-charge chutes and no throwers. Thornycroft and Yarrow, as expected, pressed to use their own designs but the Admiralty – for once – remained adamant. They wanted a standard class, to their requirements, documented by them with just a little leeway for the tenderers via propulsion alternatives with which they were still

HMS *Acasta*. The funnel bands denote the destroyer's flotilla. (Photoship uk)

'A' CLASS SPECIFICATIONS[18]

Displacement	1,520 tons (standard), 1,765 tons (full load)
LOA	323ft 0in
LBP	312ft 0in
Beam	32ft 3in
Draft	10ft 0½in (standard) 12ft 2½in (full load)
Propulsion	3 Yarrow in two @ 275lb/in² @ 600° F, 3 Thornycroft in one @ 500lb/in² @ 750° F and remainder 3 Admiralty @ 300lb/in², oil-fired, 2 shafts, Brown-Curtis single-reduction in two and Parson Impulse Reaction in remainder.
SHP	34,000 @ 350 RPM
Speed (6-hour trial)	35–36.31 knots @ 354.7–366.7 RPM @ 1,381–1,785 tons displacement
Radius of Action	4,800nm @ 15 knots
Guns	4 x BL 4.7in Mk IX on CP.XIV mountings, 2 x QF 2-pounder Mk II
TT	8 x 21in (2 x 4 QR III)

prepared to be flexible, principally boiler pressures and temperatures and any saving in machinery weights. Compared with USN machinery, RN machinery was heavy and bulky, operating less efficiently at lower pressures and temperatures.

As Norman Freidman states: 'A hostile critic could say that nearly 200 tons had bought practically no advance in speed and no advance in armament except two extra torpedo tubes.'[19] There is some confusion as to what improvement, if any, was made to the auxiliary electrical generating capacity – an area where British warships were sadly lacking.

Next year's – 1928 – Programme 'B' or *Beagle* class was, essentially, a repeat of the 'A' class and leader but with the following differences: the TSDS was deleted in favour of ASDIC, two depth-charge throwers, one depth-charge rail and twenty-five depth charges.

The 1929 Programme introduced the 'C' or *Crusader* class which was only a half-flotilla – plus leader – as either an economy measure, or as a gesture due to the naval disarmament talks taking place at the time – perhaps a politically convenient amalgam of the two. The ships were slightly larger (329ft 0in LOA) and differently armed in that they re-introduced the QF 3in 12-pounder 12 cwt and moved the two QF 2-pounder Mk IIs to the bridge after end of the foredeck.[20] The class introduced a split bridge whereby the wheelhouse with compass platform over was separated from the chartroom which had the DCT and rangefinder above it. Quite where the impetus for this came from and what it achieved is unknown. All four were transferred to the Royal Canadian Navy in 1937–8.

The Treaty For The Limitation And Reduction Of Naval Armament of 1930 – most usually called the London Naval Treaty – determined 'standard displacement' and set a limit on the Royal Navy and United States Navy of 150,000 tons total for destroyers of which individual ships were restricted to 1,500 tons with the proviso that 16 per cent of that total tonnage could be used for destroyers known as leaders displacing up to 1,850 tons. Japan had a limit of 105,000 tons. The maximum gun size that could be carried was 130mm (5.1in) calibre. Germany and the Soviet Union were not parties to the Treaty. Naturally, Britain abided by the Treaty. I think a comment from Lenton is appropriate here: '. . . the United Kingdom was unrealistically bound by naval limitation treaties which sought to provide national security on the cheap. In adhering to a smaller design to achieve numerical sufficiency [and comply with the Treaty] the Royal Navy was on firm ground, but the policy became suspect when the overall result was both smaller *and* [my emphasis] fewer vessels.'[21] But, of course, this does pose questions. If there had been no treaty, would the destroyer design have changed? Would they have become larger to take advantage of the de-restriction? Was there any need? On the face of it, it would appear that the Royal Navy was more than happy with the size and type of destroyer with which they were being supplied.

The 'D' or *Defender* class of the 1930 Programme was nine destroyers because this time the flotilla leader was not a 'special' as before but one was fitted specifically as a leader and two were fitted as divisional leaders. Apart from the economies of this change, the other benefit was that now all nine ships of the flotilla had the same performance. The previous flotillas had leaders with larger turning circles and other handling characteristics that put them at odds when manoeuvring as a unit. Without having the benefit of operational experience (because no ships of the 1929 Programme were commissioned until late 1931), the curiously designed and ergonomically awkward split bridge was abandoned. All were a repeat of the 'C' class but with the new Vickers quad 0.5in machine gun in place of the QF 2-pounder – but this time raised one level on to the bridge wings – plus ASDIC instead of TSDS and twenty depth charges with a single rail and two throwers. There is some suggestion that the Vickers might not have been available to outfit all of the ships at the time of their commissioning.[22]

The 1931 Programme saw the model of nine-ship flotillas with one leader and two divisional leaders being slightly-adapted destroyers abandoned and an enlarged leader and eight-ship flotilla re-introduced. This cannot have been due to operational experience because the ships of the 1930 Programme were not launched until April–July 1932! So, why was the model introduced in the first place and abandoned before it was even put to the test? A little like the split bridge concept of the 'C' class? The 'E' or *Eclipse* class of the 1931 Programme did see some other small but significant changes. The hull form was modified, beam and depth were

HMS *Ivanhoe* of the 'I' class, the last of what might be termed the direct descendants of the 'V & Ws' insofar as the general layout and overall appearance is concerned. The 'Tribal' class which followed with six twin 4.7in guns was a step-change. (wikivisually.com)

increased and the policy of alternating annual flotillas between anti-submarine and minesweeping capabilities was now altered to minelaying or minesweeping, although ASDIC was to be fitted to all ships. Two ships were fitted with full minelaying rails running from abreast the after funnel to the stern. The ships' boats had to be raised to a lengthened foredeck and when the full mine complement of sixty Mk XIVA mines was carried, 'A' and 'Y' guns plus both torpedo tube mounts were landed. To clear space for the minelaying tracks a tripod mainmast was fitted to remove the shrouds and stays supporting the pole mast. The 4.7in guns finally had 40° elevation via a clumsy well with a removable cover. While this gave greater range, it did not address the issue of anti-aircraft fire, something that was to plague the Royal Navy well into the coming war.

The 'F' or *Fearless* class of the 1932 Programme was a repeat of the 'E' class but with some weight savings. Since these had been in machinery and down low in the hull, they affected the stability – specifically the GM – an issue that would become important in wartime as topweight increased with armament and sensors being added. All ships were TSDS and ASDIC-equipped.

The 'G' or *Greyhound* class of the 1933 Programme returned to the LOA dimensions of the smaller 'A' and 'B' classes due to the omission of cruising turbines and with single and double boiler rooms, although beam increased. A major recognition feature was the adoption of a cruiser-like tripod mainmast. A quintuple/pentad torpedo tube mounting was tried in one ship and later adopted in the 'I' class (see below).

The 'H' or *Hero* class of the 1934 Programme and the 'I' or *Intrepid* class of the 1935 Programme were repeats of the 'G' class. The 'H' class had incremental improvements such as the new CP.XVIII mounting for the 4.7in guns permitted 40° elevation with the shallow wells and a twin mounting was tried in one ship, a redesigned bridge was tested in two ships (later adopted with changes in the 'I' class), the leader had a tripod foremast (which became essential late in the war as large radar antennae required more stable platform than that offered by a wire-supported pole mast) and all had the tripod mainmast (removed in wartime to improve anti-aircraft firing arcs). The 'I' class introduced the quintuple torpedo tube mounting and two rails for sixteen depth charges and were adaptable for minelaying. The boilers went back into separate compartments and the revised bridges of the two 'H' class were adopted in all but the flotilla leader.[23]

As David Brown, ex-Deputy Chief Naval Architect of the Royal Corps of Naval Constructors says in his book *Nelson to Vanguard: Warship Design and Development 1923-1945*:

> The 'V' and 'W' classes were world leaders, continual small improvements led to the 'I' class which had fallen well behind other contemporary designs. British designs between the wars were designed for a fleet action in the North Sea or Mediterranean. This led to requirements for a heavy torpedo armament, low silhouette (freeboard), small size and short endurance . . . Since the 'V' and 'W' classes were quite suitable for short-range fleet actions it was natural that post-war designs should follow their general design.[24]

The product of the 1936 Programme, the destroyers that changed the mould from what was, in effect, variations on a theme – the logical, step-by-measure-step, trial-and-error adjustments to the formula established by the 'V & W' destroyer – were the fabled 'Tribal' class destroyers. But, that's worthy of a book on its own.

FARRAGUTS TO *FLETCHERS*

The United States Navy ended the First World War with 41 *Caldwell*, *Wickes* and *Clemson* class ('flush-deckers') commissioned and another 232 under construction. The last of these was not commissioned until 1922 – the cessation of hostilities meaning there was no urgency to complete a destroyer fleet commenced too late to be of any significant strategical benefit to the conflict (only twenty-seven of the forty-one actually made it to the conflict zone). I mentioned the issue of block obsolescence before and here, writ large, was one confronting the USN – probably made worse by the USN's policy of 'mothballing' ships in Reserve for long periods of time as distinct from the Royal Navy's practice of

USS *Farragut*, the first new destroyer in the USN since the First World War. (en-wikipedia.org)

USS *FARRAGUT* 1934 AND BRITISH 'H & I' CLASS 1934–6

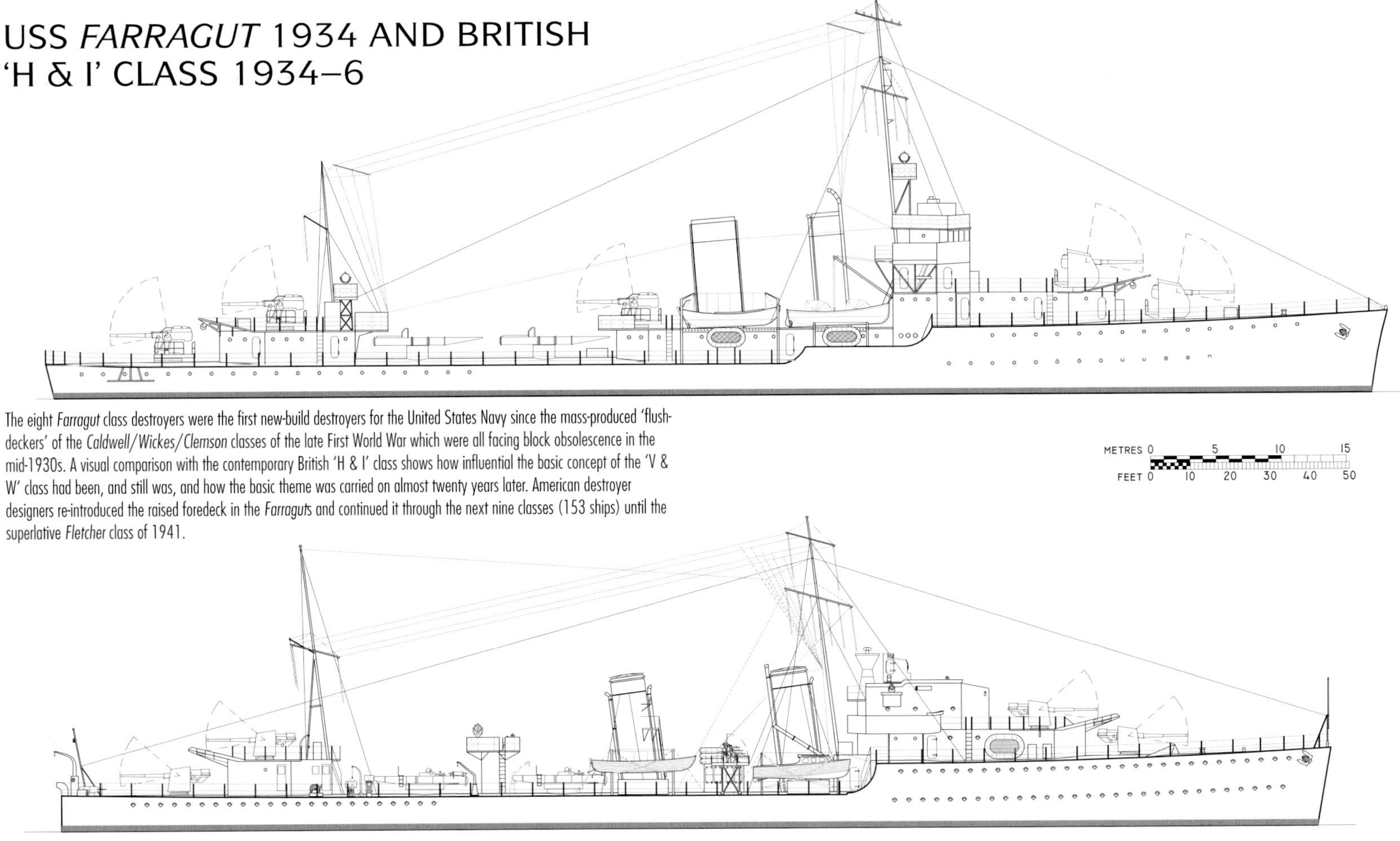

The eight *Farragut* class destroyers were the first new-build destroyers for the United States Navy since the mass-produced 'flush-deckers' of the *Caldwell/Wickes/Clemson* classes of the late First World War which were all facing block obsolescence in the mid-1930s. A visual comparison with the contemporary British 'H & I' class shows how influential the basic concept of the 'V & W' class had been, and still was, and how the basic theme was carried on almost twenty years later. American destroyer designers re-introduced the raised foredeck in the *Farraguts* and continued it through the next nine classes (153 ships) until the superlative *Fletcher* class of 1941.

decommissioning ships, placing them in reserve for short periods of time, recommissioning them and putting them back into service. For example, in 1922, half the USN destroyer fleet – presumably the ones built earliest – were mothballed and in 1930–1 fifty-six were scrapped due to poor condition (principally those with Yarrow boilers), three were expended as targets and two tested to destruction.

Rather than addressing the problem – for there was no real financial restriction in a wealthy post-war US economy until the Wall Street Crash of 1929 that prevented it – the issue of replacement was simply ignored or postponed until the *Farragut* class of 1932. Money went into aircraft carriers, the modernisation of battleships and new cruisers for very long-range operations on the premise that these would accompany the carriers rather than destroyers.[25] It's not that new designs weren't considered – they were and a general parameter of a 1,500-ton destroyer as established by the London Naval Treaty seems to have become some sort of yardstick.

A quick look at a *Farragut* – from Bethlehem Steel – shows a remarkable similarity in basic layout to contemporary British destroyers: two single superfiring guns forward on a raised foredeck, bridge, two funnels, midships gun, two sets of torpedo tubes, mainmast and two superfiring single-barrelled guns aft. At 341ft 3in LOA and 1,365 tons (standard) they were a little bigger than the British leaders, could make 35.5 knots and their 600 tons of fuel gave a useful range of 6,400 nautical miles at 12 knots. Paul Silverstone – the American equivalent of the British Lenton and Colledge – says this about the *Farraguts*: 'First post-war destroyer, enlarged version of contemporary British destroyers.'[26] So, there was nothing particularly new here except the *Farraguts* had five 5in/38 dual purpose (DP) capable of 85° elevation – something the British gun-makers had been unable to achieve for some inexplicable reason – and, as such, was capable of anti-aircraft fire. It was 'unquestionably the finest Dual Purpose gun of World War II'.[27] What was new, however, was the *Farraguts*' boilers operated at 400PSI and at 650° F (340° C). Later classes increased these pressures to 600 PSI and 850° F (450° C). Contemporary British destroyers operated inefficiently at lower pressures of 300 PSI. Also, American turbines were made smaller and lighter and more efficient. There was a marked difference in operating procedure between the RN and USN when it came to boiler maintenance. The RN preferred three-boiler destroyers so that one boiler could be out of action and still allow reasonable performance on the remaining two. Boiler cleaning was scheduled for every 750 hours in the RN and 2,000 hours in the USN – the difference due to the use of chemical additives by the USN in the boiler water. Pigheadedly, the Admiralty refused to change its position and allow the use of additives and continued to suffer the consequences of ships being out of action due to boiler cleaning that could have been reduced.

While the *Farraguts* were inclined to be top-heavy (two were lost in a cyclone), on face value they looked comparable to contemporary British destroyers but gun-wise were certainly superior. What made that gun even better was the Mk 33 dual-purpose surface/anti-aircraft director which was replaced by the even better Mk 37. However, the *Farraguts* were not cheap – at least compared with contemporary British destroyers. According to the 1939 edition of *Jane's Fighting Ships* they cost between US $3.4m–$3.75m. (£2.04m–£2.25m), whereas the 'Tribal' class were £510,000 (US $850,000) according to March.[28]

The USN continued the very similar concept of the *Farraguts* (eight ships, 1932–5) through the *Porter* class (eight ships, 1933–7) and the *Mahan* class (eighteen ships, 1934–7) – both these classes having twelve torpedo tubes arranged in two sets of beam-mounted quad tubes plus one centreline mount. The next-built, the *Gridley* class (four ships, 1935–8) had sixteen torpedo tubes with four sets of beam-mounted quad tubes and introduced a single-funnel design which continued though the next four classes – the *Bagley* class (eight ships, 1935–7), *Somers* class (five ships, 1935–9), *Benham* class (ten ships, 1936–9) and *Sims* class (twelve ships, 1937–40). The *Benson* class (twelve ships, 1938–43) re-introduced two funnels and this continued through the *Gleaves* class (sixty-six ships, 1938–43) which saw the last of what I regard as the British destroyer concept. That is, principally, as described earlier. It was not until the extraordinarily successful *Fletcher* class (175 ships, 1941–5) that the basic mould was changed and the raised foredeck was dispensed with and, somewhat paradoxically since it was the question of seaworthiness that saw the flush deck abandoned in favour of the raised foredeck, the flush deck of 1916 was re-introduced. However, like the 'Tribal' class, that is worth a book of its own.

EUROPEAN NAVIES

Some might say it's drawing a long bow to say that British destroyer design influenced other navies but, on the other hand one would have to ask if the influence did not come from that source, from where did it come? Also, one must consider timing. Anything designed and built after the first 'Tribal' class was designed in 1935 and commissioned in 1938 could be said to have been influenced by that – or *vice versa*.

Only the Swedes seem to have persisted with an exclusively flush-deck design with no superfiring guns (until after the Second World War) or Italy – with one exception (see below). But, even so, both these navys' destroyers still exhibit the same general layout of the British 'V & W' class destroyer. The only nation to remotely follow the First World War German destroyer type after that

The French Navy's light cruiser-like *Le Triomphant* which marked a totally different trend in destroyer design. (Australian War Memorial)

conflict was Japan and that is dealt with separately below.

So, in alphabetical order:

The French Navy – the *Marine Nationale* – took a contrary path to the Royal Navy, favouring a lesser number of destroyers (thirty-two built between 1926 and 1939) but significantly larger in size and armament. While they might be called super-destroyers, their official designation was *contre-torpilleurs*. As Norman Friedman summarises, they were 'intended to operate as independent strike squadrons'.[29] On the other hand, the largest of them, the *La Fantasque* and *Mogador* classes, were an intrinsic part of the *Force de Raid* (Raiding Force) centred on the fast battleships *Dunkerque* and *Strasbourg* early in the war. Their gun armament was heavier than most destroyers but lighter than that of what was generally accepted as being light cruisers, varying between carrying between five and eight guns of between 5.1in and 5.5in. So, in many respects they owed little to the British designs.

The Kriegsmarine's *Richard Beitzen*, heavily armed but overweight and not particularly seaworthy due to a low freeboard and weight forward. (en.wikipedia.org)

The German Navy – the *Kriegsmarine* – did not start building new destroyers until 1934. These were, again, like the French destroyers, large and more akin to light cruisers. While they 'borrowed' the general arrangement of the British destroyers as to armament layout, their minimum was the equivalent of the 5in gun and the 1936 Type A Class commissioned between 1940 and 1943 had no less than five guns equivalent to 6in – a calibre normally fitted to light cruisers. These turned out to be unsatisfactory and later classes reverted to the 5in guns. The German destroyers were, rather like their First World War counterparts, less seaworthy than the British destroyers and suffered particularly from their considerable topweight to which their gun armament was a major factor. It was the advent of the large German destroyers that prompted the Admiralty to pursue the successful 'Tribal' class.

The Hellenic (Greek) Navy – the *Polemikó Naftikó* – received two 'H' class destroyers from Yarrow's in 1938–9 but without armament as this was fitted in Greece to a different specification.

The Italian Navy – the *Regia Marina* – followed a similar course to the French Navy but with only one class – the '*Navigatoris*' – rated initially as *esploratori* or scouts. Not one of the Italian designs that were built could be said to resemble a British destroyer since they never embraced the superfiring guns on the foredeck, although they did tend to favour twin mounts which provided the same firepower as the two single mounts that were current until the 'Tribal' class of 1936. One design that never saw the light of day – fourteen were commenced in 1943 but never got beyond keel laying – were the '*Comandanti Medaglie d'Oro*' class which reverted to the single-barrelled guns for some reason and were to have been in the superfiring positions. These ships would have had the usual Italian single, large trunked funnel and prominent bridge structure. At just over 2,000 tons and a shade under 400ft LOA these large destroyers were more closely related to the '*Navigatori*' class.

The Polish Navy – the *Marynarka Wojenna* – placed orders with White's for two destroyers which were commissioned in 1937 and which, apart from their one large trunked funnel, were very much British destroyer look-alikes.

The Portuguese Navy – the *Marinha Portuguesa*, also known as *Marinha de Guerra Portuguesa* or as *Armada Portuguesa* – built seven destroyers to a Yarrow design based on their *Ambuscade* between 1933 and 1936.

The Romanian Navy – the *Forțele Navale Românehe* – had two destroyers built in Italy that were commissioned in 1930 that were built to designs based on the *Shakespeare* class and Thornycroft is credited with either having prepared the documentation or assisted with it.

The Royal Netherlands Navy – the *Koninklijke Marine* – built eight destroyers in two batches of four to a Yarrow design based on their *Ambuscade* between 1928 and 1931 and commenced another four very similar of which only two were completed before the German invasion in 1940.

The Spanish Navy – the *Armada Española* – built a total of eighteen destroyers (*Churruca* class) in two batches between 1927 and 1936 to a design prepared by Vickers Armstrong that was based on the *Scott* class.

The Soviet Navy – the *Voyenno-morskoy flot SSSR* – followed the French and German trends towards larger, more heavily-armed destroyers beginning with the three *Leningrad* class and its three sub-class of 1936–40. These were followed by the thirty units of the *Gvevny/Storozhevoy* class (Project 7/7U depending on which source you accept) which were commissioned between 1938 and 1942. Again, while the layout was typical of British destroyers, they owed more to the 'Tribal' class and were large and powerful ships, albeit top-heavy.

The Polish *Grom* alongside her sister-ship *Błyskawica* – both from J Samuel White of Cowes. (polishgreatness.com)

The Dutch '*Admiralen*' class was a little unusual in that they carried a small seaplane. (commons.wikimedia.org)

A Soviet *Storozhevoy* class Project 7/7U destroyer. (navypedia.org)

The Yugoslav Navy – *Jugoslavenska Ratna Mornarica* – ordered a destroyer leader-type from Yarrow's which was delivered in 1932 but with the main armament to be supplied and fitted by Skoda.

SOUTH AMERICAN NAVIES

The Argentine Navy – *Armada de la República Argentina* – also looked to Britain for its destroyers in the inter-war period, ordering three from White's that were based on the *Scott* class leader and were delivered in 1929 plus a further seven which were very similar to the contemporary 'G' class from various British builders, all delivered in 1938. Also, two of the Spanish *Churruca* class built in Spain to a British design (Vickers Armstrong, see above) were sold to Argentina.

The Brazilian Navy – *Marinha do Brasil* – ordered six 'H' class but these were under construction when war broke out and were taken over by the Royal Navy.

The Chilean Navy – *Armada de Chile* – ordered six destroyers from Thornycroft's which were delivered in 1928–9.

In summary, between the wars, more destroyers were ordered from Britain by foreign navies than in the rest of the world put together.

The Japanese *Hatsuharu* class tried to squeeze a quart into a pint pot and were unsuccessful. (wiki.wargaming.net)

THE JAPANESE NAVY

The Imperial Japanese Navy – the *Dai-Nippon Teikoku Kaigun* – persisted with the German Navy concept of the raised foredeck protecting the first bank of torpedoes in front of the bridge until 1928 when the first of the twenty-four large *Fubuki* class destroyers were completed. These did not have superfiring guns forward but favoured twin gun mounts – like the Italian ships – three of them and 5in in this case, and three triple 24in torpedo tubes and were capable of 38 knots. At just over 367ft in length and around 2,000 tons and with a large radius of action, these were large and powerful destroyers for their time. The follow-on class, the fourteen Group II or *Ayanami* class, were even more capable, in that the main armament elevated to 75° (from 40° in the *Fubukis*) giving an true DP armament. Only one class of destroyer designed and built by the Japanese featured superfiring forward guns – the *Hatsuharu* class of 1933–5 – and these were most unsuccessful having been designed to fit the Treaty limitations: a case of squeezing a quart into a pint pot. In summary, Japanese destroyers tended to be somewhat unconventional, were bigger than British destroyers by a substantial margin, favoured twin gun mounts capable of surface and anti-aircraft fire and had substantial torpedo outfits.

10: THE SECOND WORLD WAR

THE FLEET DESTROYERS

It is probably an overstatement to say that any of the 'V & Ws' in commission in the RN in September 1939 could properly be regarded as fleet destroyers, that is, being engaged in the sort of fleet tasks that would be expected of destroyers of that time – operating in cohesive flotillas of eight destroyers of the one class.

HMS *Worcester* suffered considerable damage on 12 February 1942 from the German battlecruiser *Scharnhorst* and the heavy cruiser *Prinz Eugen* during the infamous 'Channel Dash' when acting, in effect, as a fleet destroyer with the 21st Flotilla. The repairs and her conversion to an SRE took until August. (Seaforth)

Preston states that the following destroyer flotillas were in existence:

11th Destroyer Flotilla, Western Approaches Command (8 + one to join).
13th Destroyer Flotilla, North Atlantic Command (6).
15th Destroyer Flotilla, Rosyth (8).
16th Destroyer Flotilla, Portsmouth (4).
17th Destroyer Flotilla, Western Approaches Command (8).
18th Destroyer Flotilla, Western Approaches Command (3, all to join on completion of refits).[1]

He continues, 'Virtually all the old destroyers were either commissioning for service or completing refits... All the "V & W" boats and leaders in Home waters were escorting convoys and carrying out anti-submarine patrols', so, in these respects, while they were notionally formed in flotillas and had bases and came under specified commands, they were not operating in the strict sense as fleet destroyers. He goes on to make the point that they 'were not fit for front-line service',[2] and later, 'the wartime role assigned to the "V & W" destroyers was definitely a subsidiary one, as they were no longer adequate to serve as fleet destroyers. Their hand-worked guns and torpedo tubes made it unlikely that they could participate effectively with more modern destroyers against well-trained opponents. The record of the Australian destroyers in the Mediterranean showed that this was not strictly true.'[3] Preston's comment provides a perfect segue into the next section.

HMAS *Voyager, Stuart* and *Vendetta* in more peaceful times. (navy.gov.au)

THE 'SCRAP IRON FLOTILLA'

I could write a book about this alone, indeed others have and Preston devotes a chapter to it. But, I'll try to be brief and, as an Australian, objective and not biased or jingoistic.

I can claim a slight connection because my father and Surgeon Lieutenant Commander Trevor McLean of HMAS *Stuart*, the flotilla leader, were very good friends. From memory, both served as groomsmen at each other's weddings if not best men. Since I wasn't present and both have crossed the bar I can't be sure!

The *Scott* class leader *Stuart*, the 'V' class leader *Vampire*, the Admiralty 'V' class *Vendetta,* the Admiralty 'W' class *Voyager* and *Waterhen* were transferred to the Royal Australian Navy in 1932.

Five little destroyers, under the Southern Cross.

The moment war broke out the Australian government offered the services of the flotilla to the Admiralty which immediately accepted and the 10th Flotilla (as it became) was posted to the Mediterranean under Commander H M L Waller – later Captain Waller, DSO and Bar – killed while commanding the light cruiser HMAS *Perth* in the Battle of Sunda Strait, 1 March 1942 and to whom this book is dedicated. A *Collins* class submarine is named after him and many think he should have received a Victoria Cross. But that's another story.

So, why the 'Scrap Iron Flotilla'? We can thank the Nazi Propaganda Minister, Joseph Goebbels for the quote when he 'welcomed' the flotilla to the Mediterranean in December 1939 – via Lord Haw Haw's radio broadcasts apparently – as a 'consignment of old junk' and 'Australia's Scrap Iron Flotilla'.[4] Italy entered the war on Germany's side on 10 June 1940 and the complexion of the war in the Mediterranean suddenly and dramatically changed. Italy had a large and modern navy and regarded the Mediterranean as its *Mare Nostrum* – literally 'Our Sea'. It was up to the Royal Navy to prove otherwise. That was not going to be easy as its resources were stretched and its bases, Gibraltar, Malta and Alexandria, were a long way apart.

To keep the section brief, I'll address it in point form, as follows:

- 27 March: *Stuart* saved the crippled tanker *Trocas* from drifting on to a lee shore off Tripoli and towed her back to Malta.
- 14 June: *Stuart* and *Voyager* attacked an Italian submarine. The submarine surfaced then submerged and escaped.
- 17 June: *Vampire* and *Voyager* had a similar engagement with a submarine, also without success.
- 27 June: *Voyager* in company with HMS *Ilex*, *Dainty* and *Decoy*, sighted the Italian submarine *Liuzzi* which dived, was depth-charged and resurfaced and forced to surrender whereupon *Voyager* rescued some of the crew.
- 29 June: A similar occurrence west of Crete, this time involving the Italian submarine *Uebi Scebeli*.
- End June: *Stuart* bombarded Bardia in the company of the French battleship *Lorraine* and the light cruiser HMAS *Sydney*.
- 9 July 1940: *Stuart* took part in the Battle of Calabria, the first fleet engagement in the Mediterranean since Nelson's time. The handling of *Stuart* in this action resulted in Waller's DSO for 'courage, enterprise and devotion to duty'. *Voyager* was present escorting the aircraft carrier HMS *Eagle* and withstood air attacks involving near misses.
- 29–30 September: In company *Stuart* and HMS *Diamond* forced the Italian submarine *Gondar* to the surface and sank it. Waller sent a phlegmatic signal: 'On passage, detected, hunted and sank Italian submarine.'
- 25 December 1940: *Waterhen* sank the Italian supply ship *Tireremo Diritto*.
- 27–29 March 1941: In the epic Battle of Cape Matapan, *Stuart* and HMS *Havock* took part in the rarest of actions, a torpedo attack – in this case against the Italian cruiser *Zara*. For Waller's part in this action he was awarded a Bar to his DSO. *Vendetta* should have been present as part of the cruiser screening force involving HMAS *Perth* but engine problems forced her retirement. *Vampire* was officially part of the order of battle as part of Convoy AG9 (Alexandria to Greece) but saw no action.
- April 1941: *Stuart*, *Vendetta*, *Voyager* and *Waterhen* were involved in bombarding enemy position in North Africa (officially the Inshore Squadron) and the first of her twenty-four runs supplying the garrison at Tobruk. The disastrous Greek campaign saw all of the RAN destroyers active in the evacuation and subject to continual air attacks. Having no sooner effected these evacuations the same thing was repeated from Crete.
- May 1941: The commencement of the 'Tobruk Ferry Service' – a nightly run of 350 miles from Alexandria to the beleaguered garrison of mainly Australian troops which had been expected to hold out for six weeks and was not relieved for five months. All told, the 'Scrap Iron Flotilla' made 139 runs of which *Vendetta* held the record with 39.
- 29 June: *Waterhen* – AKA 'The Chook' – was bombed and sunk while under tow the next day, fortunately with no loss of life.

HMAS *Waterhen*, AKA 'The Chook', sinking after being bombed while serving on the Tobruk Ferry Run, 29 June 1941. (navy.gov.au)

HMAS *Vampire* on duty in the Indian Ocean. (navy.gov.au)

Four little destroyers, under the Southern Cross.

The Flotilla battled on with little respite and the minimum of maintenance. Captured Italian weapons augmented their First World War-standard armament – such as the quite effective Breda Model 35 20mm cannon which were mounted wherever possible together with the smaller Breda machine guns.

HMAS *Vampire*, perhaps the worst for wear – she vibrated excessively at speeds over 16 knots – was sent back to Australia in May 1941 but only made it to Singapore where she was refitted. In December she sailed to join the British Eastern Fleet based in Trincomalee Harbour, Ceylon and operating in the Indian Ocean. On 8 April 1942 *Vampire* escorted the small RN aircraft carrier HMS *Hermes* out of Trincomalee Harbour where she was expected to

HMAS *VAMPIRE*: MEDITERRANEAN 1940 AND INDIAN OCEAN, MARCH 1942

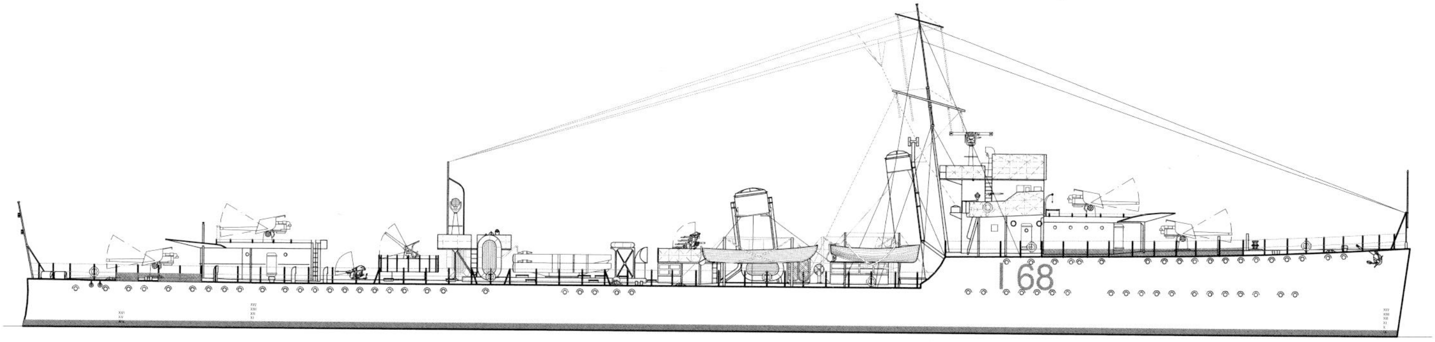

HMAS *Vampire* and the aircraft carrier HMS *Hermes* and were sunk by Japanese aircraft on 9 April 1942 in the Indian Ocean, off Ceylon. Both ships lacked adequate anti-aircraft weapons and were operating without the benefit of air cover – *Hermes* having no aircraft. More British and Commonwealth destroyers were lost to aircraft attacks than any other source due to a main armament that was incapable of providing sufficient elevation for anti-aircraft fire. Note that *Vampire* has a captured Italian Breda Model 35 20mm in 1940 supplementing the ineffective Vickers 0.50in quad HMG and the QF 12-pounder 12 cwt (which has replaced the aft torpedo tubes) and in 1942 this has been replaced by the obsolete QF 2-pounder Mk II with the searchlight moved to a position between the funnels.

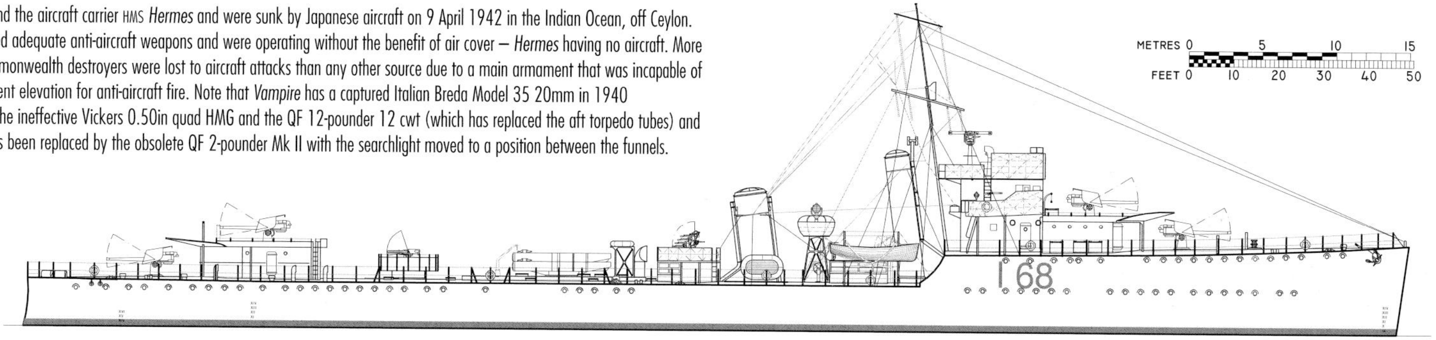

METRES 0 5 10 15

FEET 0 10 20 30 40 50

come under Japanese air attack. However, while only 65 miles from land the small force was discovered and *Hermes* was quickly sunk. *Vampire* managed to manoeuvre and avoid serious damage but a subsequent air strike broke her back in two and she quickly sank.

Three little destroyers, under the Southern Cross

HMAS *Voyager* was lost on 23 September 1942 when making a not-unfamiliar type of supply run – this time taking 250 reinforcements from Darwin to the guerrilla forces operating on the Japanese held island of Timor. Intending to land troops at last light at Betano Bay she ran aground and despite taking all possible action to re-float her, she was discovered by a Japanese reconnaissance plane and escorting fighter and attacked. Further attacks followed and it was decided that the best course of action was to set demolition charges rather than have the ship fall into enemy hands.

Two little destroyers, under the Southern Cross.

HMAS *Stuart* was released from service in the Mediterranean on 22 August 1941, and made the voyage back to Australia for an overdue refit on just the starboard engine arriving in Melbourne on 27 September. Her refit took until April 1942 and she was employed escorting convoys between Australia and New Guinea. Her next major refit in early 1945 saw a major conversion to a fast transport. Whether her No 1 boiler was beyond repair is unknown

HMS *Voyager* off Suda Bay, Crete. Note how ineffective the low-angle 4in guns would have been against the German air attacks that dominated this theatre. (navy.gov.au)

HMAS *Stuart*, or maybe still HMS *Stuart* in 1933 before her transfer to the Royal Australian Navy on 11 October. (Seaforth)

HMAS *STUART*: MEDITERRANEAN 1941

HMAS *Stuart* as she was fitted when leading the 'Scrap Iron Flotilla' in the Mediterranean in 1941. Her armament is very much non-standard and reflects the paucity of suitable anti-aircraft weapons, particularly in this theatre. Vickers quad 0.5in HMGs have been fitted to the bridge wings, there are two QF 2-pounder Mk VIIIs where there would have been a BL 4.7in Mk I between the funnels, a QF 3in 20 cwt of First World War vintage is in its normal position and there are two captured Italian Breda Model 35 20mm guns – one on the starboard side abeam the searchlight and one on the port side forward of 'X' mount – plus two single 20mm Oerlikons. There are two depth charge throwers and two tracks. The pair of Vickers .303in on the foredeck were probably 'gifts' from troops rescued on the 'Tobruk Ferry Service' complementing two pairs of Lewis .303in on the bridge. There are two smoke generators at the bow and the very basic Type 286 radar antenna is present at the masthead.

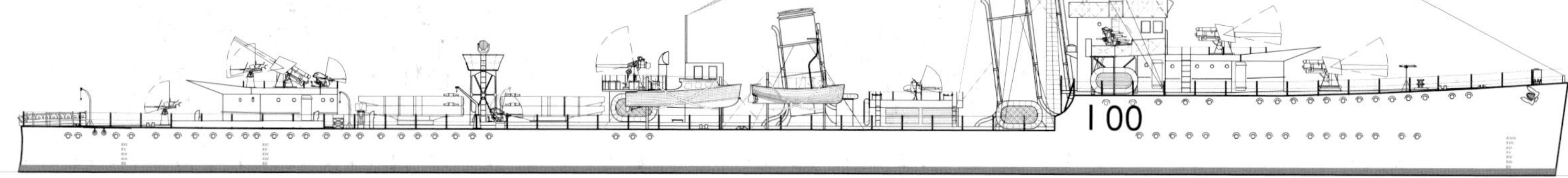

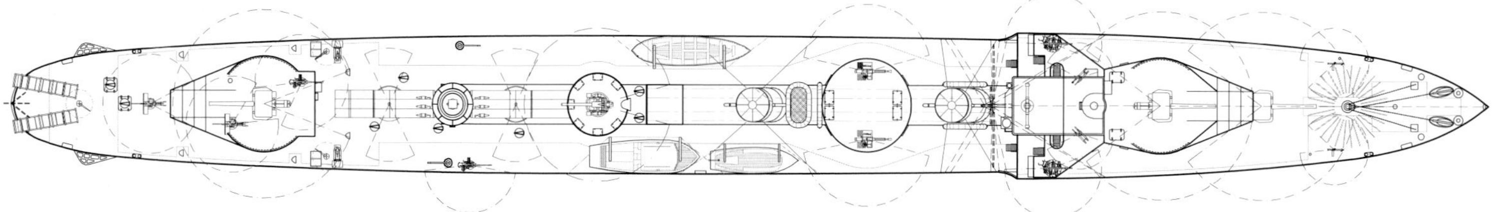

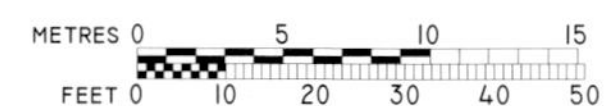

HMAS *Stuart*, with a crumpled stem and reduced armament in the later months of her service career. *(navy.gov.au)*

but, like the British Long Range Escort conversions (see below), it was removed and the foredeck extended aft and the space converted into some sort of hold and refrigerated cargo space. Since no drawings are available my drawing is based on two very vague photographs. She was decommissioned on 27 April 1946 and sold for scrapping on 3 February 1947.

One little destroyer, under the Southern Cross.

On 20 October 1941, HMAS *Vendetta* left the Mediterranean in need of a complete refit, arriving in Singapore on 12 November. She was high and dry in dock when the Japanese attacked on 8 December and a spirited defence was mounted including using the

HMAS *STUART*: SW PACIFIC 1943

HMAS *Stuart* was released from service in the Mediterranean in mid-1941 and returned to Australia on one-engine, such was her condition. This drawing shows her as refitted to serve in the South-West Pacific Theatre, mainly on convoy escort duty. She has lost 'A' gun in favour of a Hedgehog anti-submarine mortar and the bridge wings have been extended to receive single 20mm Oerlikons. Type 271 radar is now fitted to the bridge and the masthead now shows the peculiar SW1-C-looking antenna which is unexplained as she previously had Type 286. Her torpedo tubes have been landed as have the captured 20mm Bredas but not the ineffectual 2-pounders. Two more 20mm Oerlikons are now present amidships.

METRES 0 5 10 15
FEET 0 10 20 30 40 50

I 00

12-pounder and other light guns mounted dockside. With only a skeleton crew of twenty-one on board, on 2 February she was taken in tow by the tug *St. Just* and then by the 'S' class destroyer HMS *Stronghold* with the intention of getting away from Singapore as quickly as possible. Palembang (Sumatra) was reached despite further attacks and HMAS *Yarra* took over the towing duties on 8 February – destination Batavia which they reached on 10 February. Then, on 17 February, commenced the longest and most bizarre tow to Fremantle, Western Australia by the Yangtse River ferry SS *Ping Wo* – probably the most unlikely candidate you could imagine for such an exploit, a superannuated Indo-Chinese river steamer: coal-burning, wide of beam, shallow of draught, flat of bottom,

HMAS *Vendetta*, Mediterranean August 1941, 7th Destroyer Flotilla. (navy.gov.au)

HMAS *STUART*: SW PACIFIC 1945

HMAS *Stuart* spent the last months of the war as a fast transport. Like the LRE conversions of the 'V & Ws', her forward boiler was removed. Her forecastle was extended aft and the space used mainly for refrigeration. She retained the Hedgehog anti-submarine mortar despite the reduced Japanese submarine threat and 'B' gun was replaced by a QF 4in Mk V HA/LA mount. She lost the Type 271 radar but gained an Australia Type A286 or American SC at the masthead – the antennae looked similar. The obsolete QF 2-pounder Mk VIIIs were retained – this time replacing 'X' mount – and a power-operated 20mm Oerlikon Mk V was mounted above where the aft torpedo tubes had been removed in 1942.

bluff of bow and heavy of rust. Not the sort of vessel to ferry twenty-one boxes of gold bullion *and* tow a disabled destroyer to Australia! Built in Shanghai in 1922 by the New Engineering & Shipbuilding Works Limited for the Yangtze River, Shanghai–Hankou route as a passenger and freight ferry, she must have ceased being used on this route for some reason because she is recorded as being in Haiphong Harbour in 1940 as a 'store ship' – a floating warehouse. How and why she happened to be in Singapore in 1941 is not known.

A poor but historic photograph of the immobilised and partly-armed HMAS Vendetta under tow from Singapore heading to Tanjung Priok in early February 1942 prior to the tow to Australia by the Yangtse River ferry *Ping Wo*. (Australian War Memorial 301613)

Ping Wo towed *Vendetta* into Fremantle Harbour sixteen days later on 3 March – the longest continual tow ever of an Australian warship and certainly one that goes down in the annals of the Royal Navy and the Royal Australian Navy. I have seen references to the tow averaging 3.5 knots. Working backwards that means the distance travelled must have been some 1,344 nautical miles. A quick check via Google Earth confirms that this cannot be right because the distance from Christmas Island to Fremantle alone is in the order of 1,400 nautical miles. The total distance is more like 1,800 nautical miles, making the average speed something in the vicinity of 4.7 knots – still slow going allowing for parted tow lines and bad weather.

HMAS *Vendetta* as an escort destroyer, SW Pacific with a Hedgehog in 'A' position. (Seaforth)

Vendetta had her long-overdue refit in two stages and was not re-commissioned until the end of 1942. She was used as a convoy

HMAS *VENDETTA*: SEPTEMBER 1942 AND ESCORT DESTROYER 1944

HMAS *Vendetta* was under refit in Singapore when Japan first attacked there on 8 December 1941. She was towed home to Australia, an epic in itself. She is shown here as she appeared after her refit in Australia at the end of 1942 with a rather unusual secondary armament mix of two 20mm Oerlikons fitted in extended bridge wings and the near-useless Vickers quad 0.5in HMG in a raised bandstand in place of the aft torpedo tubes which have been landed, Note what looks like the Canadian SW1-C radar antenna (as appeared on HMAS *Stuart* too) probably fitted when she was in the Mediterranean. Her refit in mid to late 1944 was more comprehensive and saw the removal of the LA 4in guns in favour of the dual-purpose QF 4in Mk V fore and aft plus Hedgehog and better close-range weaponry. Type 272 SW radar was fitted amidships and either Australian Type A286 or US SC AW radar at the masthead.

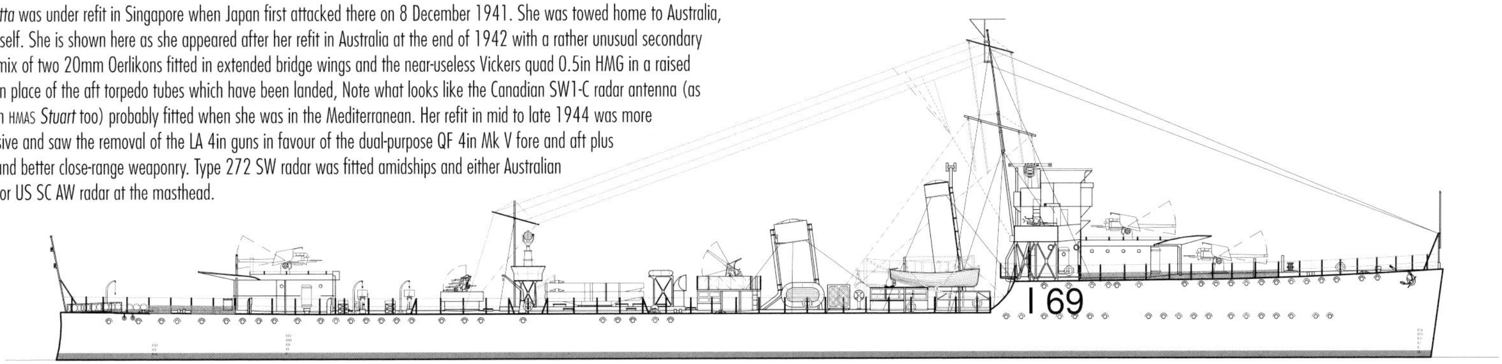

I69

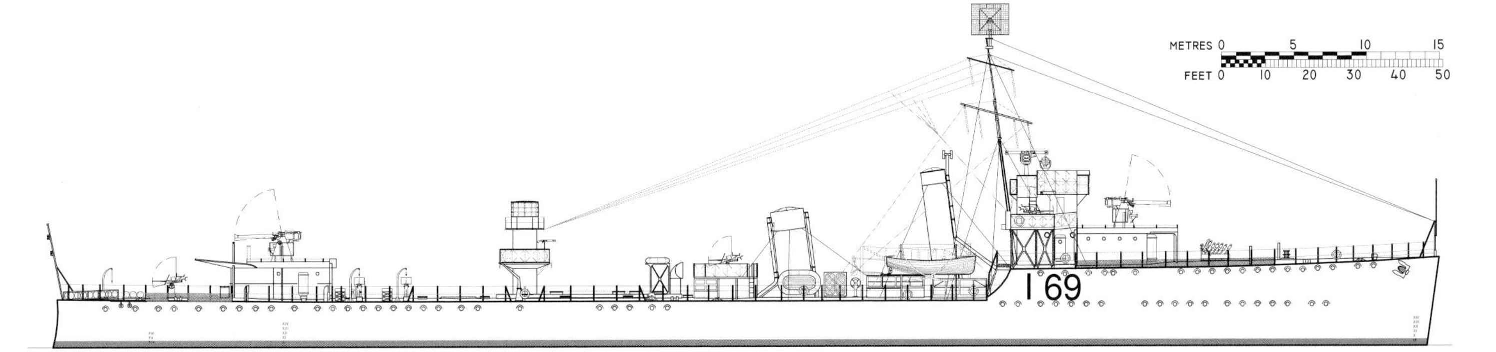

I69

METRES 0 5 10 15
FEET 0 10 20 30 40 50

HMAS *Vendetta* in her final guise, New Guinea 1944. Note the QF 4in Mk V single mounts fore and aft with Hedgehog in 'A' position and Type 272 radar in place of the searchlight. (navy.gov.au)

escort to and from Australia and New Guinea. In late 1944 she had another refit and emerged with a more appropriate armament considering the risk of attack from Japanese aircraft. Her escort duties took her further afield and at the end of hostilities the surrender of the Japanese fortress of Rabaul was signed on her quarterdeck. She was decommissioned after sailing over 120,000 miles in the Pacific campaign and eventually scuttled off Sydney on 2 July 1948.

And then there were no little destroyers under the Southern Cross.

Vale the 'Scrap Iron Flotilla'.

'WAIR' CONVERSIONS

Records do not confirm precisely where and how the term 'WAIR' originated. It is widely thought – but not proved – to stand for 'W' meaning 'W' class destroyers and 'AIR' being the reference to their intended anti-aircraft application. The authority on the subject, Preston, offers no explanation whatsoever nor do Raven and Roberts. March offers two sentences but does not even mention the term 'WAIR' except as a reference to those sentences in the Index.[5] Friedman is similarly silent.

HMS *WHITLEY*: 'WAIR' CONVERSION 1938

Fifteen of the 'V & W' destroyers were converted under the 1938 'WAIR' Programme to fast escort vessels, with an emphasis on anti-aircraft capability. To this end, they were fitted with twin QD 4in Mk XVI mountings fore and aft with good arcs of fire, with a 9ft rangefinder and only rudimentary close-range weaponry in the form of the new, but soon proved to be ineffective, Vickers quad 0.5in HMG which lacked explosive ammunition and was prone to jamming. According to Lenton, these guns were mounted en echelon but I have found no photographs to confirm this. However, HMS *Whitley*, being the first converted, is illustrated so equipped.

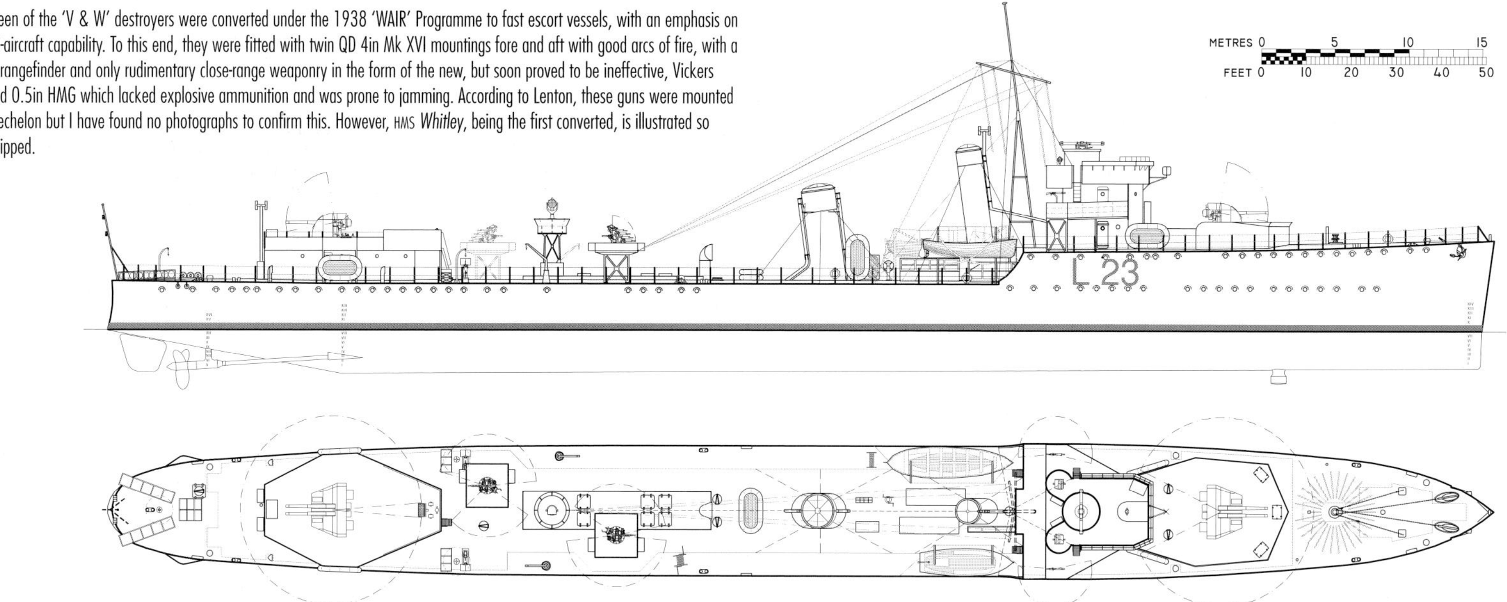

The 'WAIR' conversion HMS *Vanity*. Note the Type 285 radar fitted to the director control tower and the Type 291 GW antenna at the masthead. The ineffective Vickers quad .50in machine guns are silhouetted between the funnel and the searchlight. (seaforth)

Irrespective of the origin of the term, the origin of the species can be traced, indirectly, to the *Bittern* class sloops (and the remarkably successful follow-on *Egret* and *Black Swan* classes) which introduced the QF 4in Mk XVI and the complimentary High Angle Control System (HACS) to warships of this size (circa 1,200 tons standard) in three twin mountings offering quite formidable anti-aircraft weaponry. However, while capable warships and ideal convoy escorts, they were limited by their speed of around 19 knots. This led to the design of the 'Hunt' class escort destroyer with a similar armament but with one set of torpedo tubes for offensive action, primarily intended for East Coast operations.

Konstam says that by the 1930s it was clear that the RN needed escorts capable of providing anti-aircraft protection for convoys.[6] Although he provides no substantiation, one could assume that the Spanish Civil War and the sloop classes referred to above would

HMS *VEGA*: 'WAIR' CONVERSION 1941

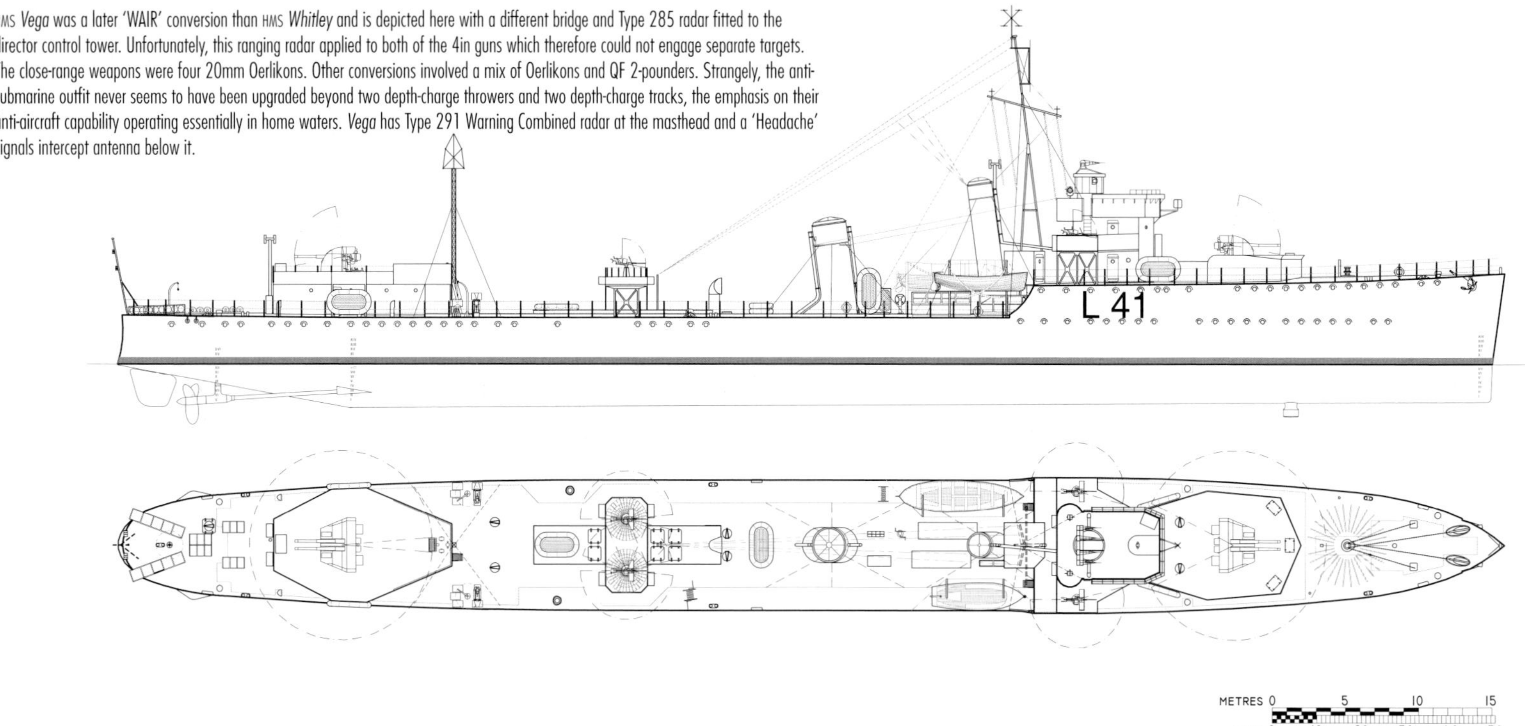

HMS *Vega* was a later 'WAIR' conversion than HMS *Whitley* and is depicted here with a different bridge and Type 285 radar fitted to the director control tower. Unfortunately, this ranging radar applied to both of the 4in guns which therefore could not engage separate targets. The close-range weapons were four 20mm Oerlikons. Other conversions involved a mix of Oerlikons and QF 2-pounders. Strangely, the anti-submarine outfit never seems to have been upgraded beyond two depth-charge throwers and two depth-charge tracks, the emphasis on their anti-aircraft capability operating essentially in home waters. *Vega* has Type 291 Warning Combined radar at the masthead and a 'Headache' signals intercept antenna below it.

bear out this assertion. Friedman states that the conversion of thirty-six 'V & W' destroyers to anti-aircraft and anti-submarine escorts was approved as early as 1936 and that the first was completed in November 1938, about the same time as the 'Hunt' class was being approved.[7] The list was reduced to twenty at some later date but one, HMS *Walrus*, was lost while under tow.[8] The Thornycroft leader HMS *Wallace* was either substituted for *Walrus* or had always been considered anyway. Being a larger ship, her conversion was somewhat non-standard. Only fifteen 'V & Ws' were finally converted, due mainly to the bottleneck of gun mounts and associated control systems. Apart from *Wallace*, they were all 4in-gunned versions which were considered less valuable than the 'Modified W' class with the 4.7in guns.

The conversions were quite drastic. Basically, the hull was stripped of superstructure and armament back to deck level. A totally new three-level bridge was built which was similar in many respects to the 'Hunt' class. It contained the fire-control room for the HACS which was located in its revolving tower at the back of the open bridge which had space for the additional air-lookouts required. A new deckhouse was built aft which had the emergency conning position at its forward end. Two twin 4in guns were located with good firing arcs – the forward one behind a substantial zareba with wind deflectors which also acted as a breakwater, the aft one on the deckhouse. A tripod foremast minimised the necessity for wire mast supports and there was no mainmast. The newly introduced quad Vickers 0.5in machine guns were mounted

This photograph of HMS *Vanity* from the port quarter shows the good firing arcs of the aft 4in mounting. Note that the camouflage is quite different from the previous photograph. (naval-history.net)

amidships – apparently *en echelon* in early completion for improved firing arcs but sided later. Lewis guns in the bridge wings completed the rather meagre close-range anti-aircraft weaponry. Strangely, considering their escort function, only two depth-charge throwers and two depth-charge rails were fitted, plus upgraded ASDIC. Ballast – some 60 tons – had to be added to compensate for the additional topweight.

Subsequent improvements included fitting Type 285 gunnery radar to the HACS, fitting Type 291 air-warning radar to the masthead, fitting 'Headache' signals-intercept antenna to the masthead, fitting single 20mm Oerlikons to the bridge wings, replacing the quad Vickers 0.5in machine guns with single 20mm Oerlikons and, according to Preston, fitting two additional single QF 2-pounders abreast the funnels.[9] I have not found any photographs to substantiate this last.

These conversions were very successful both on the East Coast and in the Mediterranean and proved that there was plenty of life still left in the old dog, as the saying goes.

LONG RANGE ESCORTS (LRE)

The complexion of the Battle of the Atlantic changed considerable when Germany gained access to the French Atlantic and Norwegian ports, thus avoiding long and perilous transit voyages to harass the convoy routes. Submarines could now range further afield and for longer periods. The advent of supply submarines – Type XIV 'Milch Cows' – in 1941 further assisted this tactical advantage.

Convoys now had to be protected port-to-port and a standard 'V & W' destroyer did not have the bunkerage necessary to achieve this, especially considering the fact that convoys did not take the most direct route (the rhumb line) and the escorts spent considerable time and distance either zigzagging, chasing up convoy stragglers or pursuing U-boat contacts, necessitating either refuelling at sea or diverting to Iceland. The former was, of course, weather permitting and was a hazardous activity in itself and hazardous as to getting the timing window right with regard to fuel state and weather forecast. Diverting to Iceland left the convoy short of escorts and became a predictable choke point for the U-boats.[10]

HMS *Woolston* at the end of the war. Note the rocket rails on the side of the forward 4in gun mount and Type 272 radar antenna aft in place of the searchlight. (vandwdestroyersassociation.org)

The answer was to convert those of the early 'V & Ws' that had the small boiler forward (the narrow funnel) by simply removing

HMS *Vanessa* was a typical LRE. She ended her service life ignominiously as an Air Target Vessel/Flying Training Target Ship. (Seaforth)

it and replacing it with a fuel tank holding about 80 tons (Brown says 450 tons)[11] plus additional fresh water tankage and using the space above for additional crew messing – very much a win-win situation as these ships were cramped with the extra complement caused by the addition of more armament and equipment. As an example, a 1940 complement of 125 rose steadily to 170 by 1944.[12] Speed was reduced to a still very useful 24.5 knots but range increased sufficiently (2,780 miles at 14 knots)[13] to be able to make the transatlantic journey unrefuelled. They were called 'long-leggers' for this reason.

The first conversion was commenced in January 1941. Like the 'WAIRs', the works were extensive and the opportunity was taken to make whatever repairs were deemed necessary at the time. Like so many conversions, no two LREs looked the same – because they usually took place at different times at different shipyards and were subject to the input of whatever happened to be the latest thinking of what was desirable at the time and what was available by way of equipment. The one distinguishing element by way of visual identification was the absence of any fore-funnel and the fact that all received the Type 271 radar in its distinctive lantern atop the bridge. Other than that, armament and its disposition varied. For instance, while the Hedgehog anti-submarine mortar was considered an

The LRE HMS *Westcott* with prominent HF/DF mast added aft. (naval-history.net)

HMS *Vansittart* was an LRE completed comparatively late in the programme but was unusual in that she retained both forward guns and had no Hedgehog fitted. (Seaforth)

essential component in the ships' armoury in 'A' position, two ships, *Vimy*, first to complete in June 1941 and probably prior to Hedgehog being available, and *Vansittart*, June 1943 (*Warwick* may have been similarly fitted) retained their guns in 'A' position. Some were 4in and some 4.7in equipped, only one retained a set of torpedo tubes for no apparent reason (*Viscount*) perhaps to launch the Mk X Heavy Depth Charge. The main anti-aircraft gun was the QF 12-pounder 12 cwt but this was removed in some ships. Some had QF 2-pounders and 20mm Oerlikons, some just Oerlikons and at least one (*Watchman*) had a 2-pounder bow-chaser which seemed strange for the mid-Atlantic. Another had a single Oerlikon on the quarterdeck. So there was little standardisation. There were four depth-charge throwers plus two depth-charge rails and a very full complement of some 100 charges (up to 150 charges according to Brown)[14] but photographs show as many as eight depth-charge throwers, probably to deliver the fourteen-charge pattern which was finally dropped in favour of the ten-charge pattern.

HMS *Vansittart* showing the two BL 4.7in guns retained in 'A' and 'B' position. (Seaforth)

HMS *VIDETTE*: LONG RANGE ESCORT 1943

In order to accompany convoys across the Atlantic without refuelling, twenty-one 'V & W' destroyers were converted to Long Range Escorts (LREs) by removing the forward boiler and converting the space into a fuel tank and extra accommodation (sadly lacking in view of the increased wartime complements occasioned by extra equipment to be manned). Speed dropped to a still useful 24.5 knots. No two conversions looked alike. Some did not receive the Hedgehog anti-submarine mortar and the secondary armament fit-out varied as to what was available at the time of conversion – as did the radar and HF/DF equipment. *Vidette* is shown better equipped than most.

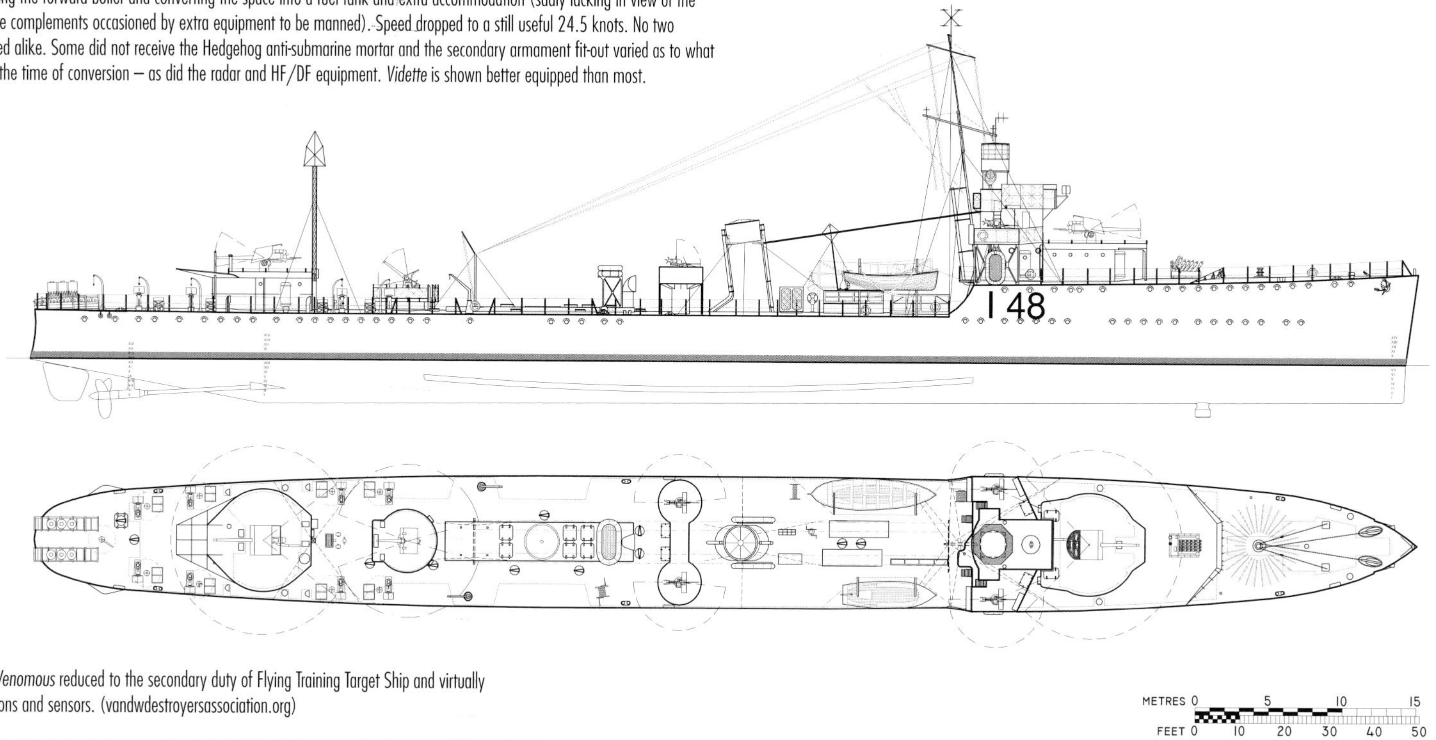

I48

METRES 0 5 10 15
FEET 0 10 20 30 40 50

The ex-LREs HMS *Venomous* reduced to the secondary duty of Flying Training Target Ship and virtually denuded of weapons and sensors. (vandwdestroyersassociation.org)

Apart from the time taken for conversion, these were considered worthwhile although by the time most were in service the Battle of the Atlantic had passed that very critical turning point – May 1943. As the very able 'River' and 'Loch' class frigates came into service, and the US-built 'Captain' and 'Colony' classes also, the need for the LREs diminished and they were gradually withdrawn to lesser uses such as Flying Training Target Ship or Air Target Vessel. In this application, they were used by the Fleet Air Arm for training their Grumman Avenger pilots in torpedo attacks against

HMS *VANSITTART*: LONG RANGE ESCORT 1943

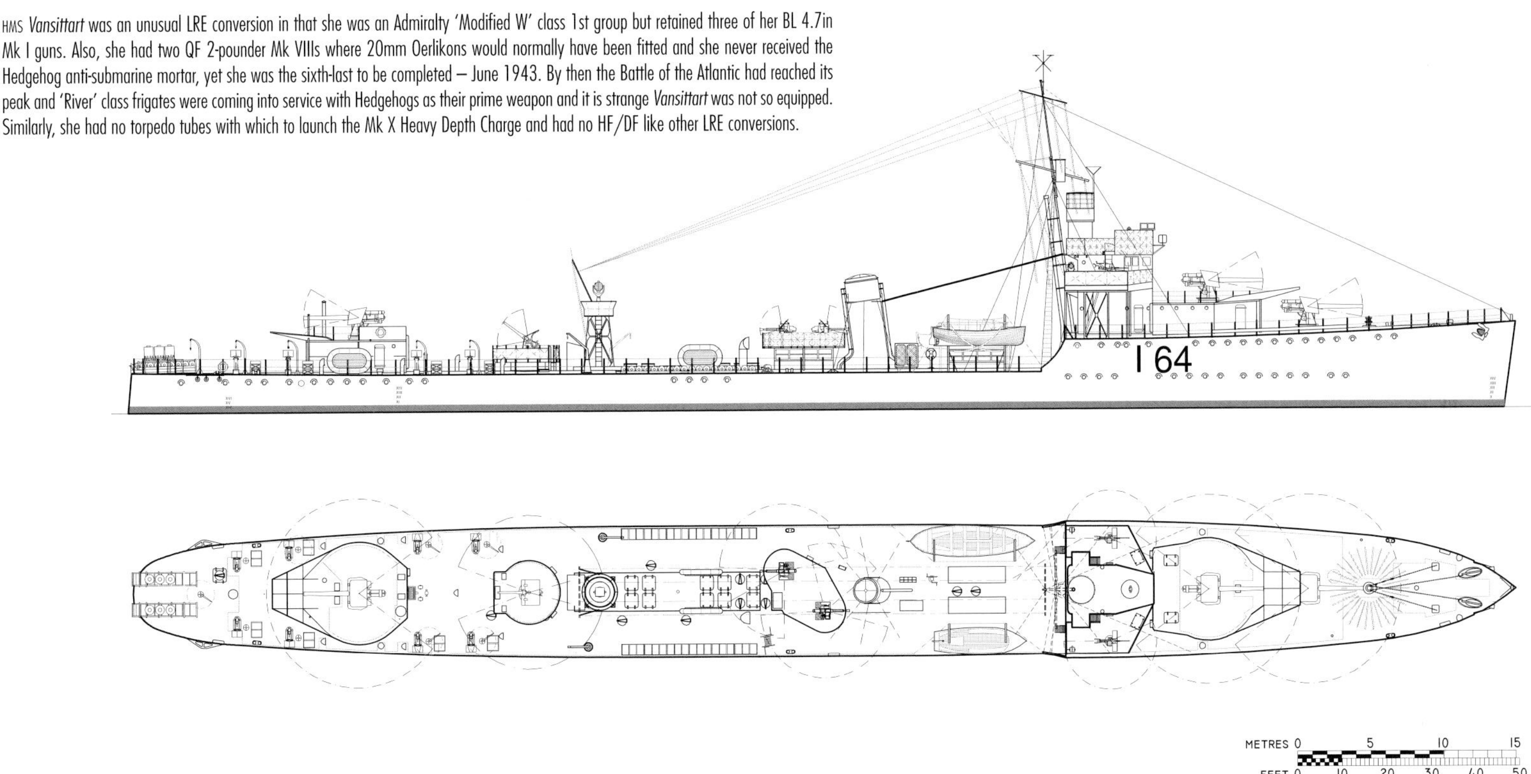

HMS *Vansittart* was an unusual LRE conversion in that she was an Admiralty 'Modified W' class 1st group but retained three of her BL 4.7in Mk I guns. Also, she had two QF 2-pounder Mk VIIIs where 20mm Oerlikons would normally have been fitted and she never received the Hedgehog anti-submarine mortar, yet she was the sixth-last to be completed – June 1943. By then the Battle of the Atlantic had reached its peak and 'River' class frigates were coming into service with Hedgehogs as their prime weapon and it is strange *Vansittart* was not so equipped. Similarly, she had no torpedo tubes with which to launch the Mk X Heavy Depth Charge and had no HF/DF like other LRE conversions.

moving warship targets in anticipation of their taking part in the Pacific war as part of the British Pacific Fleet. They carried something in the order of twelve practice torpedoes on deck – presumably recovered via the special davits fitted.

SHORT RANGE ESCORTS (SREs)

It would be simple to say that what was left over after the 'WAIRs' and the LREs must have been the Short Range Escorts (SREs). By 1942, while these were a disparate lot, one thing most of these had in common was that they had the double boiler room forward and, as such, were unsuitable for conversion to LREs and were sometimes referred to as High Speed Escorts.[15] According to Friedman, the designation of Escort Destroyer appeared in April 1943 but seems to have been applied to the post-First World War-built destroyers converted to, or being converted to, this role.[16]

Because of their range limitations, they generally found use on the East Coast although Preston refers to them being used in the Mediterranean and as far from home as West Africa.[17] For the East Coast at least, where German E-boats were a threat, slow-firing 4in and 4.7in guns proved unsatisfactory against these small, fast-moving targets. Apart from QF 2-pounder bow-chasers being fitted

HMS *VANESSA*: FLYING TRAINING TARGET SHIP 1944

HMS *Vanessa* was past her use-by-date in February 1944 as specialised anti-submarine frigates like 'River' and 'Loch' class plus the Lend-Lease 'Captain' and 'Colony' classes were becoming available in ever-increasing numbers. She was stripped of her anti-submarine equipment and sensors and used for training Fleet Air Arm torpedo aircraft – particularly those bound for service with the British Pacific Fleet. Note the torpedoes stored on deck and davits for handling them.

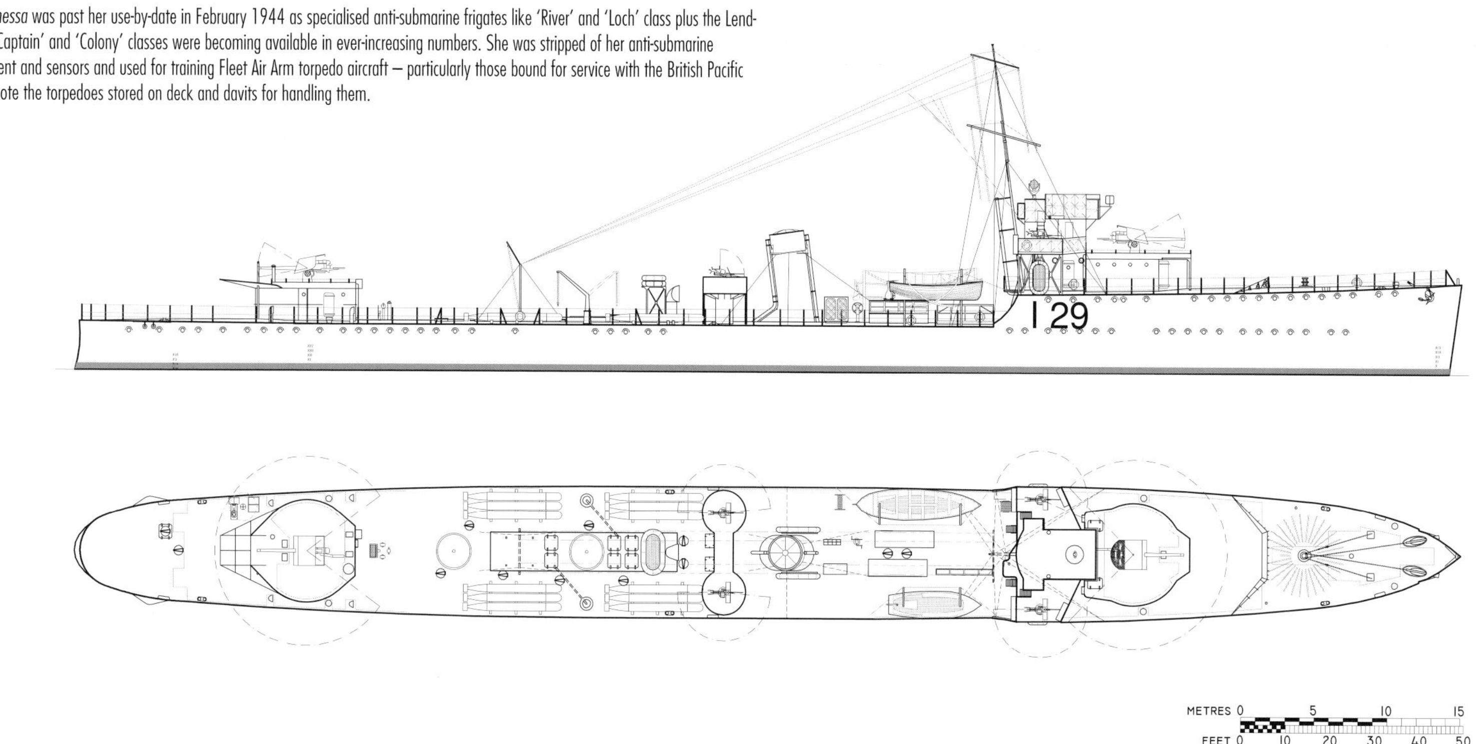

in preference to the 20mm Oerlikon because of its heavier projectile, something that was quick-firing but with an even heavier projectile was needed and this materialised in the form of a twin-barrelled 6-pounder Mk I mounted in 'A' position in four 'V & Ws'. My drawing of HMS *Whitshed* so equipped appears on page ???. Others had single 6-pounders in extended bridge wings but some sources attribute these to being fitted to deal with surfaced U-boats at close range.

Apart from augmentation of the very basic pre-war fit of depth-charge equipment by the addition of extra throwers and more or larger rails, one common upgrade was the removal of the aft bank of torpedo tubes and its replacement by either a QF 3in 20 cwt HA/LA or a QF 12-pounder 12 cwt – also a HA/LA-capable weapon and, while being the older of the two, frequently saw it replacing the former. The ineffective Vickers 0.5in quadruple machine guns were replaced as and when the superior 20mm Oerlikons became available and then these far superior, lighter, more capable anti-aircraft – and anti-surface – weapons were added as space permitted.

SOME FANCIFUL CONVERSIONS

The issue of range brought about one quite drastic possible solution which was never taken to its conclusion – the conversion of 'V & Ws'

HMS *WOLVERINE*: SHORT RANGE ESCORT 1944

HMS *Wolverine* was an Admiralty 'Modified W' class of the 2nd Group (distinguished by the fore-funnel being the more prominent of the two) and was classified as a Short Range Escort (SRE – often referred to as Fast Escorts) to distinguish her from the similarly equipped but specifically modified LREs. Despite it being 1944, note that *Wolverine* still carries twin .303in Lewis guns on the quarterdeck.

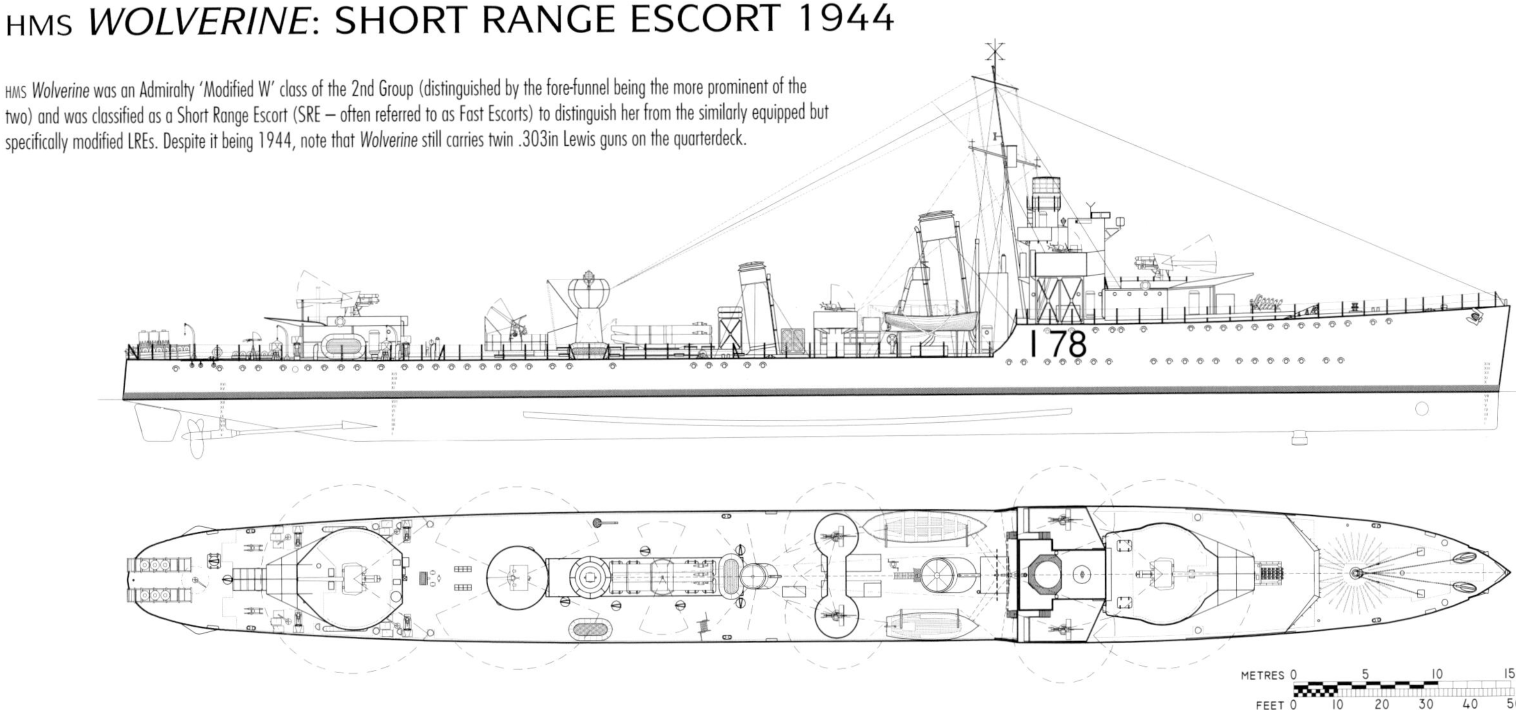

to supply destroyers, having 600–700 tons of refuelling capacity and 170–200 spare depth charges. In order to do this, the existing propulsion would be removed entirely and would be replaced by a pair of 1,600–2,000 BHP Atlas diesels to deliver 15–17 knots. The destroyer look would be maintained with dummy guns but with six Oerlikons, depth charges and ASDIC. Personally, I can't see what dummy weapons would have achieved. In order to function as a supply vessel, there would have been a need for some sort of davits at least for handling the fuel lines and for transferring the depth charges and these alone would have marked the ships as being different. Also, why confuse the escort screen by having something that looks like a fully-fledged escort being incapable of performing that role? So, I have chosen to illustrate what I believe the supply destroyer version of a 'V & W' might have looked like with one funnel only (for the Atlas diesels), six 20mm Oerlikons (which were mooted anyway) and a deckload of depth charges. The Warning Combined Type 291 radar would be all that would have been necessary for its purpose but HF/DF would have been a valuable addition and a mast has been added amidships. Knowing how long it took to convert LREs, this sort of conversion would have taken even longer and the idea was scrapped, probably for the same reason.[18] This drawing appears on page 113.

Another idea that never eventuated, but which one again shows that the 'V & Ws' were certainly never considered a spent force, was to convert some to high-speed transports, similar to the way in which the USN had converted some of its 'flush-decker' *Caldwell/Wickes/Clemson* classes for their Marine Corps as part of the Pacific war's island-hopping nature. Presumably

An interesting photograph of HMS *Vanoc* as an SRE. Note the fixed Type 286 radar antenna between the lower and upper yards. *Vanoc* was credited with being the first to use this radar successfully to detect a U-boat, *U-100* commanded by the famous Kapitänleutnant Joachim Schepke, which she rammed and sank on 17 March 1941. She was later converted to an LRE. (Seaforth)

this conversion was inspired by thoughts of a British participation in the Pacific theatre as units of the British Pacific Fleet. The conversions envisaged four Landing Craft Assault (two per side) and accommodation for 10 officers and 244 other ranks plus facilities for refuelling the landing craft. All 4in guns would be landed and only a token depth-charge outfit retained along with close-range weapons and a full radar outfit.[19] This drawing appears on page 113.

One conversion that had promise but which also failed the test was that proposed by the commanding officer of HMS *Lincoln* – a 'Town' class destroyer, one of the fifty exchanged in the 1940 Destroyers-for-Bases agreement which pre-dated the more important Lend-Lease Act of 1941. His suggestion of January 1942 was a more radical conversion: a LRE with an extended foredeck, a new 'WAIR'-like bridge but with the shelter deck retained so that there was a 4in gun in 'A' position, a Hedgehog in 'B' position (by far the better place where it could be worked in all weathers) a 12-pounder in 'X' position, and one set of torpedo tubes retained, Type 271 on a lattice mast (presumably amidships so that there could be some sort of HACS on the bridge) and a 20in searchlight on a raised platform in front of the bridge slaved to the 4in mount.[20]

My drawing of how this conversion may have appeared is on page 114. Brown refers to a similar conversion of January 1943

HMS *Veteran* was an SRE. She was torpedoed on 26 September 1942 while rescuing survivors from the American passenger ship SS *New York*. All hands were lost including those rescued from *New York* and those previously from the SS *Boston*. (Seaforth)

with two twin 4in guns ('A' and 'X' positions), Hedgehog in 'B', but only a set of twin torpedo tubes and with two twin and two single Oerlikons. Quite why a triple torpedo tube was abandoned in place of a double is curious as this would have meant replacing what already existed with tubes of the type fitted to the Type III and IV 'Hunt' class escort destroyers. Irrespective, the tubes would be required mainly to launch the Mk X and Mk X* Heavy Depth Charge. Brown also refers to a lattice mast – which was becoming standard at that time to support the new radar antennae and to accept the HF/DF antenna.[21] There is a remarkable similarity between these proposals and one cannot help wondering if apart from the date (a year apart?) they may in fact be one and the same simply re-interpreted. Nevertheless, I have chosen to draw both versions for comparison's sake.

HMS *Windsor* of the Rosyth Escort Force, escorting East Coast convoys in 1944. Notice the twin 6-pounder in 'A' position. Photographed by Lieutenant Commander John Manners RN DSC from HMS *Viceroy*. (vandwdestroyersassociation.org)

HMS *WHITSHED*: EAST COAST ESCORT 1943

Four SREs, primarily assigned to escorting East Coast convoys, had their forward BL 4.7in Mk I mounting removed and replaced with a specially developed twin 6-pounder Mk I that could fire at up to 18 rounds per minute per barrel to deal with German E-boats. The mast supports a Type 291 Warning Combined antenna, a 'Headache' signals intercept antenna below the yardarm and there is Type 272 surface-warning radar on a tower amidships.

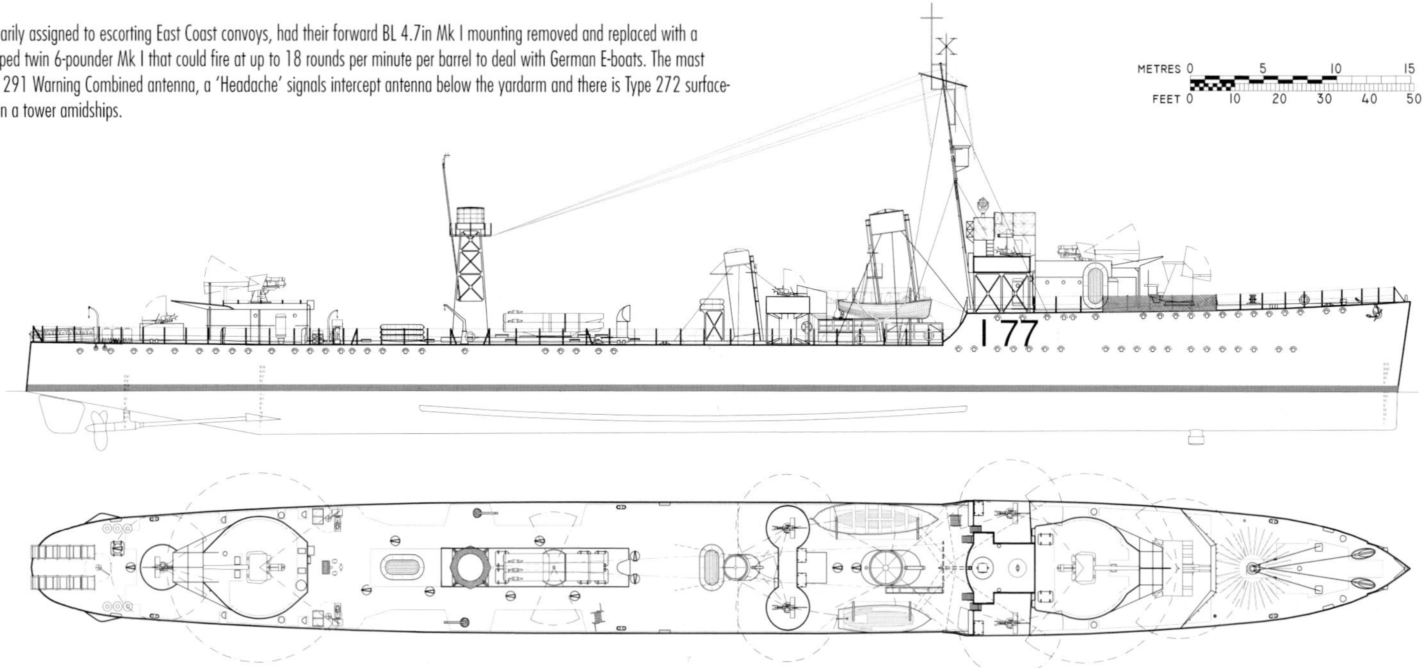

METRES 0 5 10 15

FEET 0 10 20 30 40 50

I77

The QF 6-pounder Mk I was a bulky mounting. Note the ready-use ammunition to supply the theoretical 18rpm each barrel was capable of firing. (Seaforth)

SUPPLY DESTROYER CONVERSION

A proposal that never went ahead was to convert some 'V & Ws' to supply destroyers. This conversion involved removing the existing steam propulsion and replacing it with Atlas diesels and providing 600–700 tons of fuel for refuelling escorts plus re-arming them from a store of 170–200 depth charges – although how these were to be transferred would be problematical. They were apparently to be equipped with dummy guns but I have presumed that this was a pointless exercise and have shown only a secondary and basic anti-submarine armament.

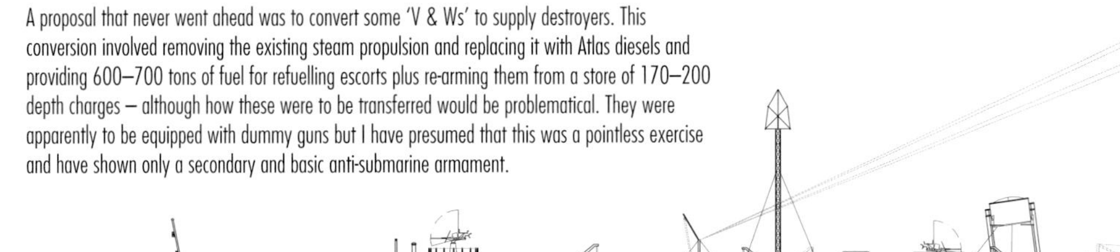

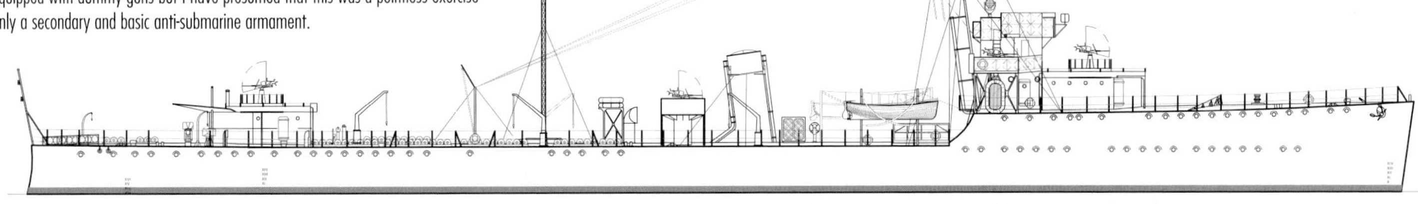

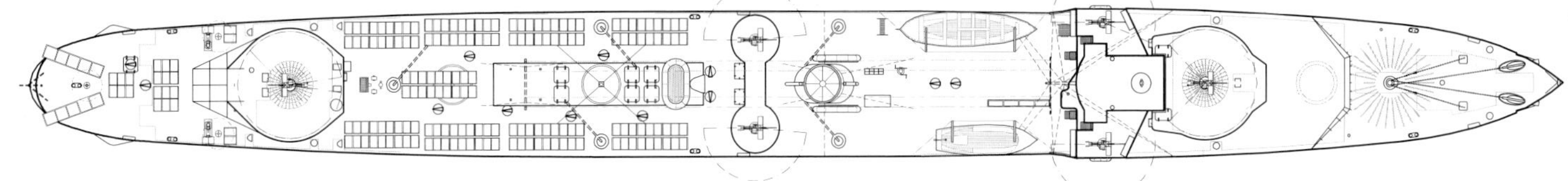

FAST TRANSPORT VERSION 1943

One of the uses for which 'V & Ws' were considered was the equivalent of the USN's conversion of their First World War-built *Caldwell/Wickes/Clemson* class 'flush-decker' destroyers into fast troop transports – in their case to support the island-hopping Pacific campaign. Details are vague as the proposals did not proceed, but to accommodate the 10 officers and 244 other ranks specified for anything other but the shortest journey it would have been necessary to remove the forward boiler room like the LRE conversions. In this representation, the main armament has been removed to reduce topweight and replaced by single 40mm Bofors with which troops would be familiar.

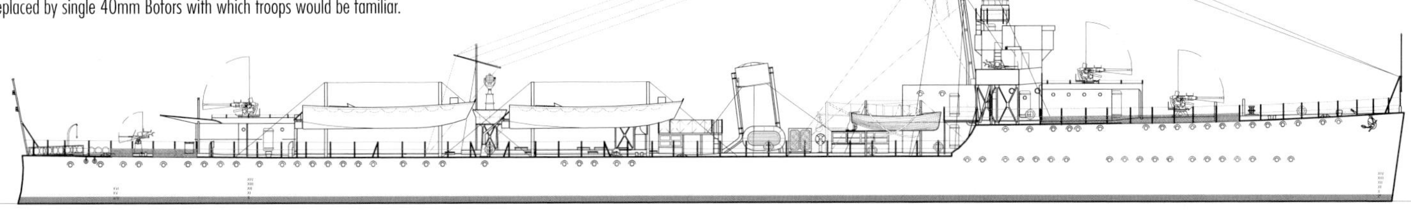

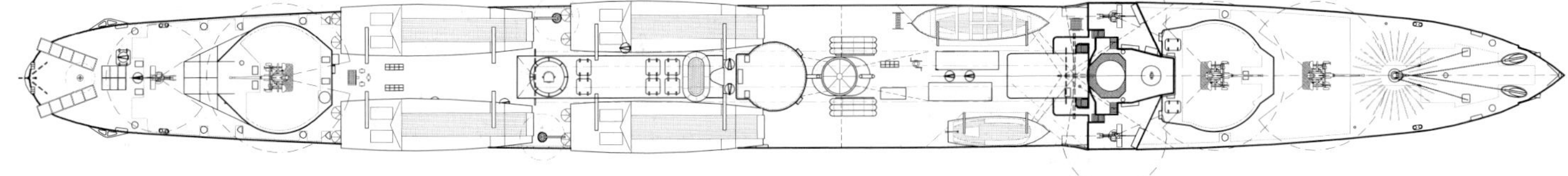

CONVERSION AS PROPOSED 1942

The captain of the 'Town' class destroyer HMS *Lincoln*, one of fifty ex-USN that were part of the 1940 Destroyers For Bases Agreement, suggested a conversion of 'V & Ws' which consisted of a basic LRE conversion but with an extended forecastle (length unknown), with a 'WAIR'-type bridge with a Hedgehog mounted on the shelter deck where it could be used in all weathers, a searchlight in front of the bridge where it could be presumably trained in conjunction with the QF 4in Mk XVI gun in 'A' position, torpedo tubes to be retained and, curiously, a QF 12-pounder 12 cwt retained aft in place of another twin 4in and two twin 20mm Oerlikons in the waist (and presumably one single on each bridge wing) and a lattice mast. No drawings exist to my knowledge so this is my interpretation of how such a conversion may have looked.

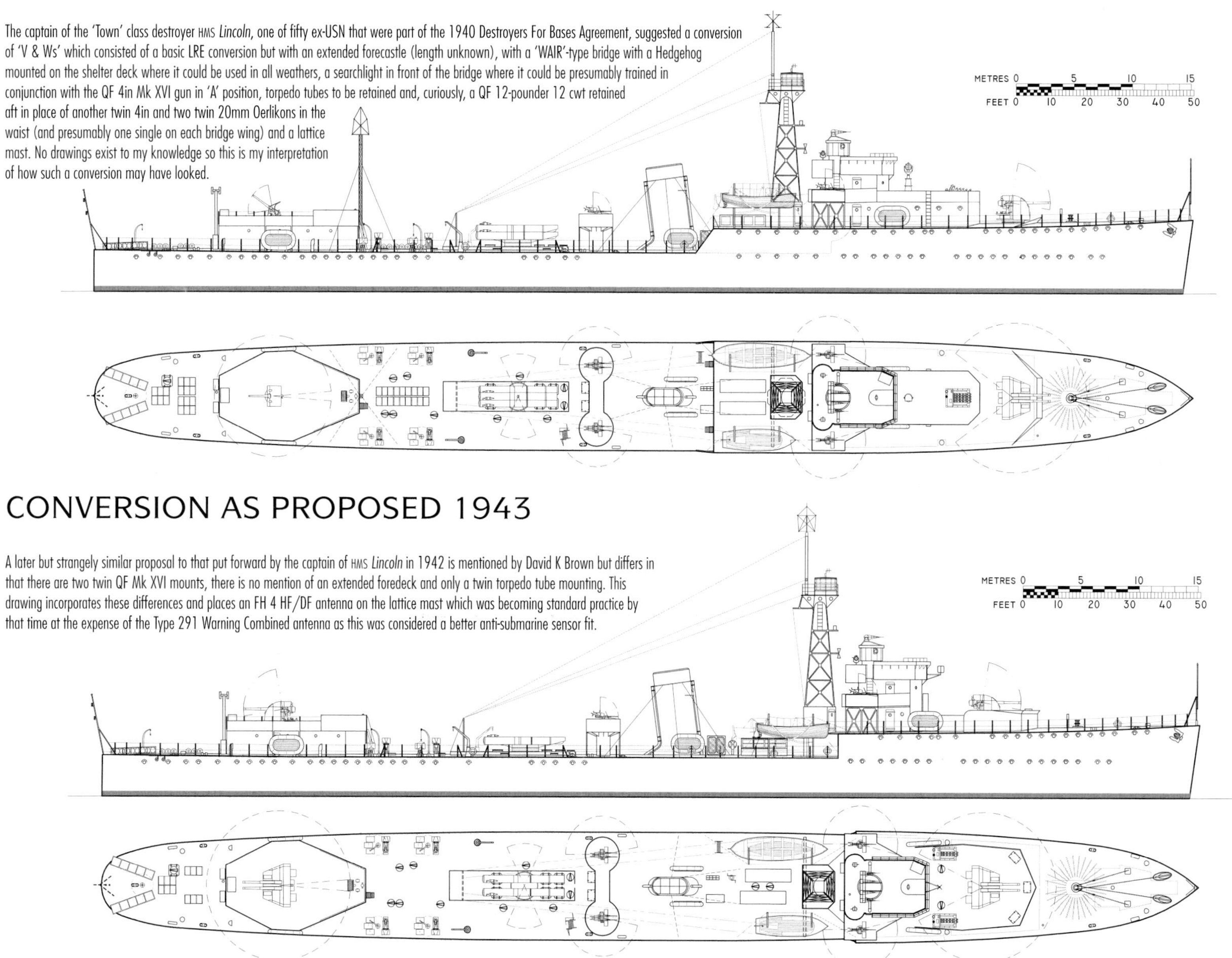

CONVERSION AS PROPOSED 1943

A later but strangely similar proposal to that put forward by the captain of HMS *Lincoln* in 1942 is mentioned by David K Brown but differs in that there are two twin QF Mk XVI mounts, there is no mention of an extended foredeck and only a twin torpedo tube mounting. This drawing incorporates these differences and places an FH 4 HF/DF antenna on the lattice mast which was becoming standard practice by that time at the expense of the Type 291 Warning Combined antenna as this was considered a better anti-submarine sensor fit.

11: Miscellany

MACHINERY

While the basic 'V & W' design set the pattern for destroyers for more than a decade following the First World War, the Royal Navy lagged behind in the design of propulsion – that is, boilers particularly. The refusal to accept higher boiler pressures and temperatures and to introduce more modern turbine design resulted in the lead that British destroyers had in overall design being squandered due to old-fashioned machinery that was heavy, bulky and gave poor endurance. Also, poor workmanship resulted in leaking pipe joints making machinery even less efficient. Undoubtedly, these issues could all have been solved – but at a price. That then poses the question of quantity versus quality. Is it better to have less ships of better quality, or more ships of a lesser quality? As Voltaire said: 'Perfect is the enemy of good enough.'

RADAR

British ship-borne warning radar can be divided into divided into four categories and principal types are shown:

Aircraft Warning: (AW)

Metric Waves	Type 79B, Type 279B, Type 281

Warning Combined: (WC)

Metric Waves	Type 286, Type 286M, Type 286P Type 291& 291Y (Destroyers), Type 291U Light Craft Type 291W Submarines
Centimetric Waves	Type 293 General Service, Type 268U Light Craft Type 267W Submarines

Warning Surface: (WS)

Centimetric Waves	Type 271, Type 271P, Type 271Q Type 272P Type 273P Type 273Q Type 276 Type 277 (WS and AW function) Type 268 Type 970 Type 971

Fire Control: Gunnery Aircraft (GA)

Decimetric Waves	Type 285P, Type 285Q

The first radar fitted to 'V & W' destroyers was the fixed-aerial Type 286. This was developed from the airborne ASV Mk 1 radar and was not particularly successful, shortcomings being poor range, problems with back-echoes, a fixed rectangular aerial which gave only a 60° picture either side of the bow requiring the destroyer to zig-zag and poor bearing accuracy. The M version (from the ASV Mk II) was more powerful and the P version introduced a manually rotated antenna with improved performance. At best, the radar could detect a submarine at 1.5 miles, a destroyer at 4 miles, an aircraft at 5,000ft at 15 miles and an aircraft at 10,000ft at 19 miles. However, they were available in quantity, could be fitted quickly and were valuable for station-keeping in convoys at night.[1]

Its successor, the Type 291, had a recognisable X-shaped antenna and offered better performance: a submarine at 3 miles, a destroyer at 6 miles, an aircraft at 1,000ft at 15 miles, an aircraft at 5,000ft at 30 miles and an aircraft at 10,000ft at 35 miles. M, P, and Q'versions had power rotation and PPI displays.[2]

The most important radars fitted to any of the 'V & W' destroyers, however, were the centimetric wave-based Type 271–273 series resulting from the breakthrough by R A Watson-Watt and his invention of the 10cm cavity magnetron in early 1940. This powered a surface-search antenna with separate transmitting and receiving antenna stacked one above the other and incorporated a crystal detector more sensitive than the usual tube type. The 'cheese' shape of the antenna gave a better fan beam irrespective of its angle to the horizontal. The first models involved the antenna being located directly above the radar 'office', the antenna rotation was manual and limited to 400° due to the use of coaxial cable and the display was via an A-scope only, requiring, as with other contemporary screen, considerable interpretation. The Type 271Q introduced higher power, wave guides to allow separation of the antenna and the radar office and a PPI display. In a corvette, not dissimilar to a 'V & W' in its antenna placement, ranges were a submarine at 4–5 miles, and a destroyer at 9 miles. The antenna was easily distinguishable in its teak-framed, Perspex-enclosed lantern.

The Type 272 allowed even greater – 40ft – separation of antenna and office allowing greater freedom for the placement of the antenna. For instance, note the placement of the antenna in the drawing of HMS *Whitshed* on page 112. Greater height improved range.[3]

Sources vary as to exactly what the Type 273 antenna looked like as it was enclosed – apparently in a sixteen-sided 'lantern'. Quite clearly, at some stage the teak-framed lantern gave way to a totally frameless opaque Perspex or glass-fibre drum. Friedman shows a drawing of a Type 273Q antenna and a description which shows a totally different antenna with two 4ft 6in (some say 3ft 0in) paraboloids side by side compared to the one-above-the-other cheese type so typical of the Type 271/272. I think it is probably fair to assume that the change in antenna type went hand-in-hand with the change in antenna cover. Friedman states that this type was introduced in 1942, had continuous rotation at 15rpm, was gyro-stabilised and ranges were a submarine at 7 miles and a destroyer at 17 miles.[4] Type 273 seems to have been only used on larger – cruiser-size – warships.

The 'WAIR' conversions had Type 285 gunnery radar fitted to the director control tower. Unfortunately, the one tower controlled both twin 4in mounts so only one target could be engaged at the same time. Accuracy was 100yds on the 15,000yd scale and 250yds on the 30,000yd scale with a bearing accuracy of 3–4°. Range against aircraft was 17,000yds at 5,000ft, 18,000yds at 2,000ft, 14,000yds at 1,000ft and 9,500yds at 600ft. It could not follow targets in elevation nor provide blind-fire capability.[5]

ASDIC

The ASD in ASDIC comes from the Anti-Submarine Division of the British Admiralty formed late in the First World War to investigate methods of detecting German submarines by the use mainly of quartz piezoelectric crystals to detect underwater sounds. The addition of the 'IC' is subject to conjecture. One school of thought is that it refers to scientif-IC, the other that the name of the organisation was changed to Allied Submarine Detection Investigation Committee without supporting evidence. Nevertheless, research did take place and the following is a list of the major developments by type.[6]

Type 112

This was a primitive passive set designed in 1920 only to listen for submarines and was fitted to some 'V & W' destroyers in 1924 (6th Flotilla).

Type 119

This was a more refined set of 1930 designed to combat the effects of bending the beams due to water density layers and was fitted to 'B' class destroyers onward.

Type 121

The Type 119 with a gyro-stabilised transducer introduced in 1931 and could operate at up to 24 knots. Fitted with a retractable dome and to 'D' to 'G' class destroyers. Like the preceding Type 119, it had a bridge loudspeaker to give the commanding officer a better idea of how the situation was developing.

Type 124

A 1934 improvement with a retractable dome, a range recorder and an improved amplifier. It had a practical range of about 2,500yds and could be controlled from the destroyer's bridge. This became the standard outfit for new destroyers and some older destroyers, possibly including 'V & Ws'.

Type 127
This was designed for the convoy sloops but was fitted to older destroyers, possibly some 'V & Ws', and was the first type to be fitted with a bearing plotter.

Type 128
This was the next development and had a range recorder, tested in 1937. This type was fitted to the 'A', 'L' and 'Hunt' class destroyers and had the dome and directing gear of the Type 121 but the electronics of the Type 127. It could be controlled from the bridge.

Type 141
This was exclusive to the 'Town' class destroyers from America and was a QCJ/QCL set modified with British range and bearing recorders. The transducer was built-in but some received a dome and became the British Type 141A type.

Type 144
This was in use from mid-1942 and had a visual bearing recorder which provided a memory of the bearing of echoes received. It was a complete re-design and was the first set specifically intended for the ahead-throwing weapons like Hedgehog. Used in any 'V & W' so equipped, such as LRE conversions. It had a normal range of about 2,500 yards but could reach 3,000yds under ideal conditions. It also introduced automatic scanning, turning 5° after each ping. This reduced the burden on the operator, allowing him to concentrate on listening for contacts. Some features were incorporated into late-production Type 127–128s.

Type 144Q
This was a variation of Type 144. With Type 147B the ultimate wartime ASDIC.

Type 147
This had a steerable beam which was broad in the horizontal plane but vertically shallow and was designed to work with the Squid ASW mortar.

Type 147B
This was a variation of Type 147. Also referred to as Sword due to the shape of the transducer which was placed ahead of the Type 147 transducer.

Q Attachment
In use from 1943, this was the opposite of Sword in that the beam was very narrow – again about 3° – but the wedge shape was in the long fore and aft plane and measured depth. It could be retro-fitted to Types 127, 128 and 144.

THE 'FIVE WIDE VIRGINS', PARSNIPS, HEDGEHOGS AND SQUIDS

The concept of a weapon mounted on the foredeck of an escort that could throw an anti-submarine missile ahead of the ship – most often thought of as a depth charge or depth charge-like missile – had considerable advantages over depth charges. No matter how good the ASDIC and its operator, contact would be lost as the escort passed over the submarine's presumed location – a blind spot. If the submarine could be held in the ASDIC's beam ahead of the escort then some sort of weapon that projected a charge into that live zone was desirable.

The crudely-named 'Bell-mouthed Bastard' had been designed, unsuccessfully, to fire quite a large projectile from a mounting sunk into, presumably, the foredeck. Another, name unknown, used rockets. A Fairlie Mortar with multiple barrels in a fore-and-aft configuration had also proved unsuccessful as had a similar, five-barrelled athwartships arrangement by the ever-inventive Thornycroft's called the 'Five Wide Virgins'. The Admiralty 'Modified W' class destroyer HMS *Whitehall* was used for trials in July 1941 but they proved unsuccessful as it was clumsy to reload on the foredeck where 'A' gun had been removed. Eight men were required for reloading and it took nine minutes to do so – under ideal conditions. The standard Mk VII depth charges were launched about 330yds ahead of the ship and the tubes were angled to provide a spread. The device was redesigned with two ten-

HMS *WHITEHALL* JULY 1941

HMS *Whitehall* was one of the 1st Group of the seven Admiralty 'Modified W' class. After serving in the evacuation at Dunkirk, she was subjected to the normal anti-submarine and anti-aircraft upgrade by the addition of extra depth-charge throwers and tracks, the removal of the aft torpedo mounting and its replacement with a QF 12-pounder 12 cwt AA gun. At some later stage, her two single QF 2-pounders (probably Mk IIs) were replaced with single 20mm Oerlikons and Type 286 radar was added. In July 1941 she was the trials ship for the 'Five Wide Virgins' – an unsuccessful attempt at a Thornycroft-designed ahead-throwing anti-submarine mortar mounted on the foredeck in place of 'A' mount. This requirement was subsequently satisfied by the Hedgehog spigot mortar and this was replaced by the superior Squid three-barrelled mortar. Whitehall was converted to a Long Range Escort in 1942.

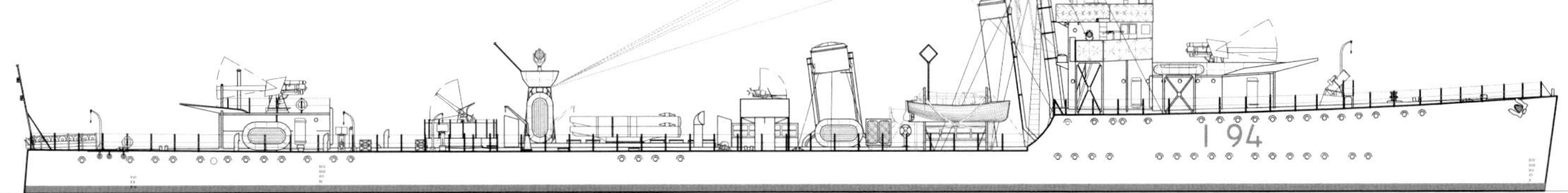

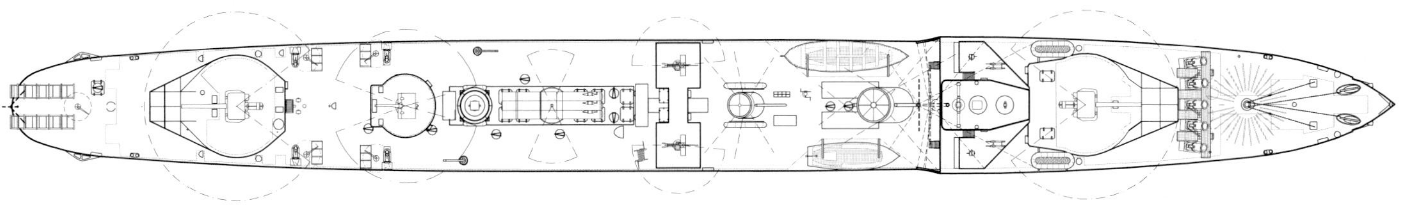

HMS *Whitehall* was an SRE (or Fast Escort) before being used as a test-bed for the 'Five Wide Virgins' anti-submarine ahead-throwing mortar mounted on her foredeck. This proved a failure and she was converted to an LRE. (Seaforth)

barrelled units known as 'Parsnip'. These fired smaller projectiles electronically delayed to deliver a semi-circular pattern but this too failed to gain acceptance.

The simple Hedgehog spigot mortar eventually won the race. It owed its beginnings to Lieutennat Colonel Stewart Blacker for use as an anti-tank weapon, the 'Blacker Bombard'. Prior to the war, Blacker had suggested the use of such a mortar to the Admiralty for attacking submarines but was rejected. The Department of Miscellaneous Weapons Development – also known as the 'Wheezers and Dodgers' – took up the concept on the basis of firing not one but a ring of twenty-four bombs. After many trials and

HMS *AMBUSCADE* WITH SQUID ASW MORTAR 1943

HMS *Ambuscade* was selected as an Air Target Ship in mid-1942 but gained a reprieve early in 1943 to be used as a trials ship for the unsuccessful Parsnip anti-submarine mortar then the brilliant three-barrelled Squid anti-submarine mortar – two of which were mounted on her foredeck in place of 'A' mount (shown here). These were superior to the Hedgehog spigot mortar and the three 390lb depth charges that each Squid fired up to 275 yards ahead of the ship could be set to explode at depth determined by the ship's Type 147 ASDIC. Note that her torpedo tubes have been removed for her intended use as an Air Target Ship but she still carries a full radar outfit.

HMS *Ambuscade* with the first two Squid anti-submarine mortars on her foredeck for testing in place of 'A' mount. They proved to be an improvement over the Hedgehog. (Seaforth)

tribulations, a successful demonstration on land before Prime Minister Winston Churchill saw it tested at sea on HMS *Westcott* in May 1941 and go into production nine months after the first drawings had been prepared. Although unpopular to begin with, mainly due to inherent conservatism, being hurried into operation and with insufficient training, the Hedgehog grew in acceptance – particularly with the USN which promoted a more rigorous training procedure and had better ASDIC/sonar. Unlike depth charges, there was no explosion underwater unless one of the twenty-four projectiles hit the target so there was no disturbance to the ASDIC signal. Also, the projectiles had a quicker sink rate than depth charges. Kill ratios for depth-charge attacks averaged 1 in 80 but with Hedgehog attacks ended up with an impressive 1 in 5 success ratio.

An even better weapon which went from the drawing board virtually straight into production and when in active service began producing immediate results was the three-barrelled Squid mortar. HMS *Ambuscade* (one of the first two destroyers to be designed and built after the First World War, see above) was used as a test bed for the prototype, two being mounted side-by-side on the foredeck in place of 'A' mount. Squid fired special depth charges whose depth

WEAPONS 1

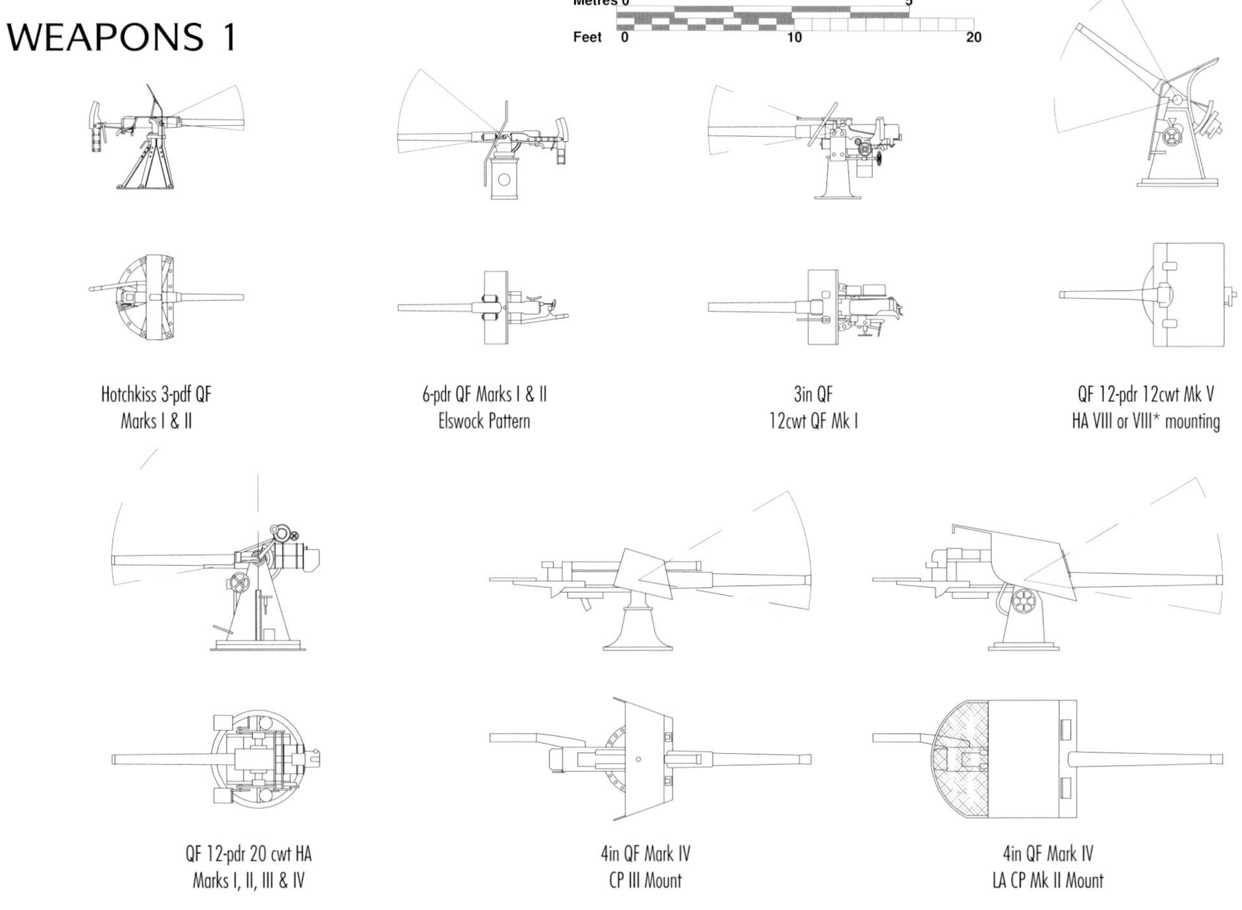

Hotchkiss 3-pdf QF
Marks I & II

6-pdr QF Marks I & II
Elswock Pattern

3in QF
12cwt QF Mk I

QF 12-pdr 12cwt Mk V
HA VIII or VIII* mounting

QF 12-pdr 20 cwt HA
Marks I, II, III & IV

4in QF Mark IV
CP III Mount

4in QF Mark IV
LA CP Mk II Mount

settings could be determined by the Type 147 ASDIC up to the very last moment before firing. Squid obtained its first kill on 31 July 1944. By trawling through the records, I was able to estimate that Squid was involved in possibly six U-boat losses in 1944 (two to 'Castle' class corvettes and four to 'Loch' class frigates) and possibly eleven in 1945 (two to 'Castle' class corvettes and nine to 'Loch' class frigates). Squid went on to become a more sophisticated mortar in Limbo in the mid-1950s but was superceded by homing torpedoes.

My drawing of HMS *Whitehall* equipped with the 'Five Wide Virgins' appears on page 118 and HMS *Ambuscade* equipped with two Squids appears on page 119.

WEAPONS 2

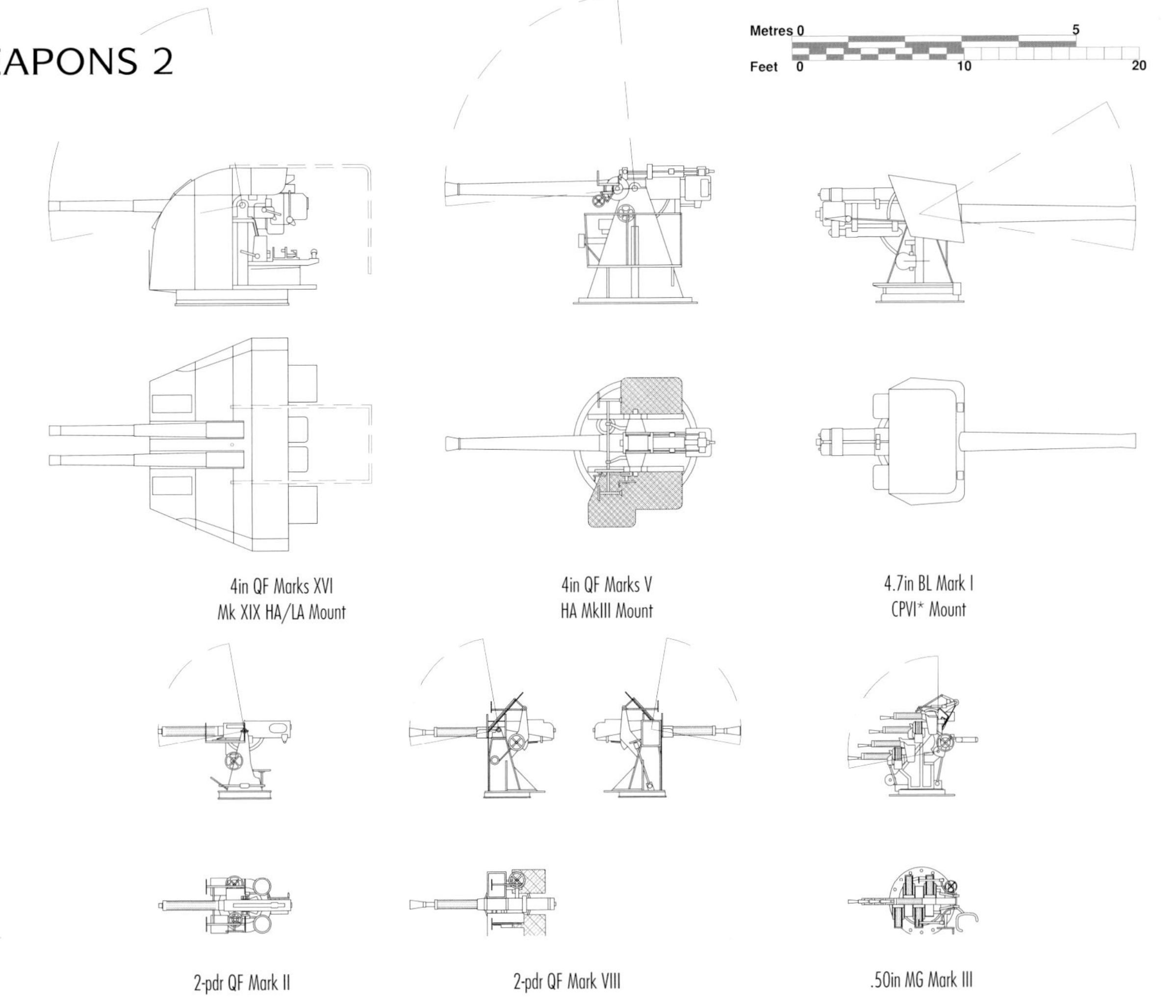

GUNNERY CONTROL

The British Destroyer Director Firing System was deployed late in the First World War to provide destroyers and flotilla leaders with the benefits of director firing. It used a crew of three at the director and a fixed elevation angle for firing on the roll.

The smaller ships of the Royal Navy were not amenable to the bulky equipment that comprised the director firing systems for the capital ships, but some simplifications and compromises were seen as helpful in preserving the basic benefit in a suitable form. The director could also signal the training angle for the ship's searchlights. The basic design proved sound enough that the

WEAPONS 3

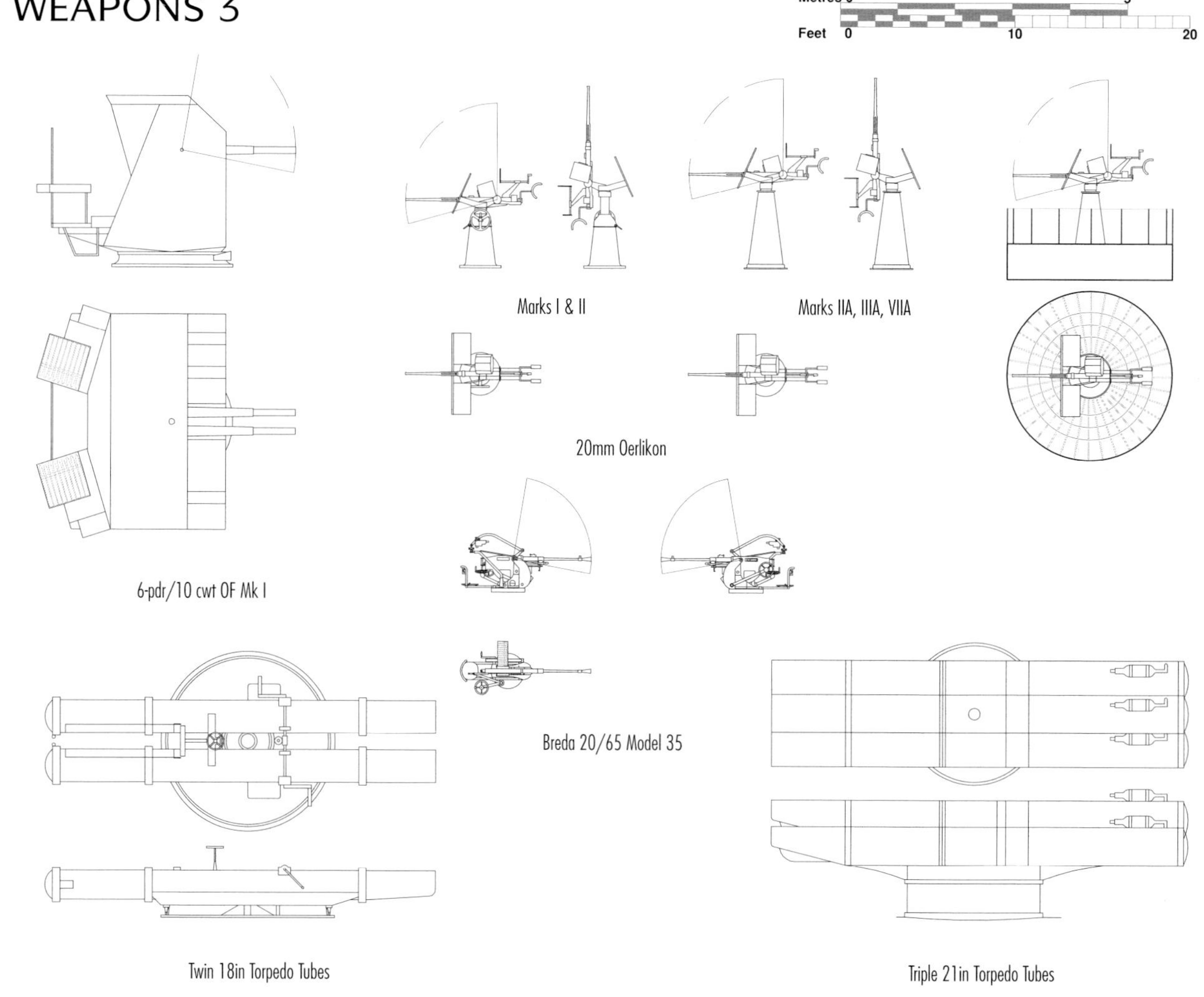

6-pdr/10 cwt OF Mk I

Twin 18in Torpedo Tubes

Triple 21in Torpedo Tubes

Handbook was receiving minor addenda as late as 1947 – and these pertained to the methods used in conducting a tilt test.

Director

The director was pedestal-mounted and, like the capital ship system, transmitted slewing and training angle to the gun mounts, and in the same step-sizes: 4 arc-minutes for training, and 2° per step for slewing. Firing impulses were likewise transmitted to the guns, always firing on the roll. Unlike the larger system, however, elevation angles were not transmitted at all; the guns were all elevated to a fixed index-mark so they would match the sighting angle of the director's telescope. Henderson firing gear was

WEAPONS 4

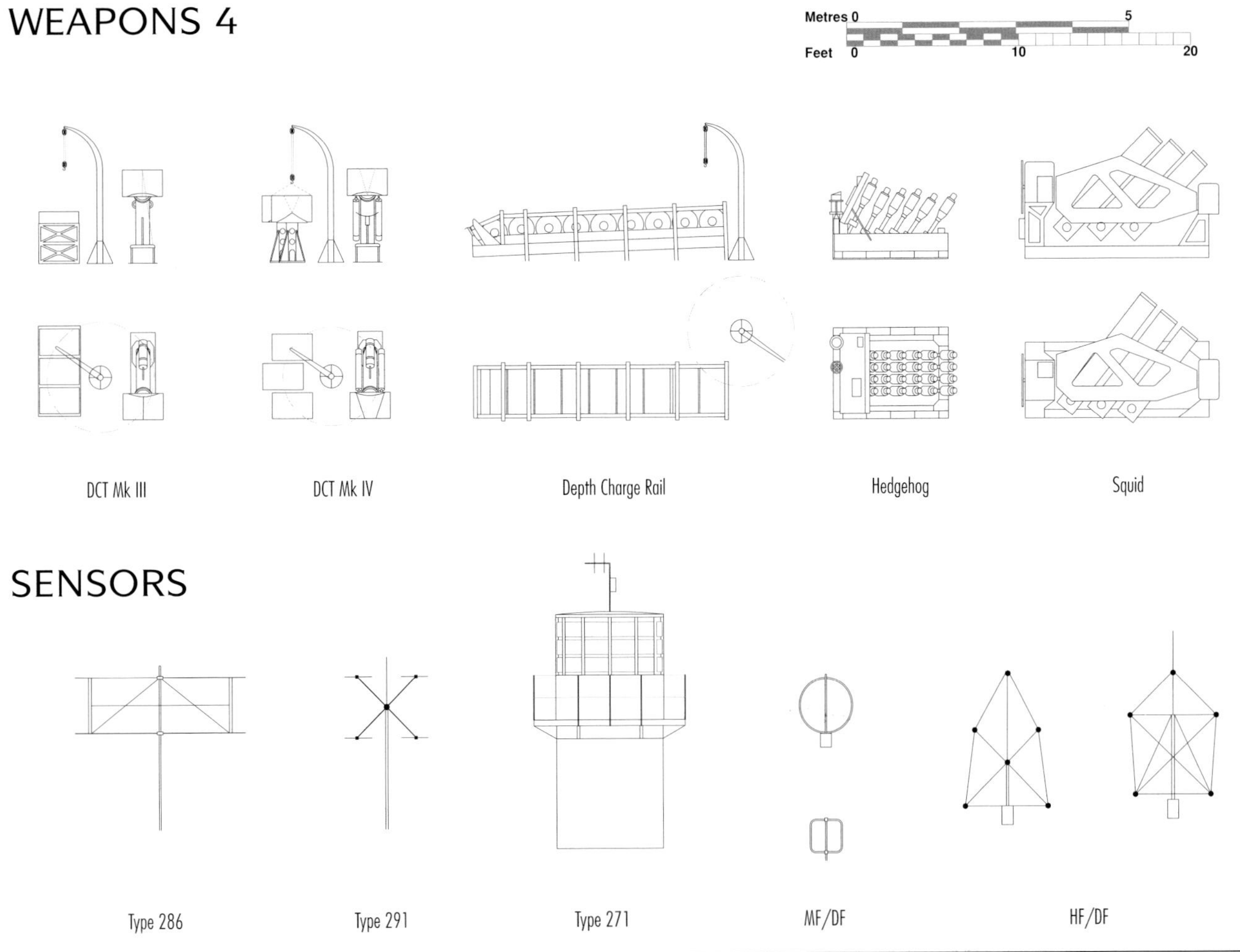

provided if the director layer wished to use it. The gearing was set up such that the slewing handle rotated the director fifteen times as fast (6° per revolution) as the training handle did (40 arc-minutes per revolution). Tilt correction was addressed in the simplest possible way: by using two wedge-shaped rings at the base of the director to neutralise a tilt of up to 1°. Dip was entirely ignored.

Director Crew

The director eventually required a crew of three after cross-level correction was added.

Director Layer

The director layer on this device both trained and elevated the director. He also worked the firing pistol and adjusted the Henderson gyroscope. Since the Henderson gear would keep his horizontal wire on the target, he could concentrate on keeping the scope always on for training. Firing by Henderson was the preferred mode, with firing by the director layer an alternative method. Firing individually at the guns was preferred for close-range night fighting.

Continuous training was to be used as far as practicable, with practice being used to allow anticipation of yaw motions to cause the minimum required number of training reversals. The second addendum to the Handbook, issued in mid-1928, specifies that the training had been sped up by 50 per cent by use of a new training worm wheel and related mechanisms.

Sight-setter

The sight-setter only set the deflection as directed; the gunsights at the guns worked in concert with the mechanical elevation indexes to establish the proper elevation for the range. The director's deflection drum featured a movable pointer which would be adjusted for the range in use, and this would correct for drift. He was required to check the deflection after adjusting the drift pointer, as it would be changed, and he verified the elevation index being used by the director's telescope to ensure common settings at the guns.

Cross-Level Operator

This man kept an open sight arranged 90° off the scopes in azimuth on the horizon by use of a handwheel. The eyepiece for his open sight could be placed on either end of the assembly to suit any constraints on physical movement about the director. He used a second handwheel to enter the range onto a graduated scale to establish the training correction on the director to provide the proper correction required by the canted trunnions. At night, this man also acted as sight-setter for the searchlight deflection dial.

Gun Crews

The gun crews functioned as usual, except as follows. Rather than keeping his crosshairs on the target and firing when they came on, the gunlayer would use his handwheel to keep a newly-fashioned pointer attached to the trunnion in line with a given index mark on an arc. The arc had a series of indices arrayed at 1° intervals numbered 6 through 14. 10 was the mark ordinarily used, and corresponded to the director's scopes being in the same plane as the guns; the other marks could allow for super-elevation or firing at different points on the roll. The trainer would use his handwheel to satisfy his FTP Training Receiver and keep its range pointer set to the range reported by his sight-setter, as this would achieve the convergence correction.

Searchlight Crew

The man training each searchlight would have a bearing receiver very similar to the training receiver used at the guns, except that the deflection sent to the training receivers would be factored out at the director from its signals. The bearing receiver also corrected for convergence.

Adoption

Although it was approved in 1917 to fit this equipment in almost all Flotilla Leaders and all destroyers of the 'V & W' class and later, no installations were completed before 1918. However, once things got underway, progress was rapid, as 118 ships were equipped during 1918.[7]

CAMOUFLAGE

Camouflage, whether it was applied to warships, aircraft or military equipment was designed to achieve one, or two, of three things:

concealment, confusion or deception.

Concealment applied more in a situation such as a ship in a harbour. At sea, this was more difficult and a scheme which made a ship harder to distinguish in one sort of light might have had the opposite effect in other lights. Reduced visibility was achieved by painting vertical surfaces to harmonise with the horizon, and horizontal surfaces to blend with the sea.

Confusion was achieved by dazzle-style camouflage that used shapes or colours, or a combination of both, to make it difficult to estimate range, speed and bearing. Other methods of achieving confusion was painting a false bow wave so that the enemy would overestimate a ship's speed. Disruptive camouflage was also designed to break up the outline of a ship, making its size and type more difficult to establish by painting obtrusive patterns on vertical surfaces

Deception was aimed at making a ship look like something it was not. For example, painting a section of the bow and stern painted black, the bow with a white dividing slash. The aim of this was to foreshorten the hull and, as such, the enemy would underestimate either the size of the ship or its range.

Some camouflage methods attempted to serve two of these purposes. However, a camouflage scheme for one theatre might not be suitable for another. Changing schemes was time consuming – even if the base surface was in good order – and expensive. Paint colours weren't consistent, relying on formulae for mixing and the application itself was often open to interpretation and amateurish when done by crew-members rather than professional dockyard workers who weren't guaranteed to get it right anyway. The TLAR – 'That Looks About Right' – formula was generally applied when it came to painting.

Malcolm Wright's excellent book, *British and Commonwealth Warship Camouflage of WWII: Destroyers, Frigates, escorts, Minesweepers, Coastal Warfare Craft, Submarines & Auxiliaries*, illustrates no less than fifty-two different schemes that applied to 'V & W' destroyers and the *Shakespeare* and *Scott* leaders. Some of these were one-off, spur-of-the-moment, using-what-was-available concepts with little science behind them. Some, as Wright says, were 'probably an invention of the wardroom using whatever was available from her paint locker'. Whatever the actual shades that were specified, the final shades of paint varied. Unlike today, when paint comes either pre-mixed and coloured from the factory or coloured at the point of sale to a shade, ships in RN had formulae with which to mix paint and these formulae were complicated using pigmented powders and liquids. Lots of things could go wrong with this, and almost certainly did. Ships were rarely camouflaged bow to stern, truck to waterline all at the one time. Often paint was applied *ad hoc* or touched up between assignments by crew members. Paint faded. Storms took their toll. It was rare for a ship to look pristine. From 1943 onwards, paint began to be pre-mixed and schemes became more standardised.

The Admiralty Western Approaches Scheme was a completely different and somewhat radical approach to camouflage – the traditional thinking being that darker was better. Peter Scott, a serving RN officer and a naturalist, suggested that ships should be painted overall white with contrasting patches – ultimately polygonal shapes were chosen – of light sea blue and light sea green. This was adopted in mid-1941 for use exclusively on destroyers and anti-submarine escort ships. This white background was sometimes used with various applications of darker colours like blue and black. The traditional pale grey was broken with darker greys, pale and dark greens and also dark blue, mainly in geometrical slashed shapes but sometimes organic waves.

The Royal Australian Navy ships operating in the SW Pacific followed United States Navy camouflage protocols since they were so closely integrated with their task forces. An overall dark blue was favoured but this was later varied by additions of grey, particularly when ships became attached to the British Pacific Fleet and adopted the two-tone blue-grey scheme.

I have chosen to illustrate six different camouflage styles of the very many variants (pages 126–7).

LIVING CONDITIONS

Lest one thinks the 'V & Ws' were just the bees knees in every respect, it might be worth considering some of the more mundane aspects of their design – indeed many aspects that applied to all destroyers and even light cruisers of the time.

Sanitary arrangements were – well, primitive would be too generous a word to those used to twenty-first century conveniences,

CAMOUFLAGE 1

Ships are drawn to demonstrate camouflage only.
They may not represent configuration at the time.

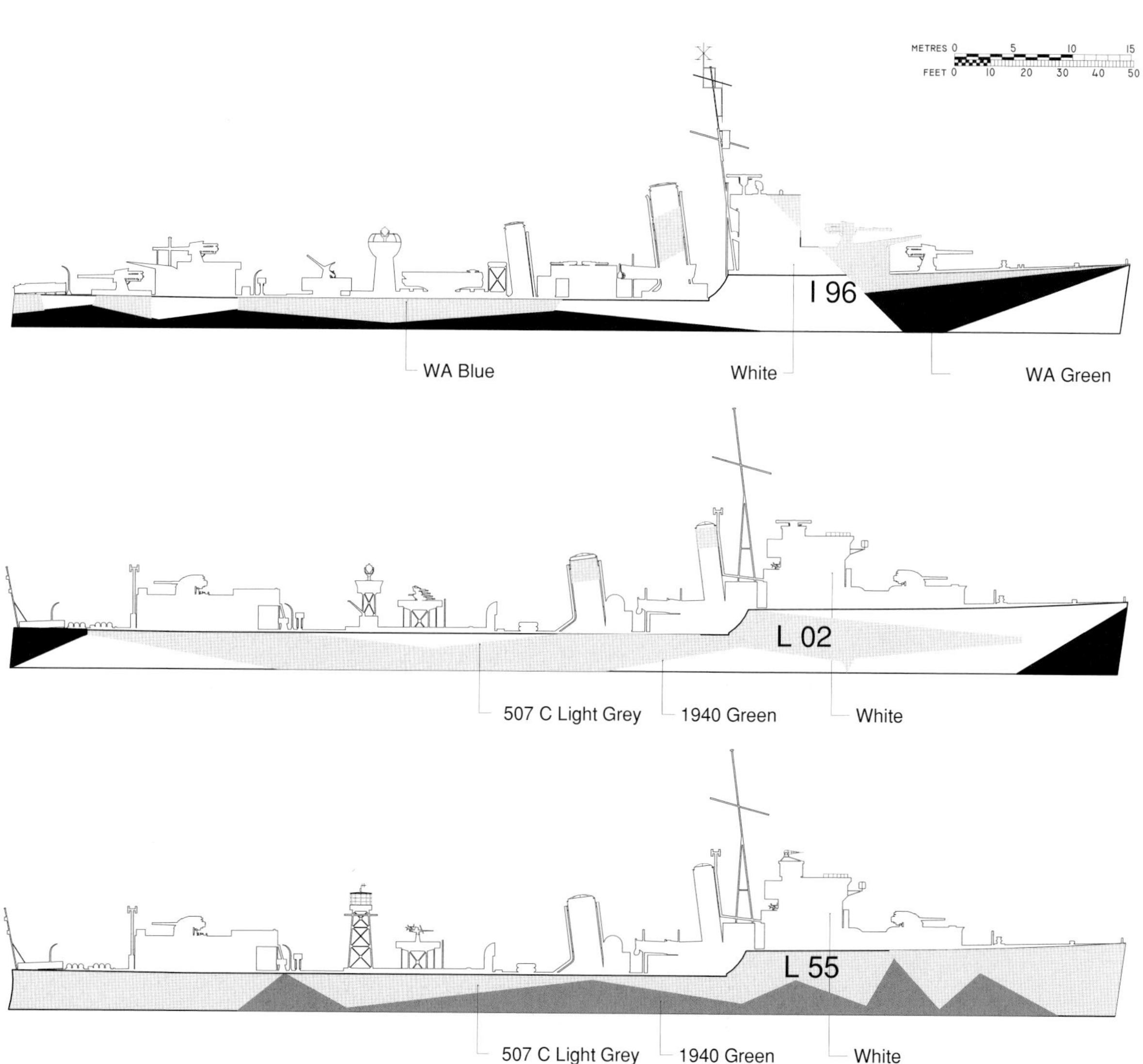

HMS *Worcester* SRE 1942
Western Approaches Scheme

HMS *Wolsey* 'WAIR' Conversion 1942
Western Approaches Scheme

HMS *Winchester* 'WAIR' Conversion 1942
Light Admiralty Disruptive Pattern – East Coast

CAMOUFLAGE 2

Ships are drawn to demonstrate camouflage only.
They may not represent configuration at the time.

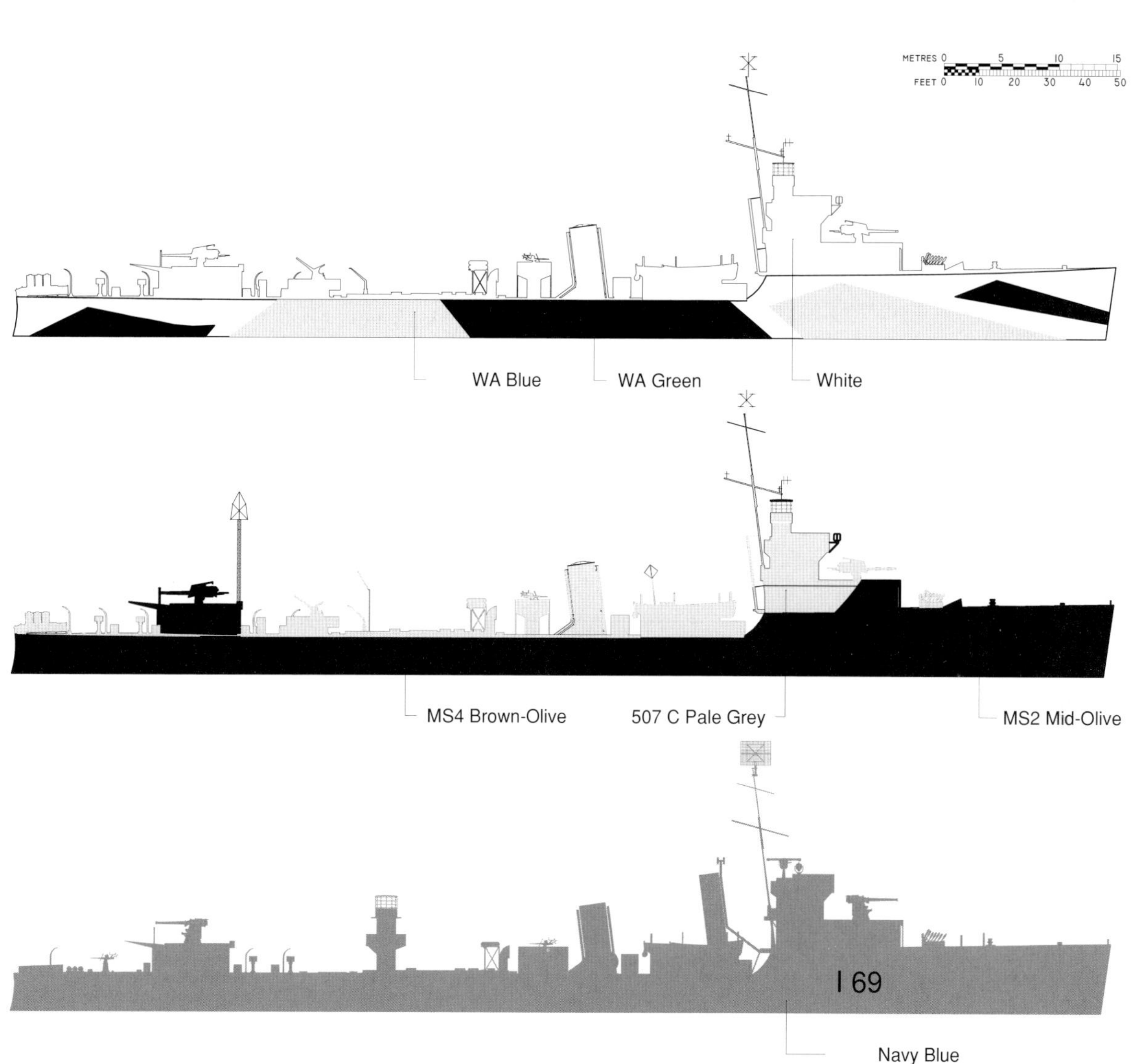

LRE Atlantic 1942
Western Approaches Scheme

HMS *Vidette* – LRE 1943
Admiralty Light Disruptive Pattern

HMAS *Vendetta* – SW Pacific 1944
US Pacific Fleet, adaptation of Measure 21,
Navy Blue (5-N) overall

SHIPS BOATS

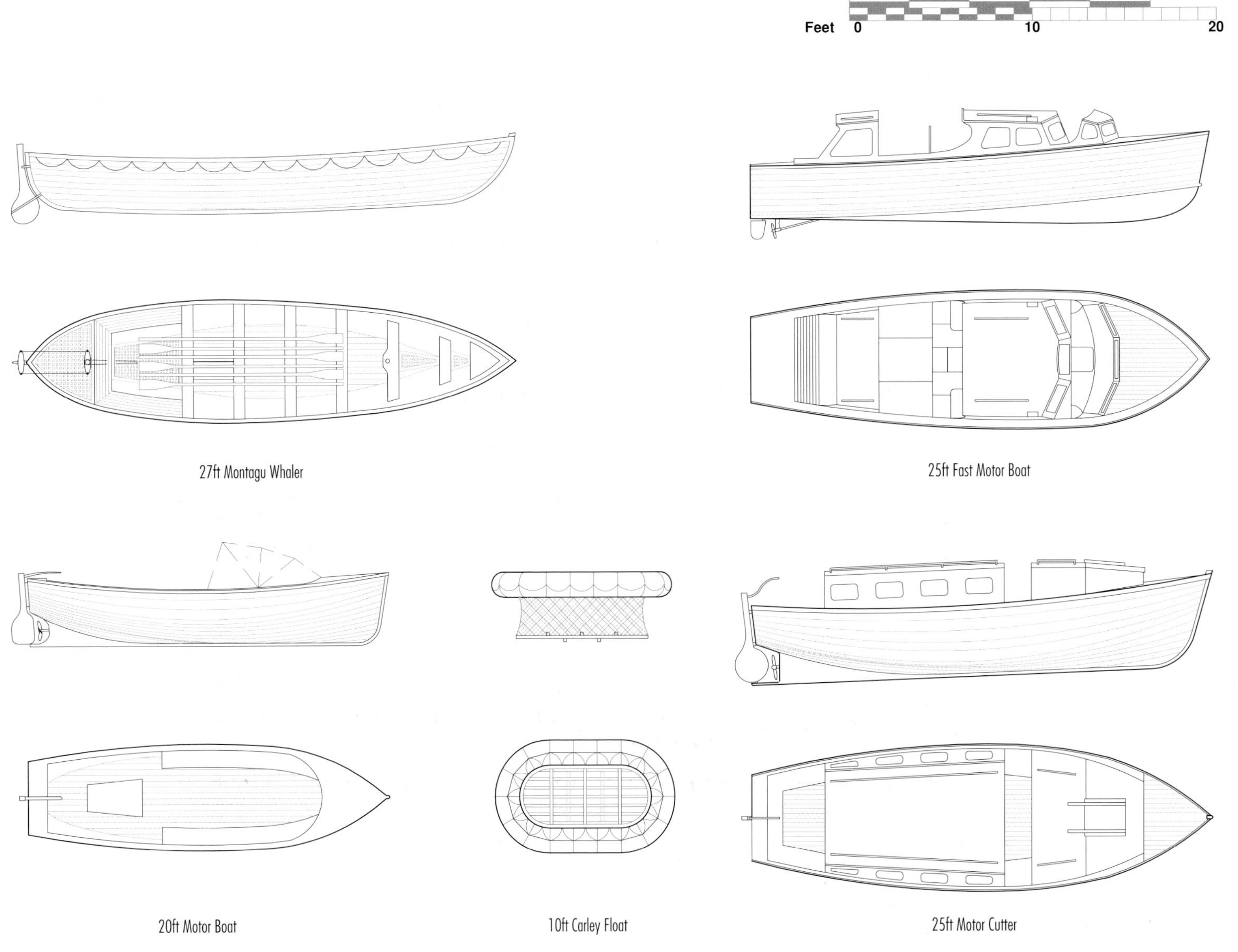

27ft Montagu Whaler

25ft Fast Motor Boat

20ft Motor Boat

10ft Carley Float

25ft Motor Cutter

and that applied almost equally to officers and the lower decks. For instance, seamen and stokers (note the class distinction) had more-or-less open wash places just under the break of the forecastle with tipping basins over a trough. The heads (water-closets or lavatories) were open cubicles flushed with seawater fed from a gravity tank filled by a hand pump each morning – or as required depending on demand – which was the responsibility of the 'captain of the heads'. Fresh water was at a premium and was also pumped by hand – sometimes from tanks used for additional fuel (peace tanks), albeit not at the same time! This also had to be stored in a gravity tank on the upper tank in order to provide a head of water. There were no baths for the lower deck – just showers. Officers fared little better with their own small circular galvanised bath hung from a deckhead hook in their small (usually shared) cabin.

The galleys were coal-fired initially then, apparently somewhat reluctantly, oil-fired. There was no refrigeration. When going away from base, enough bread and meat would be drawn for four days (meat was kept in a fly-proof safe/beef screen on the starboard side just forward of the aft funnel and is quite conspicuous in my drawings). Each man received a basic ration of the three staples of the time; bread, meat and potatoes. When these became unavailable, it was bully beef, lentils and tinned milk. But each man received an allowance to cover the purchase of bacon and other items not normally provided. A cook was appointed by each mess. Each morning, he reported to received his mess's rations of meat, bread and potatoes which he then prepared and took back to the galley for cooking. When cooked, the meals (in buckets) were carried from the galley to the messes despite the weather. Officers fared a bit better because they had their own cook and pantry, as it was called.

Electricity was generated by the ship's turbo-generator. When in port, power was supplied from the shore but the generator was inadequate as demands for electricity grew, despite the fact that many parts of the ships – the messdecks for instance – lacked electric lighting, relying on sperm whale oil lamps.

The capstan on the foredeck looked more primitive than it really was since the deck below – the seamen's mess – housed the steam capstan that drove it – the slots in the capstan for the capstan bars only being required in an emergency.

The ships were hot in the tropics and cold everywhere else, being poorly ventilated and uninsulated save some rudimentary asbestos. Condensation was a never-ending problem which became worse as ships' complements grew. Despite being well built – for their time – riveted decks 'worked' and leaked into mess decks below. It became standard practice to change into boiler suits at sea and not change out of them unless absolutely necessary, only putting normal rig back on when entering harbour.

HARD LYING MONEY

Because conditions in destroyers were considered to offer hardships not experienced in larger warships of the Royal Navy, in a union-like enterprise bargaining agreement, a special allowance termed Hard Lying Money (HLM) was instituted in 1909 applicable to both officers and men by way of compensation while serving in a variety of ships and in a variety of circumstances. HLM still exists today and is applied via a formula which weighs nine different categories that are assessable: living accommodation, eating accommodation, sleeping accommodation, other facilities, galleys, size of ship, ventilation, sanitary arrangements and stabilisers (not present of course in the period we are talking about!).

12: The scoreboard

For the data used in this scoreboard I have relied in the first instance on that provided by Preston (pages 126–7). However, since this was published in 1971 and various research activities – particularly uboat.net – have taken place in the interim, the tables are an amalgam of these. They include all 'V & W' classes and their leaders and are dealt with in chronological order.

SUCCESSES

The First World War

27 Jul 1918

HMS *Vanessa* sank *UB-107* about one mile off Flamborough Head. According to uboat.net's research, an RN trawler, *Calvis*, was also involved in the depth charge attack on 27 July but two ships, *Chloris* and *John Rettig*, were torpedoed two and a half hours later than this attack and that this could only have been by *UB-107* – apparently the only submarine operating in this area at the time. The wreck of *UB-107* was found to be underneath *Malvina* which was torpedoed by *UB -104* on 3 August off Flamborough Head but uboat.net concluded that *UB-107* 'apparently either suffered an accident of some sort or was lost on a British mine'.

The Second World War

30 Jan 1940

HMS *Whitshed* in company with HMS *Fowey* (*Shoreham* class sloop), the French destroyers *Valmy* and *Guépard* and Sunderland aircraft from 228 Squadron RAF sank *U-55* which was attacking Convoy OA-80G (River Thames to Liverpool) 100 miles off West Ushant.

30 Sep 1940

HMAS *Stuart* in company with HMS *Diamond* ('D' class destroyer) sank the Italian submarine *Gondar* (refer Scrap Iron Flotilla, above, for details)

1 Oct 1940

HMS *Wrestler* in company with HMS *Firedrake* ('F' class destroyer) depth-charged the Italian submarine *Durbo* east of Gibraltar and forced it to the surface where it was boarded and secret documents recovered before the submarine sank.

17 Mar 1941

HMS *Walker*, commanded by the famous Commander Donald Macintyre (later Captain D. Macintyre DSO and 2 Bars, DSC), in this instance depth-charged and forced to the surface *U-99* south-east of Iceland, one of Germany's most successful submarines under the command of Korvettenkapitän Otto Kretschmer. The U-boat was abandoned and scuttled and Kretschmer sent this signal to McIntyre: 'We are sunking [*sic*].'[1]

17 Mar 1941

HMS *Walker* in company with HMS *Vanoc*. *U-100* was located on the surface by radar in overcast conditions south-east of Iceland having been damaged in an earlier depth-charge attack and was rammed by *Vanoc* and sunk. Her commander was another U-boat ace, Joachim Schepke.

5 Apr 1941

HMS *Wolverine* in company with HMS *Scarborough* (*Folkestone* class sloop) sank *U-76* south of Iceland.

2 Jun 1941

HMS *Wanderer* in company with HMS *Periwinkle* ('Flower' class corvette) sank *U-147* north-west of Ireland.

27 Jun 1941

HMS *Wishart* attacked and damaged the Italian submarine *Glauco* west of Gibraltar and the submarine was scuttled by her crew.

29 Jun 1941

HMS *Malcolm* in company with HMS *Scimitar* ('S' class destroyer) and HMS *Speedwell* (*Halcyon* class minesweeper) and HMS *Arabis* and HMS *Violet* (both 'Flower' class corvettes) sank *U-651* south of Iceland.

3 Aug 1941

HMS *Wanderer* in company with HNOMS *St. Albans* ('Town' class destroyer) and HMS *Hydrangea* ('Flower' class corvette) sank *U-401* south-west of Ireland. It is of interest that u-boat.net credits this exclusively to *Hydrangea*. However, it also credits the following: '3 Aug 1941: German U-boat *U-205* was damaged in the North Atlantic south-west of Ireland, in position 50°27'N, 19°50'W, by depth charges from the British destroyer HMS *Wanderer* (Cdr. A.F.St.G. Orpen, RN) and the Norwegian destroyer *St. Albans* (Lt.Cdr. S. Storheill).'[2]

11 Sep 1941

HMS *Veteran* in company with HMS *Leamington* ('Town' class destroyer) sank *U-207* in the Denmark Strait south-east of Angmassalik, Greenland.

21 Sep 1941

HMS *Vimy* is credited by Preston with sinking the Italian submarine *Alessandra Malaspina* off Gibraltar. What seems to have been verified by later research is that the Italian submarine *Luigi Torelli* was damaged by depth charges from *Vimy* while attempting to attack Convoy HG 3 west of Gibraltar. According to uboat.net, the loss of the Italian submarine *Alessandro Malaspina* that is often credited to HMS *Vimy* is incorrect. Her fate was revised in March 2004 by Dr Axel Niestlé and Eric Zimmerman. This report concludes: 'Based on the foregoing information it is proposed to amend the loss of the Italian submarine *Alessandro Malaspina* in the way that it was sunk on 10 September 1941 by depth charges from Sunderland "U" (serial # W3986) of 10 Squadron RAAF, piloted by Flight Lieutenant Athol Galway Hope Wearne, in position 46°23'N / 11°22'W.'[3]

2 Feb 1942

HMS *Westcott* sank *U-581* south-east of Horta, Azores.

27 Mar 1942

HMS *Volunteer* in company with HMS *Leamington* ('Town' class destroyer), HMS *Aldenham* and HMS *Grove* (both 'Hunt' class destroyers) sank *U-587* south-west of Ireland while escorting Convoy WS-17. The submarine was discovered after a HF/DF fix from HMS *Keppel*.

2 May 1942

HMS *Wishart* in company with HMS *Wrestler* and a Catalina from 202 Squadron RAF sank *U-74* east-south-east of Cartagena, Spain. Subsequent research in 2012 seems to indicate that the Catalina was not involved but that it was involved in an attack on *U-375* which escaped undamaged.[4]

12 Aug 1942

HMS *Wolverine* rammed and sank the Italian submarine *Dagabur* south of the Balearic Islands. This is reported as 12 May by Preston.

3 Sep 1942

HMS *Vimy* in company with HMS *Pathfinder* ('P' class destroyer) and HMS *Quentin* ('Q' class destroyer) sank *U-162* after a depth-charge and ramming attack north-east of Trinidad.

15 Oct 1942

HMS *Viscount*. Preston places the sinking of *U-619* by *Viscount* simply as N. Atlantic. Later research by uboat.net seems to indicate that it was a Hudson from 269 Squadron RAF that sank the submarine south-west of Iceland and it was *U-661* that was sunk by *Viscount* on 15 October.[5]

15 Nov 1942

HMS *Wrestler*. Preston places the sinking of *U-411* by *Wrestler* simply as off Bone. Later research by uboat.net seems to indicate a scenario similar to *Viscount* above, in that a Hudson was responsible, this time from 500 Squadron RAF and the U-boat was sunk west of Gibraltar. *Wrestler* apparently sank *U-98* in a similar location on the same date.[6]

26 Dec 1942

HMS *Vanessa* in company with HMS *Hesperus* ('H' class destroyer) sank *U-357* north-west of Ireland.

4 Feb 1943

HMS *Vimy* in company with HMS *Beverley* ('Town' class destroyer) sank *U-187* east-south-east of Cape Farewell, Greenland.

17 Feb 1943

HMS *Viscount*. Preston attributes the sinking of *U-69* to *Viscount* simply as N. Atlantic. Later research by uboat.net attributes this submarine to HMS *Fame* ('F' class destroyer) but gives *Viscount* credit for *U-201* in a similar location on the same date.[7]

6 May 1943

HMS *Vidette*. Preston attributes the sinking of *U-125* to *Vidette* simply as ESE Newfoundland. According to the records of uboat.net, *U-125* was sunk by HMS *Oribi* ('O' class destroyer) and HMS *Snowflake* ('Flower' class corvette) on this date and north-east of Newfoundland and provides a detailed account of the action.[8]

The entry for *Vidette* in the navalhistory.net would seem to bear this out, as follows:

> May 6th Detected U125 on surface and attacked by Hedgehog mortar forcing it to submerge.
> (Note: This submarine was later sunk by depth charges from HMS SNOWFLAKE after it had been again caught on the surface and rammed by HMS ORIBI).[9]

23 Oct 1943

HMS *Vidette* in company with HMS *Duncan* ('D' class destroyer) and a Liberator from 224 Squadron RAF sank *U-274* south-east of Cape Farewell, Greenland.

29 Oct 1943

HMS *Vidette* in company with HMS *Duncan* ('D' class destroyer) and HMS *Sunflower* ('Flower' class corvette) sank *U-282* south-east of Cape Farewell.

31 Oct 1943

HMS *Whitehall* in company with HMS *Geranium* ('Flower' class corvette) sank *U-306* north-east of the Azores.

31 Oct 1943

HMS *Douglas* in company with HMS *Imperialist* (anti-submarine trawler) sank *U-732* in the Strait of Gibraltar, north of Tangier.

1 Nov 1943

HMS *Witherington* in company with HMS *Active* ('A' class destroyer), HMS *Fleetwood* (*Grimsby* class sloop) and a Wellington from 179 Squadron RAF sank *U-340* a few miles south-east of Punta Almina, Spanish Morocco.

17 Jan 1944

HMS *Wanderer*. Preston attributes the sinking of *U-305* to *Wanderer* in company with HMS *Glenarm* ('River' class frigate) north-east of the Azores, but later research by uboat.net indicates that this was *U-377* and that *U-305* was probably sunk by its own torpedo as confirmed by a radio signal.[10]

30 Jan 1944

HMS *Whitehall*. Preston attributes the sinking of *U-314* to *Whitehall* in company with HMS *Meteor* ('M' class destroyer) simply as being in the Barents Sea, but later research by uboat.net indicates that it was HMS *Inconstant* ('I' class destroyer) that sank *U-314* south-east of Bear Island and that *Whitehall* and *Meteor*'s attack was probably directed, unsuccessfully, at *U-965*.[11]

24 Feb 1944

HMS *Keppel* sank *U-713* north-west of Narvik.

24 Feb 1944

HMS *Wishart* in company HMS *Anthony* ('A' class destroyer) and a Catalina from 202 Squadron RAF, a Ventura VB-127 USN and two Catalinas from VP-63 USN sank *U-761* in the Strait of Gibraltar, North of Tangier.

16 Mar 1944

HMS *Vanoc* in company with HMS *Affleck* ('Captain' class frigate) and three Catalinas from VP-63 USN sank *U-392* in the Strait of Gibraltar.

2 Apr 1944

HMS *Keppel* sank *U-360* in the Norwegian Sea, south-west of Bear Island.

5 July 1944

HMS *Wanderer* in company with HMS *Tavy* ('River' class frigate) sank *U-390* in Seine Bay, English Channel.

20 Aug 1944

HMS *Vidette* in company with HMS *Forester* ('F' class destroyer) and HMS *Wensleydale* ('Hunt' class destroyer) sank *U-413* in the English Channel, south of Brighton.

24 Aug 1944

HMS *Keppel*. Preston credits *Keppel* in company with HMS *Mermaid*, HMS *Peacock* (both Modified *Black Swan* class sloops) and HMS *Loch Dunvegan* ('Loch' class frigate) with sinking *U-354* in the Barents Sea, north-east of North Cape. However, uboat.net only credits *Mermaid* and *Loch Dunvegan*. Naval-history.net credits the same warships as Preston plus a Swordfish from HMS *Vindex* (*Nairana* class escort aircraft carrier). Uboat-net further muddies the waters by attributing *U-344* to the Swordfish from 825 Squadron FAA on *Vindex*.

2 Sep 1944

HMS *Keppel* in company with HMS *Whitehall*, HMS *Mermaid* and HMS *Peacock* (as above) and a Swordfish from 825 Squadron FAA on HMS *Vindex* sank *U-394* in the Norwegian Sea, south-East of Jan Mayen Island. However, records indicate that this was primarily the Swordfish's kill with rockets and depth charges.

14 Mar 1945

HMS *Wivern* in company with HMSAS *Natal* ('Loch' class frigate) sank *U-714* in the North Sea near the Firth of Forth.

6 Apr 1945

HMS *Watchman* sank *U-1195* in the English Channel, South-East of Spithead Roads.

10 Apr 1945

HMS *Vanquisher* in company with HMS *Tintagel Castle* ('Castle' class corvette) sank *U-878* not south of Iceland as Preston asserts but in the Bay of Biscay, off St. Nazaire.

16 Apr 1945

HMS *Viceroy* sank *U-1274* in the North Sea, North of Newcastle.

NOTE: For readers wanting more detailed particulars, uboat.net gives the precise latitude and longitude of U-boat sinkings. I have not included details of aircraft shot down although I know claims have been made. These are always suspect as claims exceed the number of aircraft actually shot down.

LOSSES

The First World War

1 Aug 1918

HMS *Vehement* mined and sunk by gunfire, North Sea.

The Baltic Campaign 1918–1920

1 Sep 1919

HMS *Vittoria* was torpedoed by the Bolshevik submarine *Pantera* off Seiskari Island, Gulf of Finland.

3–4 Sep 1919

HMS *Verulam* was mined and sunk off Seiskari Island, Gulf of Finland

Between The Wars

While not strictly losses in the same sense of the three ships above, when one considers the ridiculous circumstances that related to the next five I think it is fair to consider them as losses.

17 Dec 1931

HMS *Valhalla* was sold for scrapping. Friedman says this was 'an unusual fate for a V class destroyer, which the Admiralty seems to have considered far more valuable than the S class'.[12] I can only concur.

24 Aug 1936

HMS *Valkyrie*, HMS *Vectis*, HMS *Venturous* and HMS *Violent* were 'traded-in', in effect, on a convoluted deal that involved a German passenger liner, the SS *Bismarck,* a war reparation being sold by the British Government to the White Star Line which renamed her SS *Majestic* but which was then sold to Thos W Ward for scrapping in 1936 when she was retired. However, because of the war prize arrangements being compensation for lost tonnage, virtual ownership remained with the British government who assigned her to the Royal Navy for conversion to a repair ship, thus leaving Ward's without the contract value of the *Majestic* for scrapping. Enter the four 'V & W' destroyers and a number of old destroyers in place of the *Majestic*. *Majestic* became HMS *Caledonia*, a training ship for Boys and Artificers, and was burnt out and sank in September 1939. Thos Ward did the scrapping, proving that what goes around comes around.

2 Feb 1938

HMS *Walrus*. As mentioned earlier, *Walrus* was one of the 'V & Ws' earmarked for conversion to a 'WAIR' escort destroyer. She was under tow on passage from Rosyth to Chatham Dockyard for the conversion when her towline broke in a storm in the North Sea and she was driven ashore on Mascus Rocks in Scarborough's North Bay. She was re-floated in October but found to be beyond economical repair and was scrapped.

The Second World War

15 May 1940

HMS *Valentine* was damaged by attack by Ju 87 dive-bombers in the North Sea off Terneuzen on the Schelde Estuary while providing naval gunfire support to the left flank of the Belgian Army and beached.[13]

19 May 1940

HMS *Whitley* was struck by two bombs while in the English Channel, two miles off Nieuport and beached. Later destroyed by gunfire from HMS *Keith*.[14]

24 May 1940

HMS *Wessex* succumbed to repeated air attacks while supporting the Guards Brigade and the Rifle Brigade off Calais. HMS *Vimiera* was also damaged this day.[15]

29 May 1940

HMS *Wakeful* was torpedoed 13 miles north-east of Nieuport by German E-boat *S-30* while returning to Dover from Bray Beach off Dunkirk with 600 evacuated troops on board. Only twenty-six survivors.[16]

5 Jul 1940

HMS *Whirlwind* was torpedoed by *U-34* 120 miles west of Lands End but did not sink immediately. Considered beyond repair, she was scuttled four hours later by her sister-ship, HMS *Wescott*.[17]

27 Jul 1940

HMS *Wren*, while providing anti-aircraft cover for minesweeping operations in the North Sea off Aldeburgh, was singled out and bombed until sunk.[18]

19 Oct 1940

HMS *Venetia*, although in a swept channel in the Thames off the Knob Buoy, ran over a magnetic mine laid by German aircraft the previous evening.[19]

27 Apr 1941

HMS *Wryneck*. During the evacuation of Greece, *Wryneck* and HMS *Diamond* ('D' class destroyer) were attacked by German Ju 87 aircraft south of Nauplia while coming to the aid of the Dutch transport *Slamat* with 700 evacuated troops on board. All three ships were sunk.[20]

30 Jun 1941

HMAS *Waterhen*. While taking part in the Tobruk Ferry Run, *Waterhen* in company with HMS *Defender* ('D' class destroyer) was attacked by German aircraft at 20.00 on 29 June 100 miles east of Tobruk and 'The Chook' sustained damaged that brought her to a standstill. An Italian submarine was sighted and engaged by *Defender* who later took *Waterhen* in tow but at 01.50 on 30 June she rolled over and sank.[21]

9 Jan 1942

HMS *Vimiera* was mined in the Thames Estuary off the East Spile Buoy.[22]

15 Mar 1942

HMS *Vortigern* was torpedoed by a German E-boat, probably *S-104*, while escorting Convoy FS 749 in the North Sea off Cromer.[23]

9 Apr 1942

HMAS *Vampire*. After Japanese aircraft sank the aircraft carrier HMS *Hermes* which *Vampire* was escorting in the Indian Ocean off Batticaloa, Ceylon, the fifteen aircraft turned their attention on *Vampire* which sustained a number of hits and broke in half.[24]

17 Jun 1942

HMS *Wild Swan* had been escorting Convoy HG 74 and parted company to return to harbour due to low fuel state and was attacked by twelve Ju 88 bombers while passing through a fleet of Spanish fishing boats which was also attacked by the Germans in the belief that it was the convoy. *Wild Swan* suffered direct hits and damage from four near misses which caused flooding and then collided with a Spanish fishing boat in the fleet – three of which were sunk by the German attack. *Wild Swan* sank several hours later and her survivors and the Spanish fishermen were picked up by her sister-ship HMS *Vansittart*.[25]

25 Sep 1942

HMAS *Voyager* grounded in Betano Bay, Timor Island while landing reinforcements to the guerrilla forces (Australian and Dutch) operating on Timor. She was sighted by Japanese aircraft and attacked and, unable to be re-floated, was scuttled.[26]

26 Sep 1942

HMAS *Veteran*, while re-joining Convoy RB 1 with survivors

rescued from two sinkings, was torpedoed by *U-404*. There were no survivors.[27]

8 Nov 1942

HMS *Broke*. The loss of *Broke* is worth recounting in some detail: she was charged with landing US Rangers in the Vichy French-held port of Algiers. Two RN ships – *Walney* and *Hartland* (ex-USCG cutters) – had earlier tried to break through the protecting boom. *Broke* made three unsuccessful attempts at night then waited until dawn. On the fourth attempt, *Broke* smashed through the boom at 26 knots and, despite being fired upon by shore batteries, berthed at the Quai de Falaise as if 'she were being berthed at the Gladstone Dock in Liverpool', letting the Rangers ashore who were then recalled because *Broke*'s position was untenable, being under fire from field guns and she was on fire. She foundered off Algiers and was scuttled.[28]

20 Feb 1944

HMS *Warwick* was torpedoed by *U-413* in the English Channel, 20 miles south-west of Trevose Head and sank rapidly.[29]

6 Jun 1944

HMS *Wrestler* struck a mine in the English Channel while shepherding landing craft through a mine barrage in bad weather. *Wrestler* was towed to Portsmouth but was declared a constructive total loss and never repaired.[30]

10 Jun 1944

HMS *Montrose* collided with a USN Landing Ship Tank (number unknown) off Arromanches and was towed to Immingham and declared a constructive total loss.[31]

6 Jan 1945

HMS *Walpole* struck a mine in the North Sea off Flushing while escorting a cross-Channel convoy. She was towed back to Sheerness but declared a constructive total loss and never repaired.[32]

For disposals, refer various Appendices depending on classes

Conclusion

I don't think it is an exaggeration to say that the 'V & W' class destroyers were to destroyer design what the *Dreadnought* was to battleship design. The *Dreadnought* was so radical that it created two distinct classes of battleship – those that came before it, the pre-Dreadnought, and those that came after it, simply Dreadnoughts. The same could be said of the 'V & W' class – there were to my mind pre-'V & W' types and then simply 'V & Ws' and the many variations to the basic design fundamentals they introduced and which held true for the next 20 years – well after Dreadnoughts had ceased to be relevant and aircraft carriers ruled the waves.

The 'V & W' class set the benchmark in destroyer design that established a design formula that was followed, not just by the Royal Navy but by other navies including the United States Navy – until their *Fletcher* class of 1939. While perhaps not quite so radical as the *Dreadnought* which introduced geared turbines and an all-big-gun armament, the 'V & Ws' did not so much introduce new or radical innovations as they did combine all of the best features learnt over the previous 20 years into one highly successful package. They were not so much a revolutionary breakthrough as they were the logical or perhaps fortunate culmination of a number of totally sensible and evolutionary processes. Moving the bridge a little further back from the bow, having a little more freeboard forward may seem logical for good sea-keeping, but it had to happen to prove just how beneficial such small improvements could be. With the bridge further back, superfiring guns, common to larger ships, then became possible in destroyers.

As David K Brown (ex-deputy Chief Naval Architect, Royal Corps of Naval Constructors) says in his book, *Nelson to Vanguard: Warship Design and Development 1923-1945*;

> Evolutionary design, in which each class is a small improvement on its predecessor, is an almost foolproof method of avoiding serious problems but, if continued too long, will inevitably lead to mediocrity or worse.[1]

The word serendipity comes to mind – that is, the occurrence and development of events by chance in a happy or beneficial way – although, of course the end result did not happen by chance. A lot of work went into producing the 'V' leader from which sprang the 'V & W' class. But hard work alone is no guarantee of success. Sometimes the Gods have to look kindly upon you. Sometimes the dice have to fall just the right way. Sometimes you just have to be . . . well, serendipitous. For instance, what if the decision had been only to press on with more 'R' and 'S' class destroyers? How, when and by whom would a destroyer with the sort of attributes the 'V & Ws' possessed been developed? What sort of destroyer might the Royal Navy then have had in its fleet at the beginning of the Second World War and the United States Navy in its fleet in December 1941? Might Japan or an inter-war Germany have introduced the superfiring armament first then the RN and USN would have been on the back foot and have had to catch up?

What makes the difference between good and great? For instance, there have been plenty of good aircraft but ones such as the Douglas DC-3 – the Dakota – must be regarded as 'Great Planes'. Similarly, cars: the Volkswagen 'Beetle', the Willys 4x4 Jeep or the Mini-Minor. to mention but three must fit into the 'Great' category. And, in my opinion, the 'V & W' destroyer can wear the title of 'Great'. I was tempted to make the book's sub-title Venerable and Watershed reflecting their longevity and the turning point they represented in destroyer evolution – surely two ingredients of greatness. The DC-3s were both venerable and watersheds, as were the Volkswagen Beetle the Jeep and the Mini. Each in their own way introduced something entirely new which led to better aeroplanes and vehicles and they stood the test of time. Only the fact that the 'V & Ws' were built quickly for a purpose, were hard-used under wartime conditions and were eventually outmoded by newer versions of what was essentially the same basic concept led them to being scrapped when the DC-3s, Volkswagen Beetles and Minis still exist albeit in ever depleted numbers.

Preston sums up the 'V & Ws' reasons for success better than I can:

> Looking back, one wonders what combination of factors made the 'V & W' design so successful. We have seen how well their increased gun power and performance compared with previous destroyers, but the 'V & W' boats had something more: the detailed design work was good, and so the major improvements were properly evaluated. The paradoxical answer is that the design of the 'Vs' and the 'Ws' was both progressive and conservative; it met an important criterion of any design in not introducing too many innovations, but rather concentrating on new combinations of tried components. Thus, their geared turbines had already been tested in the 'R' class, the superimposed gun had been introduced in the *Seymour* class leaders, and their method of construction used the well-tired transverse framing. Where British destroyer designers looked far ahead was in combining these proven ideas, and the expertise acquired in twenty years of building destroyers, with a larger hull, to accommodate greater armament and seaworthiness. In addition, the D.N.C. had for years insisted on sturdy construction and a good margin of stability as prerequisites for destroyers.[2]

To quote Brown again:

> The V&W classes, with their leaders, were the finest destroyers of World War I. Others may have been more heavily armed or faster but the V & Ws seem to have achieved the best balance of military qualities. Their design by C.D. Hannaford shows how rearrangement of conventional features can lead to a step change in capability.[3]
>
> At the end of the First World War the V&W classes of destroyers were the best destroyers in the world, at least for a North Sea war; seaworthy, well armed and with adequate endurance.[4]
>
> Post-war destroyers did not enter service until the thirties, so for a decade the V&W class were indisputably the best. Even in the thirties the new destroyers of the A-I classes were of only slightly greater capability than the V&Ws, and the older classes were said to be more robust.[5]

Yet another author, Angus Konstam:

> In November 1918, the Royal Navy had the largest destroyer fleet in the world, which included the latest V- & W-class vessels, which was arguably the best destroyer design of the war.[6]

The second sentence of Lenton's Introduction in *British Fleet & Escort Destroyers Vol 1* states:

> . . . with the 'V' and 'W' classes, British design had a commanding lead and was universally copied.[7]

From someone who served on a 'V & W':

> When they first came into service towards the end of World War I these ships were widely acclaimed and marked the high point in destroyer design up to that time. Many other navies followed the design closely in their own new buildings. Although towards the end of the interwar period faster ships were being built, and others with heavier armament, this class had sea keeping qualities and an all round performance that was unrivalled. Their sturdy construction stood the test, not only of enemy action, but also of the relentless buffeting of the North Atlantic and Arctic Oceans.[8]

Two more quotes from Brown;

> The 'V' class destroyer leaders, designed by Hannaford in 1915–16, and the later 'V' and 'W' class destroyers set the style for destroyers of many navies in the 1920s and early 1930s. They had geared turbines, advanced for its day, four guns (4in, later ships having 4.7in), four, later six torpedo tubes and, with a high forecastle and bridge well aft, they were the best sea boats of their size anywhere.[9]

> The 'V' and 'W' classes were superior to earlier ships in stability, seakeeping, strength and other aspects of naval architecture.[10]

As I said in the opening paragraph of Chapter 6, the 'V & W' destroyers gave 'the most bang for your buck'. While not especially economical to build in that there were no special or inherent economies built into their design – and certainly not an intrinsic part of the design brief as was the sheerless flush-deck of the USN's four-piper counterparts – the facts remains that the overall success of the basic design and its variations, that when past their prime as fleet destroyers they leant themselves so readily to conversions to 'WAIR', Short or Long Range Escorts must surely qualify them as having been exceedingly good value for money.

But warships are built for war and it is in this environment that they must be judged. The exploits of the 'Scrap Iron Flotilla' speak for themselves in the cauldron of the eastern Mediterranean where they were the oldest destroyers deployed. But it was in the Battle of the Atlantic where the 'V & Ws' serving as escort destroyers in one form or another, or on the East Coast in the North Sea were participants in the sinking of forty-four submarines[11] and in doing so this places them ahead of the next most successful class of U-boat killer, the 'Flower' class corvettes with thirty-eight kills.[12] Considering there were considerably more 'Flowers' than 'V & Ws' then the success rate of the 'V & Ws' – that is, the ratio of U-boats sunk to the number of 'V & W destroyers involved – would be considerably greater. But, of course, they had cost much more to build – originally – and they had much bigger crews to operate them. And, given their turn of speed, they were given greater freedom of action to pursue and maintain contacts with U-boats – something the slower corvettes simply could not afford to do, at least for any extended period.

However, it is misleading to view these sorts of metrics simply in terms of submarines sunk. The primary aim of the escorts, no matter their type, was the safe and timely arrival of the convoys. To this end, keeping the U-boats submerged, keeping them clear of the convoys – where their slow submerged speed prevented them from maintaining contact with the convoy – was a victory in itself. Sinking U-boats was a distinct bonus. Certainly, that is the opinion of Professor A J Marder in his five-volume work, *From the Dreadnought to Scapa Flow*. What mattered was that ships delivered their cargoes regularly and adequately, that it did not matter how many submarines the Germans had, providing they were forced to keep out of the way and the ships got through without being delayed by fear of attack.[13] It's an interesting concept because it assumes that the advantages of one to override the disadvantages of the other, that the volume of the logistics delivered, the materiel to sustain war and the people who wage it would eventually be the determining factor, not the enemy's submarine losses. Other historians, particularly viewed through the American prism where materiel and manpower were more plentiful and could be spread more widely, tend to view the contest more offensively believing, typically, that 'any submarine not sunk will sooner or later return and sink more ships'.[14] However, slow, basic, uncomfortable as they were, the ubiquitous 'Flower' class corvettes certainly achieved the role of deterrence and, in this respect, I think it is fair to say they were more effective than the 'V & Ws' simply by their very presence, their sheer weight of numbers.

So, I leave it to you, the reader, as to how you judge the 'V & Ws'.

V for Venerable – they truly were, and **W** for Watersheds – insofar as they represented a turning point in destroyer design.

If I wear my heart on my sleeve for these fine old warships – well, so be it. I know I am not alone.

Appendices

Appendix A

'A' CLASS DESTROYERS

NAME	BUILDER	LAID DOWN	LAUNCHED	COMPLETED	FATE
Havock	Yarrow & Co Ltd	Jul 1892	12 Aug 1893	Jan 1894	Broken up May 1912
Hornet	Yarrow & Co Ltd	Jul 1892	23 Dec 1893	Jul 1894	Broken up Oct 1909
Daring	John I Thornycroft & Co Ltd	Jul 1892	25 Nov 1893	Feb 1895	Broken up Apr 1912
Decoy	John I Thornycroft & Co Ltd	Jul 1892	2 Feb 1894	Jun 1895	Collision 13 Aug 1904
Ferret	Laird Bros Ltd	Jul 1893	9 Dec 1893	Mar 1895	Sunk as target 1911
Lynx	Laird Bros Ltd	Jul 1893	24 Jan 1894	Aug 1895	Broken up Apr 1912
Ardent	John I Thornycroft & Co Ltd	Dec 1893	16 Oct 1894	Apr 1895	Broken up Oct 1911
Boxer	John I Thornycroft & Co Ltd	Mar 1894	28 Nov 1894	Jun 1895	Collision 8 Feb 1918
Bruizer	John I Thornycroft & Co Ltd	Apr 1894	27 Feb 1895	Jun 1895	Broken up May 1914
Charger	Yarrow & Co Ltd	Nov 1893	15 Sep 1894	Feb 1896	Broken up May 1912
Dasher	Yarrow & Co Ltd	Dec 1893	28 Nov 1894	Mar 1896	Broken up May 1912
Hasty	Yarrow & Co Ltd	Dec 1893	16 Jun 1894	May 1896	Broken up Jul 1912
Hardy	William Doxford & Sons Ltd	4 Jun 1894	16 Dec 1895	Aug 1896	Broken up Jul 1911
Haughty	William Doxford & Sons Ltd	28 May 1894	18 Sep 1895	Aug 1896	Broken up Dec 1912
Janus	Palmer Shipbuilding & Iron Co Ltd	28 Mar 1894	12 Mar 1895	Nov 1895	Broken up 1914
Lightning	Palmer Shipbuilding & Iron Co Ltd	28 Mar 1894	10 Apr 1895	Jan 1896	Mined 30 Jun 1915
Porcupine	Palmer Shipbuilding & Iron Co Ltd	28 Mar 1894	19 Sep 1895	Mar 1896	Broken up Apr 1920
Salmon	Earle's Shipbuilding & Engineering Co Ltd	12 Mar 1894	15 Jan 1895	Jan 1896	Broken up May 1912
Snapper	Earle's Shipbuilding & Engineering Co Ltd	2 Apr 1894	30 Jan 1895	Jan 1896	Broken up May 1912
Banshee	Laird Bros Ltd	Mar 1894	17 Nov 1894	Jul 1895	Broken up Apr 1912
Contest	Laird Bros Ltd	Mar 1894	1 Dec 1894	Jul 1895	Broken up Jul 1911
Dragon	Laird Bros Ltd	Mar 1894	15 Dec 1894	Jun 1895	Broken up Jul 1912
Conflict	J Samuel White & Co Ltd	3 Jan 1894	13 Dec 1894	Jul 1899	Broken up May 1920
Teazer	J Samuel White & Co Ltd	3 Feb 1894	9 Feb 1895	Mar 1899	Broken up Jul 1912
Wizard	J Samuel White & Co Ltd	3 Apr 1894	26 Feb 1895	Jul 1899	Broken up May 1920
Fervent	Hanna, Donald & Wilson	27 Mar 1894	28 Mar 1895	Jun 1900	Broken up Apr 1920
Zephyr	Hanna, Donald & Wilson	23 Apr 1894	10 May 1895	Jul 1901	Broken up Feb 1920
Handy	Fairfield Shipbuilding and Engineering Co Ltd	7 Jun 1894	9 Mar 1895	Oct 1895	Broken up 1916
Hart	Fairfield Shipbuilding and Engineering Co Ltd	7 Jun 1894	27 Mar 1895	Jan 1896	Broken up 1912
Hunter	Fairfield Shipbuilding and Engineering Co Ltd	7 Jun 1894	28 Dec 1895	May 1896	Broken up Apr 1912
Opossum	R & W Hawthorn, Leslie & Co Ltd	17 Sep 1894	9 Aug 1895	Mar 1896	Broken up Jul 1920
Ranger	R & W Hawthorn, Leslie & Co Ltd	17 Sep 1894	4 Oct 1895	Jun 1896	Broken up May 1920
Sunfish	R & W Hawthorn, Leslie & Co Ltd	29 Aug 1894	23 May 1895	Feb 1896	Broken up Jun 1920
Rocket	J & G Thomson	14 Feb 1894	14 Aug 1894	Jul 1895	Broken up Apr 1912
Shark	J & G Thomson	14 Feb 1894	22 Sep 1894	Jul 1895	Broken up Jul 1911
Surly	J & G Thomson	14 Feb 1894	10 Nov 1894	Jul 1895	Broken up Mar 1920
Skate	Vickers Armstrongs Ltd	20 Mar 1894	13 Mar 1895	Jan 1896	Broken up Apr 1907
Starfish	Vickers Armstrongs Ltd	22 Mar 1894	26 Jan 1895	Jan 1896	Broken up May 1912
Sturgeon	Vickers Armstrongs Ltd	1 Mar 1894	21 Jul 1894	Jan 1896	Broken up May 1912
Spitfire	Sir W G Armstrong, Whitworth & Co Ltd	4 Jun 1894	7 Jun 1895	Nov 1896	Broken up Apr 1912
Swordfish	Sir W G Armstrong, Whitworth & Co Ltd	4 Jun 1894	27 Mar 1895	Dec 1896	Broken up Oct 1910
Zebra	Thames Ironworks & Shipbuilding Co Ltd	Jul 1894	3 Dec 1895	Jan 1900	Broken up Jul 1914

'B' CLASS DESTROYERS

NAME	BUILDER	LAID DOWN	LAUNCHED	COMPLETED	FATE
Quail	Laird Bros Ltd	28 May 1895	24 Sep 1895	Jun 1897	Broken up Jul 1919
Sparrowhawk	Laird Bros Ltd	30 May 1895	8 Oct 1895	Jun 1897	Wrecked 17 Jun 1904
Thrasher	Laird Bros Ltd	30 May 1895	5 Nov 1895	Jun 1897	Broken up Nov 1919
Virago	Laird Bros Ltd	13 Jun 1895	19 Nov 1895	Jun 1897	Broken up Oct 1919
Earnest	Laird Bros Ltd	2 Mar 1896	7 Nov 1896	Nov 1897	Broken up Jul 1920
Griffon	Laird Bros Ltd	7 Mar 1896	21 Nov 1896	Nov 1897	Broken up Jul 1920
Locust	Laird Bros Ltd	20 Apr 1896	5 Dec 1896	Jul 1898	Broken up Jun 1919
Panther	Laird Bros Ltd	19 May 1896	21 Jan 1897	Jan 1898	Broken up Jun 1920
Seal	Laird Bros Ltd	17 Jun 1896	6 Mar 1897	May 1898	Broken up Mar 1921
Wolf	Laird Bros Ltd	12 Nov 1896	2 Jun 1897	Jul 1898	Broken up Jul 1921
Express	Laird Bros Ltd	1 Dec 1896	11 Dec 1897	Feb 1902	Broken up Mar 1921
Orwell	Laird Bros Ltd	9 Nov 1897	29 Sep 1898	Jan 1900	Broken up Jul 1920
Lively	Laird Bros Ltd	20 Jun 1899	14 Jul 1900	Apr 1902	Broken up Jul 1920
Sprightly	Laird Bros Ltd	20 Jun 1899	25 Sep 1900	Mar 1902	Broken up Jul 1920
Success	William Doxford & Sons	18 Sep 1899	21 Mar 1901	May 1902	Wrecked 27 Dec1914
Spiteful	Palmer Shipbuilding and Iron Company Ltd	12 Jan 1898	11 Jan 1899	Feb 1900	Broken up Sep 1920
Peterel	Palmer Shipbuilding and Iron Company Ltd	29 Jul 1898	30 Mar 1899	Jul 1900	Broken up Aug 1919
Myrmidon	Palmer Shipbuilding and Iron Company Ltd	23 Oct 1899	26 May 1896	May 1901	Collision 26 Mar 1917
Syren	Palmer Shipbuilding and Iron Company Ltd	24 Nov 1899	20 Dec 1900	Feb 1902	Broken up Sep 1920
Kangaroo	Palmer Shipbuilding and Iron Company Ltd	29 Dec 1899	8 Sep 1900	Jul 1901	Broken up Mar 1920
Arab	J & G Thomson	5 Mar 1900	9 Feb 1901	Jan 1903	Broken up 1919
Cobra	Sir W G Armstrong, Whitworth & Company Ltd	n/a	28 Jun 1899	1901	Foundered 17 Sep 1901
Albacore	Palmer Shipbuilding and Iron Company Ltd	1 Sep 1905	19 Sep 1906	27 Mar 1909	Broken up Aug 1919
Bonetta	Palmer Shipbuilding and Iron Company Ltd	1 Sep 1905	14 Jan 1907	27 Mar 1909	Broken up Jun 1920

'C' CLASS DESTROYERS

NAME	BUILDER	LAID DOWN	LAUNCHED	COMPLETED	FATE
Star	Palmer Shipbuilding and Iron Company Ltd	23 Mar 1896	11 Aug 1896	Sep 1898	Broken up Jun 1919
Whiting	Palmer Shipbuilding and Iron Company Ltd	13 Apr 1896	26 Aug 1896	Jun 1897	Broken up Nov 1919

Bat	Palmer Shipbuilding and Iron Company Ltd	28 May 1896	7 Oct 1896	Aug 1897	Broken up Nov 1919
Chamois	Palmer Shipbuilding and Iron Company Ltd	28 May 1896	9 Nov 1896	Nov 1897	Foundered 26 Sep 1904
Crane	Palmer Shipbuilding and Iron Company Ltd	2 Aug 1896	17 Dec 1896	Apr 1898	Broken up Jun 1919
Flying Fish	Palmer Shipbuilding and Iron Company Ltd	9 Aug 1896	4 Mar 1897	Jun 1898	Broken up Aug 1919
Fawn	Palmer Shipbuilding and Iron Company Ltd	5 Sep 1896	13 Apr 1897	Dec 1898	Broken up Jul 1919
Flirt	Palmer Shipbuilding and Iron Company Ltd	5 Sep 1896	15 May 1897	Apr 1899	Sunk 27 Oct 1916
Bullfinch	Earle's Shipbuilding & Engineering Co Ltd	17 Sep 1896	10 Feb 1898	Jun 1901	Broken up Jun 1919
Dove	Earle's Shipbuilding & Engineering Co Ltd	17 Sep 1896	21 Mar 1898	Jul 1901	Broken up Jan 1920
Violet	William Doxford & Sons Ltd	13 Jul 1896	3 May 1897	Jun 1898	Broken up Jun 1920
Sylvia	William Doxford & Sons Ltd	13 Jul 1896	3 Jul 1897	Jan 1899	Broken up Jul 1919
Lee	William Doxford & Sons Ltd	4 Jan 1898	27 Jan 1899	Mar 1901	Wrecked 5 Oct 1909
Avon	Vickers Armstrongs Ltd	17 Feb 1896	10 Oct 1896	Feb 1899	Broken up Jul 1920
Bittern	Vickers Armstrongs Ltd	18 Feb 1896	1 Feb 1897	Apr 1897	Collision 4 Apr 1918
Otter	Vickers Armstrongs Ltd	9 Jun 1896	23 Nov 1896	Mar 1900	Broken up Oct 1916
Leopard	Vickers Armstrongs Ltd	10 Jun 1896	20 Mar 1897	Jul 1899	Broken up Jun 1919
Vixen	Vickers Armstrongs Ltd	7 Sep 1899	29 Mar 1900	Mar 1902	Broken up Mar 1921
Brazen	J & G Thomson	18 Oct 1895	3 Jul 1896	Jul 1900	Broken up Nov 1919
Electra	J & G Thomson	18 Oct 1895	14 Jul 1896	Jul 1900	Broken up Apr 1920
Recruit	J & G Thomson	18 Oct 1895	22 Aug 1896	Oct 1900	Torpedoed 1 May 1915
Vulture	J & G Thomson	26 Nov 1895	22 Mar 1898	May 1900	Broken up May 1919
Kestrel	J & G Thomson	2 Sep 1896	25 Mar 1898	Apr 1900	Broken up Mar 1921
Cheerful	R & W Hawthorn, Leslie & Co Ltd	7 Sep 1896	14 Jul 1897	Feb 1900	Mined 3 Jun 1917
Mermaid	R & W Hawthorn, Leslie & Co Ltd	7 Sep 1896	22 Feb 1898	Jun 1899	Broken up Jul 1919
Greyhound	R & W Hawthorn, Leslie & Co Ltd	18 Jul 1899	6 Oct 1900	Jan 1902	Broken up Jun 1919
Racehorse	R & W Hawthorn, Leslie & Co Ltd	23 Oct 1899	8 Nov 1900	Mar 1902	Broken up Mar 1920
Roebuck	R & W Hawthorn, Leslie & Co Ltd	2 Oct 1899	4 Jan 1901	Mar 1902	Broken up 1919
Gipsy	Fairfield Shipbuilding and Engineering Co Ltd	1 Oct 1896	9 Mar 1897	Jul 1898	Broken up 1921
Fairy	Fairfield Shipbuilding and Engineering Co Ltd	19 Oct 1896	29 May 1897	Aug 1898	Foundered 5 Jul 1920
Osprey	Fairfield Shipbuilding and Engineering Co Ltd	14 Nov 1896	17 Apr 1897	Jul 1898	Broken up Nov 1919
Leven	Fairfield Shipbuilding and Engineering Co Ltd	24 Jan 1898	28 Jun 1898	Jul 1899	Broken up Sep 1920
Falcon	Fairfield Shipbuilding and Engineering Co Ltd	28 Jun 1899	1899	Dec 1901	Collision 1 Apr 1918
Ostrich	Fairfield Shipbuilding and Engineering Co Ltd	28 Jun 1899	22 Mar 1900	Dec 1901	Broken up Apr 1920
Thorn	John Brown & Co.	n/a	17 Mar 1900	Jun 1901	Broken up 1919
Tiger	John Brown & Co.	n/a	19 May 1900	Jun 1901	Collision 2 Apr 1908
Vigilant	John Brown & Co.	n/a	16 Aug 1900	Jun 1901	Broken up Feb 1920
Albatross	John I Thornycroft & Co Ltd	27 Nov 1896	19 Jul 1898	Jul 1900	Broken up Jul 1920
Viper	C A Parsons & Company Hull by R & W Hawthorn, Leslie & Co Ltd	1898	6 Sep 1899	1900	Wrecked 3 Aug 1901
Velox	C A Parsons & Company Hull by R & W Hawthorn, Leslie & Co Ltd	10 Apr 1901	11 Feb 1902	Feb 1904	Mined 25 Oct 1915

'D' CLASS DESTROYERS

Desperate	John I Thornycroft & Co Ltd	1 Jul 1895	15 Feb 1896	Feb 1897	Broken up May 1920
Fame	John I Thornycroft & Co Ltd	4 Jul 1895	15 Apr 1896	Jun 1897	Broken up Aug 1921
Foam	John I Thornycroft & Co Ltd	16 Jul 1895	8 Oct 1896	Jul 1897	Broken up May 1914
Mallard	John I Thornycroft & Co Ltd	13 Sep 1895	19 Nov 1896	Oct 1897	Broken up Feb 1920
Angler	John I Thornycroft & Co Ltd	21 Feb 1896	2 Feb 1897	Jul 1898	Broken up May 1920
Ariel	John I Thornycroft & Co Ltd	23 Apr 1896	5 Mar 1897	Oct 1898	Wrecked 19 Apr 1907
Coquette	John I Thornycroft & Co Ltd	8 Jun 1896	25 Nov 1897	Nov 1899	Mined 7 Mar 1916
Cynthia	John I Thornycroft & Co Ltd	16 Jul 1896	8 Jan 1898	Jun 1899	Broken up Apr 1920
Cygnet	John I Thornycroft & Co Ltd	25 Sep 1896	3 Sep 1898	Feb 1900	Broken up Apr 1920
Stag	John I Thornycroft & Co Ltd	16 Apr 1898	18 Nov 1899	Sep 1900	Broken up Mar 1921
*Taku**	Schichau-Werke	n/a	1898	n/a	Broken up 25 Oct 1916

* Ex-Chinese, captured 17 Jun 1900.
Note: 'D' class had 2 funnels

APPENDIX B

RIVER CLASS – by laid down date

NAME	BUILDER	LAID DOWN	LAUNCHED	COMPLETED	FATE
Erne	Palmer Shipbuilding & Iron Co Ltd	3 Jul 02	14 Jan 03	1 Feb 04	Wrecked 6 Feb 15
Ettrick	Palmer Shipbuilding & Iron Co Ltd	9 Jul 02	28 Feb 03	Feb 1904	Sold May 1919 for scrapping
Exe	Palmer Shipbuilding & Iron Co Ltd	14 Jul 02	27 Apr 03	Mar 1904	Sold Feb 1920 for scrapping
Ribble	Yarrow & Co Ltd	4 Jul 02	19 Mar 04	Jun 1904	Sold Jul 1920 for scrapping
Teviot	Yarrow & Co Ltd	10 Jul 02	7 Nov 03	Apr 1904	Sold for Jun 1919 for scrapping
Usk	Yarrow & Co Ltd	30 Jul 02	25 Jul 03	Mar 1904	Sold Jul 1920 for scrapping
Derwent	R & W Hawthorn, Leslie & Co Ltd	12 Jun 02	14 Feb 03	Jul 1904	Mined 2 May 17
*Eden**	R & W Hawthorn, Leslie & Co Ltd	12 Jun 02	13 Mar 03	Jun 1904	Collision 18 Jun 16
Foyle	Laird Bros Ltd	15 Aug 02	25 Feb 03	Mar 1904	Mined 15 Mar 17
Itchen	Laird Bros Ltd	18 Aug 02	17 Mar 03	Jan 1904	Torpedoed 6 Jul 17
Kennet	John I Thornycroft & Co Ltd	5 Feb 02	4 Dec 03	Jan 1905	Sold Dec 1919 for scrapping
Jed	John I Thornycroft & Co Ltd	27 Feb 03	16 Feb 04	Jan 1905	Sold for scrapping 1920
Welland	Yarrow & Company	1 Oct 02	14 Apr 04	Jul 1904	Sold Jun 1920 for scrapping
Cherwell	Palmer Shipbuilding & Iron Co Ltd	20 Jan 03	23 Jul 03	Mar 1904	Sold Jun 1919 for scrapping
Dee	Palmer Shipbuilding & Iron Co Ltd	5 Mar 03	10 Sep 03	May 1904	Sold 23 Jul 1919 for scrapping
Arun	Laird Bros Ltd	27 Aug 02	29 Apr 03	Feb 1904	Sold Jun 1920 for scrapping
Blackwater	Laird Bros Ltd	27 Aug 02	25 Jul 03	Mar 1904	Collision 6 Apr 1909
Waveney	R & W Hawthorn, Leslie & Co Ltd	20 Oct 02	16 Mar 03	14 Jun 04	Sold Feb 1920 for scrapping

Chelmer	John I Thornycroft & Co Ltd	11 Dec 04	8 Dec 04	Jun 1905	Sold Jun 1920 for scrapping
Colne	John I Thornycroft & Co Ltd	21 Mar 04	21 May 05	Jul 1905	Sold Nov 1919 for scrapping
Gala	Yarrow & Co Ltd	1 Feb 04	7 Jan 05	n/a	Collision 27 Apr 08
Garry	Yarrow & Company	25 Apr 04	21 Mar 05	Sep 1905	Sold Oct 1920 for scrapping
Ness	J Samuel White	5 May 04	5 Jan 05	Aug 1905	Sold Jun 1919 for scrapping
Nith	J Samuel White	5 May 04	7 Mar 05	Oct 1905	Sold Jun 1919 for scrapping
Swale	Palmer Shipbuilding & Iron Co Ltd	23 Feb 04	20 Apr 05	Sep 1905	Sold Jun 1919 for scrapping
Ure	Palmer Shipbuilding & Iron Co Ltd	1 Mar 04	25 Oct 04	Jun 1905	Sold May 1919 for scrapping
Wear	Palmer Shipbuilding & Iron Co Ltd	7 Mar 04	21 Jan 05	Aug 1905	Sold Nov 1919 for scrapping
Liffey	Laird Bros Ltd	22 Mar 04	23 Sep 04	24 May 05	Sold Jun 1919 for scrapping
Moy	Laird Bros Ltd	22 Mar 04	10 Nov 04	Jun 1905	Sold May 1919 for scrapping
Ouse	Laird Bros Ltd	22 Mar 04	7 Jan 05	Sep 1905	Sold Oct 1919 for scrapping
Boyne	Laird Bros Ltd	16 Feb 04	12 Sep 04	May 1905	Sold Aug 1919 for scrapping
Doon	R & W Hawthorn, Leslie & Co Ltd	16 Feb 04	8 Nov 04	Jun 1905	Sold May 1919 for scrapping
Kale	R & W Hawthorn, Leslie & Co Ltd	16 Feb 04	8 Nov 04	Aug 1905	Mined 27 Mar 18
Rother	Palmer Shipbuilding & Iron Co Ltd	23 Mar 03	5 Jan 04	May 1905	Sold Jun 1919 for scrapping
*Stour**	Laird Bros Ltd	5 Dec 04	3 Jun 05	Mar 1910**	Sold Aug 1919 for scrapping
*Test**	Laird Bros Ltd	5 Dec 04	6 May 05	Mar 1910**	Sold Aug 1919 for scrapping

* Turbine-engined
** These dates are questionable and may be October 1910
Source: Friedman, *British Destroyers*, p 304, the dreadnoughtproject.org

APPENDIX C

'*TRIBAL*' CLASS – by laid down date

NAME	BUILDER	LAID DOWN	LAUNCHED	COMPLETED	FATE*
Cossack	Cammell Laird	13 Nov 05	16 Feb 07	Apr 08	Sold Dec 1919 for scrapping
Tartar	John I Thornycroft & Company	13 Nov 05	25 Jun 07	Apr 08	Sold May 1921 for scrapping
Ghurka	Hawthorn Leslie & Company	6 Feb 06	29 Apr 07	Dec 08	Mined 8 Feb 17
Mohawk	J Samuel White	1 May 06	15 Mar 07	Jun 08	Sold Sep 1919 for scrapping
Afridi	Armstrong, Whitworth & Company	9 Aug 06	8 May 07	Sep 09	Sold Dec 1919, used as target Apr 1930
Amazon	John I Thornycroft & Company	24 Jun 07	29 Jul 08	Apr 09	Sold Oct 1919 for scrapping
Saracen	J Samuel White	12 Jul 07	31 Mar 08	Jun 09	Sold Oct 1919 for scrapping
Nubian	John I Thornycroft & Company	18 May 08	21 Apr 09	Sep 09	Torpedoed 27 Oct 16
Viking	Palmer Shipbuilding and Iron Company	11 Jun 08	14 Sep 09	Jun 10	Sold Dec 1919 for scrapping
Crusader	J Samuel White	22 Jun 08	20 Mar 09	Oct 09	Sold Jun 1920 for scrapping
Zulu	Hawthorn Leslie & Company	18 Aug 08	16 Sep 09	Mar 10	Mined 8 Nov 16
Maori	William Denny & Brothers	6 Aug 09	24 May 09	Nov 09	Mined 7 May 15

Source: Friedman, *British Destroyers*, p 305.

APPENDIX D

BEAGLE CLASS – by laid down date

NAME	BUILDER	LAID DOWN	LAUNCHED	COMPLETED	FATE*
Savage	John I Thornycroft & Company	2 Mar 09	10 Mar 10	Aug 1910	May 1921
Scourge	Hawthorn Leslie & Company	9 Mar 09	11 Feb 10	Aug 1910	May 1921
Beagle	John Brown & Company	17 Mar 09	16 Oct 09	Jun 1910	1 Nov 21
Bulldog	John Brown & Company	30 Mar 09	13 Nov 09	7 Jul 10	21 Sep 20
Foxhound	John Brown & Company	1 Apr 09	11 Dec 09	Sep 1910	1 Nov 21
Nautilus	Thames Ironworks, Shipbuilding and Engineering Company	14 Apr 09	30 Mar 10	Sep 1910	Sep 1920
Grasshopper	Fairfield Shipbuilding and Engineering Company	17 Apr 09	23 Nov 09	Jul 1910	Nov 1921
Renard	Cammell Laird	20 Apr 09	30 Nov 09	Sep 1910	Aug 1920
Mosquito	Fairfield Shipbuilding and Engineering Company	22 Apr 09	27 Jan 10	Aug 1910	Aug 1920
Harpy	J Samuel White	23 Apr 09	27 Nov 09	Jul 1910	Nov 1921
Wolverine	Cammell Laird	26 Apr 09	15 Jan 10	Sep 1910	Collision 12 Dec 1917
Rattlesnake	London & Glasgow	29 Apr 09	14 Mar 10	Aug1910	May 1921
Racoon	Cammell Laird	1 May 09	15 Feb 10	Oct 1910	Wrecked 9 Jan 1918
Scorpion	Fairfield Shipbuilding and Engineering Company	3 May 09	19 Feb 10	Aug1910	Oct 1921
Basilisk	J Samuel White	11 May 09	9 Feb 10	Sep 1910	Nov 1921
Pincher	William Denny & Brothers	20 May 09	15 Mar 10	Sep 1910	Wrecked 24 Jul 1918

* Dates refer to being sold for scrapping unless otherwise specified.
Source: Friedman, *British Destroyers*, pp 305–6.

APPENDIX E

ACORN CLASS – by laid down date

NAME	BUILDER	LAID DOWN	LAUNCHED	COMPLETED	FATE*
Nemesis	Hawthorn Leslie & Company	24 Nov 09	9 Aug 10	1 Mar 11	To Japan Jun 1917
Nereide	Hawthorn Leslie & Company	3 Dec 09	6 Sep 10	1 Apr 11	Dec 1921

Cameleon	Fairfield Shipbuilding and Engineering Company	6 Dec 09	1 Jun 10	1 Dec 10	Nov 1921
Nymphe	Hawthorn Leslie & Company	8 Dec 09	31 Jan 11	1 May 11	May 1921
Larne	John I Thornycroft & Company	8 Dec 09	23 Aug 10	1 Feb 11	May 1921
Lyra	John I Thornycroft & Company	8 Dec 09	4 Oct 10	1 Feb 11	May 1921
Hope	Swan Hunter	9 Dec 09	6 Sep 10	1 Mar 11	Feb 1920
Redpole	J Samuel White	10 Dec 09	24 Jun 10	1 Feb 11	May 1921
Martin	John I Thornycroft & Company	21 Dec 09	15 Dec 10	1 Mar 11	Aug 1920
Rifleman	J Samuel White	21 Dec 09	22 Aug 10	1 Mar 11	May 1921
Acorn	John Brown & Company	12 Jan 10	1 Jul 10	1 Dec 10	Nov 1921
Sheldrake	William Denny & Brothers	15 Jan 10	18 Jan 11	19 May 11	Nov 1921
Staunch	William Denny & Brothers	15 Jan 10	29 Oct 10	1 Mar 11	Torpedoed 11 Nov 1917
Comet	Fairfield Shipbuilding and Engineering Company	1 Feb 10	23 Jun 10	1 Jun 11	Torpedoed 6 Aug 1918***
Alarm	John Brown & Company	7 Feb 10	29 Aug 10	1 Mar 11	May 1921
Ruby	J. Samuel White	15 Feb 10	4 Nov 10	7 Apr 11	May 1921
*Brisk***	John Brown & Company	21 Feb 10	20 Sep 10	1 Jun 11	Nov 1921
Goldfinch	Fairfield Shipbuilding and Engineering Company	23 Feb 10	12 Jul 10	1 Feb 11	Wrecked 19 Feb 1915
Fury	A & J Inglis	3 Mar 10	25 Apr 11	1 Feb 12	Nov 1921
Minstrel	John I Thornycroft & Company	11 Mar 10	2 Feb 11	1 May 11	To Japan Jun 1917

* Dates refer to being sold for scrapping unless otherwise specified
** Two shafts.
*** Unconfirmed, also reported as lost under tow from collision.
Source: Friedman, *British Destroyers*, p 306.

APPENDIX F

ACHERON CLASS DESTROYERS – by laid down date

NAME	BUILDER	LAID DOWN	LAUNCHED	COMPLETED	FATE*
Sandfly	Swan Hunter	23 Aug 10	26 Jul 11	Nov 1911	9 May 21
Archer	Yarrow & Company	1 Sep 10	21 Oct 11	Mar 1912	9 May 21
Ferret	J. Samuel White	6 Sep 10	12 Apr 11	Oct 1911	9 May 21
Forester	J. Samuel White	7 Sep 10	01 Jun 11	Jan 1912	4 Nov 21
Attack	Yarrow & Company	10 Sep 10	21 Dec 11	May 1912	Mined 30 Dec 17
Acheron	John I Thornycroft & Company	30 Sep 10	27 Jun 11	Nov 1911	9 May 21
Jackal	Hawthorn Leslie & Company	6 Oct 10	9 Sep 11	Jan 1912	28 Sep 20
Ariel	John I Thornycroft & Company	10 Oct 10	26 Sep 11	Mar 1912	Mined 2 Aug 18
Beaver	William Denny & Brothers	18 Oct 10	6 Oct 11	Nov 1912	9 May 21
Defender	William Denny & Brothers	7 Nov 10	30 Aug 11	Jan 1912	4 Nov 21
Druid	William Denny & Brothers	8 Nov 10	4 Dec 11	Apr 1912	9 May 21
Hind	John Brown & Company	21 Nov 10	28 Jul 11	Dec 1911	9 May 21
Phoenix	Vickers	4 Jan 11	9 Oct 11	May 1912	Torpedoed 14 May 18
Hornet	John Brown & Company	7 Jan 11	20 Dec 11	Mar 1912	9 May 21
Goshawk	William Beardmore & Company	30 Jan 11	18 Oct 11	Jun 1912	4 Nov 21
Hydra	John Brown & Company	7 Feb 11	19 Feb 12	Jun 1912	9 May 21
Tigress	Hawthorn Leslie & Company	13 Feb 11	20 Dec 11	Apr 1912	9 May 21
Lapwing	Cammell Laird	17 Feb 11	29 Jul 11	Apr 1912	26 Oct 21
Lizard	Cammell Laird	23 Feb 11	10 Oct 11	Jun 1912	4 Nov 21
Firedrake	Yarrow & Company	1 Jul 11	9 Apr 12	Sep 1912	10 Oct 21
Lurcher	Yarrow & Company	1 Jul 11	1 Jun 12	Oct 1912	9 Jun 22
Oak	Yarrow & Company	6 Jul 11	5 Sep 12	Nov 1912	9 May 21
Badger	William Denny & Brothers	17 Oct 10	11 Jul 11	Aug 1912	9 May 21
Huon	Cockatoo Dockyard	25 Jan 13	19 Dec 14	14 Dec 15	Sunk as target 10 Apr 31
Torrens	Cockatoo Dockyard	25 Jan 13	28 Aug 15	3 Jul 16	Scuttled 24 Nov 30
Swan	Cockatoo Dockyard	22 Jan 15	11 Dec 15	16 Aug 16	Broken up Sep 1929
Parramatta	Fairfield Shipbuilding and Engineering Company	n/a	9 Feb 10	10 Sep 10	Dismantled Oct 1929
Warrego	Fairfield Shipbuilding and Engineering Company and Cockatoo Dockyard	n/a	4 Apr 11	01 Jun 12	Broken up in 1930
Yarra	William Denny & Brothers	n/a	9 Apr 10	10 Sep 10	Scuttled 11 Jun 31

* Dates relate to being sold for scrapping unless otherwise stated.
Source: Friedman, *British Destroyers*, p 308; thedreadnoughtproject.org

APPENDIX G

ACASTA CLASS – by laid down date

NAME	BUILDER	LAID DOWN	LAUNCHED	COMPLETED	FATE*
Christopher	Hawthorn Leslie & Company	16 Oct 11	29 Aug 12	Nov 1912	May 1921
Sparrowhawk	Swan Hunter	17 Oct 11	12 Oct 12	May 1913	War loss 1 Jun 16
Cockatrice	Hawthorn Leslie & Company	23 Oct 11	8 Nov 12	Mar 1913	May 1921
Shark	Swan Hunter	27 Oct 11	30 Jul 12	Apr 1913	War loss 31 May 16
Hardy	John I Thornycroft & Company	13 Nov 11	10 Oct 12	Sep 1913	May 1921
Acasta	John Brown & Company	1 Dec 11	10 Sep 12	Nov 1912	May 1921
Spitfire	Swan Hunter	18 Dec 11	23 Dec 12	Jun 1913	May 1921
Contest	Hawthorn Leslie & Company	26 Dec 11	7 Jan 13	Jun 1913	Torpedoed 18 Sep 17
Achates	John Brown & Company	15 Jan 12	14 Nov 12	Mar 1913	May 1921
Lynx	London & Glasgow	18 Jan 12	20 Mar 13	Jan 1914	Mined 9 Aug 15
Ambuscade	John Brown & Company	7 Mar 12	25 Jan 13	Jun 1913	Sep 1921
Paragon	John I Thornycroft & Company	14 Mar 12	21 Feb 13	Dec 1913	Torpedoed 18 Mar 17
Porpoise	John I Thornycroft & Company	14 Mar 12	21 Jul 13	Jan 1914	Mar 1921
Midge	London & Glasgow	1 Apr 12	22 May 13	Mar 1914	Nov 1921
Owl	London & Glasgow	1 Apr 12	7 Jul 13	Apr 1914	Nov 1921
Unity	John I Thornycroft & Company	1 Apr 12	18 Sep 13	Mar 1914	Oct 1922
Victor	John I Thornycroft & Company	1 Apr 12	28 Nov 13	Jun 1914	Jan 1923
Fortune	Fairfield Shipbuilding and Engineering Company	24 Jun 12	17 May 13	Dec 1913	War loss 31 May 16
Garland	Cammell Laird	15 Jul 12	23 Apr 13	Dec 1913	Sep 1921
Ardent	William Denny & Brothers	9 Oct 12	08 Sep 13	Feb 1914	War loss 1 Jun 16

* Dates refer to sold for scrapping unless otherwise specified.
Source: Friedman, *British Destroyers*, pp 306–7.

APPENDIX H

LAFOREY CLASS – by laid down date

NAME	BUILDER	LAID DOWN	LAUNCHED	COMPLETED	FATE*
Lark	Yarrow & Company	28 Jun 12	26 May 13	1 Oct 13	Jan 1923

Linnet	Yarrow & Company	28 Jun 12	16 Aug 13	1 Dec 13	Nov 1921
Laertes	Swan Hunter, Wigham Richardson	6 Jul 12	5 Jun 13	1 Oct 13	Dec 1921
Landrail	Yarrow & Company	24 Jul 12	7 Feb 14	1 Jun 14	1 Dec 21
Laverock	Yarrow & Company	24 Jul 12	19 Nov 13	1 Oct 14	May 1921
Lance	John I Thornycroft & Company	1 Aug 12	25 Feb 14	1 Jun 14	Nov 1921
Lysander	Swan Hunter, Wigham Richardson	8 Aug 12	18 Aug 13	1 Dec 13	Jun 1922
Laurel	J Samuel White	17 Aug 12	6 May 13	1 Mar 14	Nov 1921
Lookout	John I Thornycroft & Company	29 Aug 12	27 Apr 14	1 Aug 14	Aug 1922
Liberty	J Samuel White	31 Aug 12	15 Sep 13	1 Mar 14	Nov 1921
Laforey	Fairfield Shipbuilding and Engineering Company	9 Sep 12	28 Mar 13	1 Feb 14	Mined 25 Mar 17
Loyal	William Denny & Brothers	16 Sep 12	11 Nov 13	1 May 14	Nov 1921
Legion	William Denny & Brothers	19 Sep 12	3 Feb 14	1 Jul 14	May 1921
Lawford	Fairfield Shipbuilding and Engineering Company	28 Sep 12	30 Oct 13	1 Mar 14	Aug 1922
Lennox	William Beardmore & Company	14 Oct 12	17 Mar 14	1 Jul 14	Oct 1921
*Leonidas***	Palmer Shipbuilding and Iron Company	26 Oct 12	30 Oct 13	1 Aug 14	May 1921
*Lucifer***	Palmer Shipbuilding and Iron Company	26 Oct 12	29 Dec 13	1 Aug 14	Dec 1921
Llewellyn	William Beardmore & Company	14 Nov 12	30 Oct 13	1 Mar 14	Mar 1922
Louis	Fairfield Shipbuilding and Engineering Company	5 Dec 12	30 Dec 13	1 Mar 14	Mined 31 Oct 15
Lydiard	Fairfield Shipbuilding and Engineering Company	14 Dec 12	26 Feb 14	1 Jun 14	Nov 1921
Lochinvar	William Beardmore & Company	9 Jan 15	9 Oct 15	1 Dec 15	Nov 1921
Lassoo	William Beardmore & Company	24 Jan 15	24 Aug 15	11 Oct 15	Mined 13 Aug 16

*Sold for scrapping date unless stated otherwise
**Geared turbines

APPENDIX I

ADMIRALTY 'M' CLASS – by completion date

NAME	BUILDER	LAID DOWN	LAUNCHED	COMPLETED	FATE
Mandate	Fairfield Shipbuilding & Engineering Co Ltd	29 Oct 14	27 Apr 15	13 Aug 15	Sold Sep 1921 for scrapping
Manners	Fairfield Shipbuilding & Engineering Co Ltd	14 Nov 14	15 Jun 15	21 Sep 15	Sold Oct 1921 for scrapping
Matchless	Swan Hunter Wigham Richardson Ltd	n/a	5 Oct 14	8 Nov 15	Sold Oct 1921 for scrapping
Mindful	Fairfield Shipbuilding & Engineering Co Ltd	29 Dec 14	12 Oct 15	10 Nov 15	Sold Sep 1921 for scrapping
Mystic	William Denny & Brothers Ltd	27 Oct 14	26 Jun 15	11 Nov 15	Sold Nov 1921 for scrapping
Maenad	William Denny & Brothers Ltd	10 Nov 14	10 Aug 15	12 Nov 15	Sold Nov 1921 for scrapping
Mischief	Fairfield Shipbuilding & Engineering Co Ltd	3 Feb 15	12 Oct 15	16 Dec 15	Sold Nov 1921 for scrapping
Nestor	Swan Hunter Wigham Richardson Ltd	n/a	9 Oct 15	22 Dec 15	War loss, sunk 31 May 16
Marvel	William Denny & Brothers Ltd	11 Jan 15	7 Oct 15	28 Dec 15	Sold May 1921 for scrapping
Magic	J Samuel White & Co Ltd	1 Jan 15	10 Sep 15	8 Jan 16	Sold Sep 1921 for scrapping
Noble	Alexander Stephen & Sons Ltd	2 Feb 15	25 Nov 15	15 Feb 16	Sold Nov 1921 for scrapping
Onslaught	Fairfield Shipbuilding & Engineering Co Ltd	5 Feb 15	4 Dec 15	3 Mar 16	Sold Oct 1921 for scrapping
Obdurate	Scotts Shipbuilding & Engineering Co Ltd	Jan 1915	21 Jan 16	3 Mar 16	Sold Nov 1921 for scrapping
Moresby	J Samuel White & Co Ltd	15 Jan 15	20 Nov 15	7 Apr 16	Sold May 1921 for scrapping
Nicator	William Denny & Brothers Ltd Ltd	21 Apr 15	3 Feb 16	15 Apr 16	Sold May 1921 for scrapping
Narwhal	William Denny & Brothers Ltd	21 Apr 15	3 Dec 15	15 Apr 16	Damaged in collision 1919, scrapped 1920
Pelican	William Beardmore & Co Ltd	25 Jun 15	18 Mar 16	1 May 16	Sold Nov 1921 for scrapping
Petard	William Denny & Brothers Ltd	5 Jul 15	24 Mar 16	23 May 16	Sold May 1921 for scrapping
Pigeon	R W Hawthorn Leslie & Co Ltd	Jul 1915	3 Mar 16	2 Jun 16	Sold May 1921 for scrapping
Nonpareil	Alexander Stephen & Sons	22 May 15	16 May 16	28 Jun 16	Sold May 1921 for scrapping
Nizam	Alexander Stephen & Sons Ltd	12 Feb 15	6 Apr 16	29 Jun 16	Sold May 1921 for scrapping
Peyton	William Denny & Brothers Ltd	12 Jul 15	2 May 16	29 Jun 16	Sold May 1921 for scrapping
Pellew	William Beardmore & Co Ltd	25 Jun 15	18 May 16	30 Jun 16	Sold May 1921 for scrapping
Plover	R W Hawthorn Leslie & Co Ltd	30 Jul 15	19 Apr 16	30 Jun 16	Sold May 1921 for scrapping
Medina	J Samuel White & Co Ltd	23 Sep 15	8 Mar 16	30 Jun 16	Sold May 1921 for scrapping
Offa	Fairfield Shipbuilding & Engineering Co Ltd	6 Jul 15	7 Jun 16	31 Jul 16	Sold Oct 1921 for scrapping
Medway	J Samuel White & Co Ltd	2 Nov 15	19 Apr 16	2 Aug 16 scrapping	Sold May 1921 for
Prince	Alexander Stephen & Sons Ltd	27 Jul 15	26 Jul 16	21 Sep 16	Sold May 1921 for scrapping
Orcadia	Fairfield Shipbuilding & Engineering Co Ltd	24 Jun 15	26 Jul 16	29 Sep 16	Sold Oct 1921 for scrapping
Oriana	Fairfield Shipbuilding & Engineering Co Ltd	n/a	23 Sep 16	4 Nov 16	Sold Oct 1921 for scrapping
Pylades	Alexander Stephen & Sons Ltd	n/a	28 Sep 16	30 Dec 16	Sold May 1921 for scrapping
Mansfield	R W Hawthorn Leslie & Co Ltd	9 Jul 13	3 Dec 14	Apr 1915	Sold Oct 1921 for scrapping
Menace	Swan Hunter Wigham Richardson Ltd	17 Nov 14	9 Nov 15	Apr 1916	Sold May 1921 for scrapping
Onslow	Fairfield Shipbuilding & Engineering Co Ltd	5 Feb 15	15 Feb 16	Apr 1916	Sold Nov 1921 for scrapping
Narborough	John Brown & Co Ltd	May 1915	2 Mar 16	Apr 1916	Wrecked 12 Jan 18
Nomad	Alexander Stephen & Sons Ltd	n/a	07 Feb 16	Apr 1916	War loss, sunk 31 May 16

Nugent	Palmer Shipbuilding & Iron Co Ltd	Apr 1915	23 Jan 17	Apr 1917	Sold May 1921 for scrapping
Opal	William Doxford & Sons Ltd	1 Dec 15	11 Sep 15	Apr 1916	Wrecked 21 Jan 18
Miranda	Yarrow & Co Ltd	6 May 13	27 May 14	Aug 1914	Sold Oct 1921 for scrapping
Morning Star	Yarrow & Co Ltd	18 Oct 14	26 Jun 15	Aug 1915	Sold Dec 1921 for scrapping
Michael	John I Thornycroft & Co Ltd	12 Nov 14	19 May 15	Aug 1915	Sold Sep 1921 for scrapping
Oracle	William Doxford & Sons Ltd	Feb 1915	23 Dec 15	Aug 1916	Sold Oct 1921 for scrapping
Patrician	John I Thornycroft & Co Ltd	Jun 1915	5 Jun 16	Aug 1916	Transferred to RCN 1920, Sold 1929 for scrapping
Norman	Palmer Shipbuilding & Iron Co Ltd	n/a	20 Mar 16	Aug 1916	Sold May 1921 for scrapping
Northesk	Palmer Shipbuilding & Iron Co Ltd	n/a	5 Jul 16	Aug 1916	Sold May 1921 for scrapping
Murray	Palmer Shipbuilding & Iron Co Ltd	4 Dec 13	6 Aug 14	Dec 1914	Sold May 1921 for scrapping
Milne	John Brown & Co Ltd	18 Dec 13	5 Oct 14	Dec 1914	Sold Sep 1921 for scrapping
Morris	John Brown & Co Ltd	20 Jan 14	19 Nov 14	Dec 1914	Sold Nov 1921 for scrapping
Musketeer	Yarrow & Co Ltd	18 Oct 14	12 Nov 15	Dec 1915	Sold Nov 1921 for scrapping
Osiris	Palmer Shipbuilding & Iron Co Ltd	n/a	28 Sep 16	Dec 1916	Sold May 1921 for scrapping
Oberon	William Doxford & Sons Ltd	n/a	29 Sep 16	Dec 1916	Sold May 1921 for scrapping
Pheasant	Fairfield Shipbuilding & Engineering Co Ltd	n/a	23 Oct 16	Dec 1916	War loss, mined 1 Mar 17
Phoebe	Fairfield Shipbuilding & Engineering Co Ltd	n/a	20 Nov 16	Dec 1916	Sold Nov 1921 for scrapping
Myngs	Palmer Shipbuilding & Iron Co Ltd	31 Dec 13	24 Sep 14	Feb 1915	Sold May 1921 for scrapping
Moorsom	John Brown & Co Ltd	15 Jan 14	21 Dec 14	Feb 1915	Sold Nov 1921 for scrapping
Obedient	Scotts Shipbuilding & Engineering Co Ltd	n/a	6 Nov 15	Feb 1916	Sold Nov 1921 for scrapping
North Star	Palmer Shipbuilding & Iron Co Ltd	n/a	9 Nov 16	Feb 1917	War loss 23 Apr 18
Mentor	R.W. Hawthorn Leslie & Co Ltd	9 Jul 13	21 Aug 14	Jan 1915	Sold May 1921 for scrapping
Munster	John I Thornycroft & Co Ltd	2 Dec 14	24 Nov 15	Jan 1916	Sold Nov 1921 for scrapping
Napier	John Brown & Co Ltd	24 Mar 15	27 Nov 15	Jan 1916	Sold Nov 1921 for scrapping
Mons	John Brown & Co Ltd	30 Sep 14	1 May 15	Jul 1915	Sold Nov 1921 for scrapping
Peregrine	John Brown & Co Ltd	9 Jun 15	29 May 16	Jul 1916	Sold Nov 1921 for scrapping
Plucky	Scotts Shipbuilding & Engineering Co Ltd	Aug 1915	21 Apr 16	Jul 1916	Sold May 1921 for scrapping
Pasley	Swan Hunter Wigham Richardson Ltd	Jul 1915	15 Apr 16	Jul 1916	Sold May 1921 for scrapping
Moon	Yarrow & Co Ltd	18 Oct 14	23 Apr 15	Jun 1915	Sold May 1921 for scrapping
Observer	Fairfield Shipbuilding & Engineering Co Ltd	1 Jun 15	1 May 16	Jun 1916	Sold Oct 1921 for scrapping
Opportune	William Doxford & Sons Ltd	Feb 1915	20 Nov 15	Jun 1916	Sold Nov 1921 for scrapping
Partridge	Swan Hunter Wigham Richardson Ltd	Jul 1915	4 Mar 16	Jun 1916	War loss 12 Dec 17
Patriot	John I Thornycroft & Co Ltd	Jul 1915	20 Apr 16	Jun 1916	Transferred to RCN 1920, sold 1929 for scrapping
Orestes	William Doxford & Sons Ltd	1 Mar 15	17 Jun 16	Jun 1916	Sold Oct 1921 for scrapping
Mary Rose	Swan Hunter Wigham Richardson Ltd	17 Nov 14	8 Oct 15	Mar 1916	War loss, sunk 17 Oct 17
Nepean	John I Thornycroft & Co Ltd	Feb 1915	22 Jan 16	Mar 1916	Sold Nov 1921 for scrapping
Nonsuch	Palmer Shipbuilding & Iron Co Ltd	Jan 1915	8 Dec 15	Mar 1916	Sold May 1921 for scrapping
Nerissa	Yarrow & Co Ltd	Mar 1915	9 Feb 16	Mar 1916	Sold Nov 1921 for scrapping
Penn	John Brown & Co Ltd	9 Jun 15	8 Apr 16	May 1916	Sold Oct 1921 for scrapping
Ophelia	William Doxford & Sons Ltd	1 Dec 15	13 Oct 15	May 1916	Sold Nov 1921 for scrapping
Relentless	Yarrow & Co Ltd	Aug 1915	15 Apr 16	May 1916	Sold Nov 1921 for scrapping
Negro	Palmer Shipbuilding & Iron Co Ltd	Jan 1915	8 Mar 16	May 1916	Lost in collision 21 Dec 16
Nereus	John I Thornycroft & Co Ltd	Mar 1915	24 Feb 16	May 1916	Sold Nov 1921 for scrapping
Paladin	Scotts Shipbuilding & Engineering Co Ltd	May 1915	27 Mar 16	May 1916	Sold May 1921 for scrapping
Manly	Yarrow & Co Ltd	12 May 13	12 Oct 14	Nov 1914	Sold Oct 1921 for scrapping
Mastiff	John I Thornycroft & Co Ltd	24 Jul 13	5 Sep 14	Nov 1914	Sold May 1921 for scrapping
Ossory	John Brown & Co Ltd	23 Dec 14	9 Oct 15	Nov 1915	Sold Nov 1921 for scrapping
Minion	John I Thornycroft & Co Ltd	27 Nov 14	11 Sep 15	Nov 1915	Sold Sep 1921 for scrapping
Nessus	Swan Hunter Wigham Richardson Ltd	n/a	24 Aug 15	Nov 1915	Lost in collision 8 Sep 18
Octavia	William Doxford & Sons Ltd	n/a	21 Jun 16	Nov 1916	Sold Nov 1921 for scrapping
Oriole	Palmer Shipbuilding & Iron Co Ltd	n/a	31 Jul 16	Nov 1916	Sold May 1921 for scrapping
Norseman	William Doxford & Sons Ltd	n/a	15 Aug 16	Nov 1916	Sold May 1921 for scrapping
Mounsey	Yarrow & Co Ltd	18 Oct 14	11 Sep 15	Oct 1915	Sold Nov 1921 for scrapping
Martial	Swan Hunter Wigham Richardson Ltd	22 Oct 14	1 Jul 15	Oct 1915	Sold May 1921 for scrapping
Milbrook	John I Thornycroft & Co Ltd	20 Nov 14	12 Jul 15	Oct 1915	Sold Sep 1921 for scrapping
Mameluke	John Brown & Co Ltd	23 Dec 14	14 Aug 15	Oct 1915	Sold Sep 1921 for scrapping
Portia	Scotts Shipbuilding & Engineering Co Ltd	n/a	10 Aug 16	Oct 1916	Sold May 1921 for scrapping
Ready	John I Thornycroft & Co Ltd	n/a	26 Aug 16	Oct 1916	Sold July 1926 for scrapping

Marne	John Brown & Co Ltd	30 Sep 14	29 May 15	Sep 1915	Sold Sep 1921 for scrapping
Marmion	Swan Hunter Wigham Richardson Ltd	22 Oct 14	28 May 15	Sep 1915	Lost in collision 21 Oct 17
Orpheus	William Doxford & Sons Ltd	1 Mar 15	17 Jun 16	Sep 1916	Sold Nov 1921 for scrapping
Rival	Yarrow & Co Ltd	Aug 1915	14 Jun 16	Sep 1916	Sold in 1926 for scrapping
Rapid	John I Thornycroft & Co Ltd	Aug 1915	15 Jul 16	Sep 1916	Sold Apr 1927 for scrapping
Parthian	Scotts Shipbuilding & Engineering Co Ltd	Jul 1915	3 Jul 16	Sep 1916	Sold Nov 1921 for scrapping
Orford	William Doxford & Sons Ltd	n/a	19 Apr 16	Sep 1916	Sold Oct 1921 for scrapping
Minos	Yarrow & Co Ltd	9 May 13	6 Aug 14	Sep 1914	Sold Aug 1920 for scrapping
Meteor	John I Thornycroft & Co Ltd	17 May 13	24 Jul 14	Sep 1914	Sold May 1921 for scrapping

Source: Friedman, *British Destroyers*, pp 308–10; thedreadnoughtproject.org

APPENDIX J

ADMIRALTY 'R' CLASS AND IMPROVED 'R' CLASS – by completion date

NAME	BUILDER	LAID DOWN	LAUNCHED	COMPLETED	FATE
Sarpedon	Hawthorn Leslie & Company	27 Sep 15	1 Jun 16	2 Sep 16	Sold 13 Jul 26 for scrapping
Rocket	William Denny & Brothers	28 Sep 15	2 Jul 16	7 Oct 16	Sold 16 Dec 26 for scrapping
Sable	J. Samuel White	20 Dec 15	28 Jun 16	30 Nov 16	Sold Aug 1927 for scrapping
Rob Roy	William Denny & Brothers	15 Oct 15	28 Aug 16	15 Dec 16	Sold 13 Jul 26 for scrapping
Starfish	Hawthorn Leslie & Company	26 Jan 16	27 Sep 16	16 Dec 16	Sold 21 Apr 28 for scrapping
Stork	Hawthorn Leslie & Company	Apr 1916	15 Nov 16	1 Feb 17	Sold 7 Oct 27 for scrapping
Satyr	William Beardmore & Company	15 Apr 16	27 Dec 16	2 Feb 17	Sold 16 Dec 26 for scrapping
Red Gauntlet	William Denny & Brothers	30 Sep 15	23 Nov 16	7 Feb 17	Sold Jul 1927 for scrapping
Sylph	Harland & Wolff	30 Aug 16	15 Nov 16	10 Feb 17	Sold 16 Dec 26 for scrapping
Sturgeon	Alexander Stephen & Sons	10 Nov 15	11 Jan 17	26 Feb 17	Sold 16 Dec 26 for scrapping
Tempest	Fairfield Shipbuilding and Engineering Company	n/a	26 Jan 17	20 Mar 17	Handed over 28 Jan 37
Thruster	Hawthorn Leslie & Company/ C A Parsons & Company	2 Jun 16	10 Jan 17	30 Mar 17	Sold 1937 for scrapping
Sharpshooter	William Beardmore & Company	23 May 16	27 Feb 17	02 Apr 17	Sold 29 Apr 27 for scrapping
Springbok	Harland & Wolff	28 Jan 16	9 Mar 17	30 Apr 17	Sold 16 Dec 26 for scrapping
Trenchant	J Samuel White	17 Jul 16	23 Dec 17	30 Apr 17	Sold 15 Nov 28 for scrapping
Sceptre	Alexander Stephen & Sons	10 Nov 15	18 Apr 17	26 May 17	Sold 16 Dec 26 for scrapping
Undine	Fairfield Shipbuilding and Engineering Company	2 Aug 16	22 Mar 17	26 May 17	Sold Apr 1938 for scrapping
Tetrarch	Harland & Wolff	26 Jul 16	20 Apr 17	2 Jun 17	Sold 28 Jul 34 for scrapping
Thisbe	Hawthorn Leslie & Company	13 Jun 16	8 Mar 17	6 Jun 17	Sold 31 Aug 36 for scrapping
Skilful	Harland & Wolff	20 Jan 16	03 Feb 17	23 Jun 17	Sold 13 Jul 26 for scrapping
Tristram	J Samuel White	23 Sep 16	24 Feb 17	30 Jun 17	Sold 9 May 21 for scrapping
Tenacious	Harland & Wolff	25 Jul 16	21 May 17	12 Aug 17	Sold 26 Jun 28 for scrapping
Tormentor	Alexander Stephen & Sons	1 May 16	22 May 17	22 Aug 17	Sold 19 Nov 29 for scrapping
Tancred	William Beardmore & Company	6 Jul 16	30 Jun 17	1 Sep 17	Sold 17 May 28 for scrapping
Ulster	William Beardmore & Company	19 Jun 16	10 Oct 17	21 Nov 17	Sold Apr 1938 for scrapping
Salmon	Harland & Wolff	27 Aug 15	7 Oct 16	20 Dec 16	Handed over 28 Jan 37
Recruit	William Doxford & Sons	n/a	9 Dec 16	Apr 1917	Mined 9 Aug 17
Tarpon	John Brown & Company	12 Apr 16	10 Mar 17	Apr 1917	Sold 4 Aug 27 for scrapping
Romola	John Brown & Company	25 Aug 15	14 May 16	Aug 1916	Sold 13 Mar 30 for scrapping
Tower	Swan Hunter	Sep 1916	5 Apr 17	Aug 1917	Sold 17 May 28 for scrapping
Umpire	William Doxford & Sons	21 Aug 16	9 Jun 17	Aug 1917	Sold 7 Jan 30 for scrapping
Urchin	Palmer Shipbuilding and Iron Company	Sep 1916	7 Jun 17	Aug 1917	Sold 7 Jan 30 for scrapping
Sorceress	Swan Hunter	Nov 1915	29 Aug 16	Dec 1916	Sold 29 Apr 27 for scrapping
Simoom	John Brown & Company	n/a	30 Oct 16	Dec 1916	Torpedoed 23 Jan 17
Rosalind	John I Thornycroft & Company	Oct 1915	14 Oct 16	Dec 1916	Sold 13 Jul 26 for scrapping
Setter	J Samuel White	n/a	18 Aug 16	Feb 1917	Collision 17 May 17
Skate	John Brown & Company	12 Jan 16	11 Jan 17	Feb 1917	Sold 4 Mar 47 for scrapping
Torrent	Swan Hunter	n/a	26 Nov 16	Feb 1917	Mined 23 Dec 17
Radiant	John I Thornycroft & Company	Dec 1915	25 Nov 16	Feb 1917	Sold 21 Jun 20 for scrapping
Sybille	Yarrow & Company	Aug 1915	5 Feb 17	Feb 1917	Sold 5 Nov 26 for scrapping
Surprise	Yarrow & Company	n/a	25 Nov 16	Jan 1917	Mined 23 Dec 17
Teazer	John I Thornycroft & Company	Apr 1916	21 Apr 17	Jul 1917	Sold 6 Feb 31 for scrapping
Tyrant	Yarrow & Company	Jun 1916	19 May 17	Jul 1917	Sold Apr 1938 for scrapping
Tirade	Scotts Shipbuilding and Engineering Company	May 1916	21 Apr 17	Jul 1917	Sold 15 Nov 21 for scrapping
Telemachus	John Brown & Company	12 Apr 16	21 Apr 17	Jun 1917	Sold 26 Jul 27 for scrapping
Ulysses	William Doxford & Sons	1 Aug 16	24 Mar 17	Jun 1917	Collision 29 Oct 18
Redoubt	William Doxford & Sons	n/a	28 Oct 16	Mar 1917	Sold 13 Jul 26 for scrapping

Retriever	John I Thornycroft & Company	Jan 1916	15 Jan 17	Mar 1917	Sold 26 Jul 27 for scrapping
Torrid	Swan Hunter	Jul 1916	10 Feb 17	May 1917	Handed over 27 Jan 37
Taurus	John I Thornycroft & Company	Mar 1916	10 Mar 17	May 1917	Sold 18 Feb 30 for scrapping
Truculent	Yarrow & Company	Jun 1916	24 Mar 17	May 1917	Sold 29 Apr 27 for scrapping
Rigorous	John Brown & Company	22 Sep 15	30 Sep 16	Nov 1916	Sold 5 Nov 26 for scrapping
Strongbow	Yarrow & Company	n/a	30 Sep 16	Nov 1916	Sunk 17 Oct 17
Tornado	Alexander Stephen & Sons	n/a	4 Aug 17	Nov 1917	Mined 23 Dec 17
Raider	Swan Hunter	n/a	17 Jul 16	Oct 1916	Sold 29 Apr 27 for scrapping
Restless	John Brown & Company	22 Sep 15	12 Aug 16	Oct 1916	Handed over 23 Nov 36
Ursa	Palmer Shipbuilding and Iron Company	n/a	23 Jul 17	Oct 1917	Sold 13 Jul 26 for scrapping
Radstock	Swan Hunter	Sep 1915	3 Jun 16	Sep 1916	Sold 29 Apr 27 for scrapping
Rowena	John Brown & Company	25 Aug 15	01 Jul 16	Sep 1916	Handed over 21 Jul 37
Sabrina	Yarrow & Company	Nov 1915	24 Jul 16	Sep 1916	Sold 5 Nov 26 for scrapping
Ulleswater	Yarrow & Company	Jul 1916	4 Aug 17	Sep 1917	Torpedoed 15 Aug 18
Ursula	Scotts Shipbuilding and Engineering Company	Sep 1916	2 Aug 17	Sep 1917	Sold 19 Nov 29 for scrapping

Source: Friedman, *British Destroyers*, pp 310–11; thedreadnoughtproject.org

APPENDIX K

ADMIRALTY 'S' CLASS DESTROYERS – by launch date

NAME	BUILDER	LAID DOWN	LAUNCHED	COMPLETED	FATE
Simoom	John Brown & Co	30 May 17	26 Jan 18	? Mar 1918	Sold Jan 1931 for breaking up
Scimitar	John Brown & Co	30 May 17	27 Feb 18	13 Apr 18	Sold Jun 1947 for breaking up
Torbay	John I Thornycroft & Co Ltd	Nov 1917	6 Mar 18	17 Jul 19	Broken up 1937
Torch	Yarrow & Co Ltd	Apr 1917	16 Mar 18	11 May 18	Sold Nov 1929 for breaking up
Stonehenge	Palmer Shipbuilding & Iron Co Ltd	1918	19 Mar 18	Sep 1919	Wrecked 6 Nov 20
Tribune	J. Samuel White & Co Ltd	21 Aug 17	28 Mar 18	16 Jul 1918	Sold Dec 1931 for breaking up
Scotsman	John Brown & Co	10 Dec 17	30 Mar 18	21 May 18	Sold Jul 1937 for breaking up
Senator	Wm Denny & Bros Ltd	10 Jul 17	2 Apr 18	7 Jun 18	Broken up 1937
Trinidad	J. Samuel White & Co Ltd	15 Sep 17	8 Apr 18	9 Sep 18	Sold Mar 1932 for breaking up
Shark	Swan, Hunter & Wigham Richardson Ltd	Sep 1917	9 Apr 18	10 Jul 18	Sold Feb 1931 for breaking up
Scythe	John Brown & Co.	1918	25 Apr 18	Jul 1918	Sold Nov 1931 for breaking up
Scout	John Brown & Co.	25 Oct 17	27 Apr 18	15 Jun 18	Sold Mar 1946 for breaking up
Sikh	Fairfield Shipbuilding & Engineering Co Ltd	Aug 1917	7 May 18	29 Jun 18	Sold Feb 1927 for breaking up
Sparrowhawk	Swan, Hunter & Wigham Richardson Ltd	Sep 1917	14 May 18	4 Sep 18	Sold Feb 1931 for breaking up
Tomahawk	Yarrow & Co Ltd	Apr 1917	16 May 18	8 Jul 1918	Sold Jun 1928 for breaking up
Sepoy	Wm Denny & Bros Ltd	6 Aug 17	22 May 18	6 Aug 18	Sold Jul 1932 for breaking up
Speedy	John I Thornycroft & Co Ltd	May 1917	1 Jun 18	14 Aug 18	Sunk in collision 24 Sep 22
Tilbury	Swan, Hunter & Wigham Richardson Ltd	Nov 1917	13 Jun 18	17 Sep 18	Sold Feb 1931 for breaking up
Tryphon	Yarrow & Co Ltd	31 Mar 05	22 Jun 18	Sep 1918	Sold Sep 1920 for breaking up
Success	Wm Doxford & Sons Ltd	n/a	29 Jun 18	Apr 1918	Sold June 1937 for breaking up
Sirdar	Fairfield Shipbuilding & Engineering Co Ltd	Aug 1917	6 Jul 18	6 Sep 18	Sold May 1934 for breaking up
Seabear	John Brown & Co	13 Dec 17	6 Jul 18	Sep 1918	Sold Feb 1931 for breaking up
Seraph	Wm Denny & Bros Ltd	4 Oct 17	8 Jul 18	25 Dec 18	Sold May 1934 for breaking up
Splendid	Swan, Hunter & Wigham Richardson Ltd	Sep 1917	10 Jul 18	Oct 1918	Sold Jan 1931 for breaking up
Tobago	John I Thornycroft & Co Ltd	May 1917	15 Jul 18	2 Oct 1918	Broken up 1922
Trojan	J Samuel White & Co Ltd	3 Jan 18	20 Jul 18	6 Dec 1918	Broken up 1936
Swallow	Scotts Shipbuilding & Engineering Co Ltd	Sep 1917	1 Aug 18	29 Sep 18	Sold Sep 1936 for breaking up
Tactician	W Beardmore & Co Ltd	21 Nov 17	7 Aug 18	23 Oct 18	Sold Feb 1931 for breaking up
Steadfast	Palmer Shipbuilding & Iron Co Ltd	Oct 1917	8 Aug 18	Mar 1919	Sold Jul 1934 for breaking up
Tintagel	Swan, Hunter & Wigham Richardson Ltd	Dec 1917	9 Aug 18	Dec 1918	Sold Mar 1932 for breaking up
Seafire	John Brown & Co	27 Feb 18	10 Aug 18	Nov 1918	Broken up 1936
Shamrock	Wm Doxford & Sons Ltd	Nov 1917	26 Aug 18	16 Sep 19	Broken up 1937
Somme	Fairfield Shipbuilding & Engineering Co Ltd	Nov 1917	10 Sep 18	4 Nov 18	Sold Aug 1932 for breaking up
Searcher	John Brown & Co	30 Mar 18	11 Sep 18	Nov 1918	Sold Mar 1938 for breaking up
Serapis	Wm Denny & Bros Ltd	4 Dec 17	17 Sep 18	21 Mar 1919	Sold Jan 1934 for breaking up
Tumult	Yarrow & Co Ltd	Jun 1917	17 Sep 18	Dec 1918	Sold Oct 1928 for breaking up
Truant	J Samuel White & Co Ltd	14 Feb 18	18 Sep 18	17 Mar 1919	Sold Nov 1931 for breaking up
Sportive	Swan, Hunter & Wigham Richardson Ltd	Feb 1918	19 Sep 18	Dec 1918	Broken up 1936
Sabre	Alex Stephen & Sons Ltd	10 Sep 17	23 Sep 18	Oct 1918	Sold Nov 1945 for breaking up
Sterling	Palmer Shipbuilding & Iron Co Ltd	Sep 1917	8 Oct 18	Mar 1919	Sold Aug 1932 breaking up
Tara	W Beardmore & Co Ltd	21 Nov 17	12 Oct 18	9 Dec 18	Sold Dec 1931 for breaking up
Tenedos	R & W Hawthorn, Leslie & Co Ltd	6 Dec 17	21 Oct 18	Jun 1919	Bombed and sunk 5 Apr 42
Stalwart	Swan, Hunter & Wigham Richardson Ltd	Apr 1918	23 Oct 18	Apr 1919	Sold Jun 1937 for breaking up

Seawolf	John Brown & Co.	30 Apr 18	2 Nov 18	Jan 1919	Sold Feb 1931 for breaking up
Thanet	R & W Hawthorn, Leslie & Co Ltd	13 Dec 17	5 Nov 18	n/a	Bombed and sunk 27 Jan 42
Trusty	J. Samuel White & Co Ltd	11 Apr 18	6 Nov 18	9 May 19	Broken up 1936
Strenuous	Scotts Shipbuilding & Engineering Co Ltd	1918	9 Nov 18	Jan 1919	Sold Aug 1932 for breaking up
Turquoise	Yarrow & Co Ltd	Jun 1917	9 Nov 18	Mar 1919	Sold Jan 1932 for breaking up
Tasmania	W Beardmore & Co Ltd	18 Dec 17	22 Nov 18	29 Jan 19	Sold Jun 1937 for breaking up
Serene	Wm Denny & Bros Ltd	2 Feb 18	30 Nov 18	30 Apr 19	Broken up 1936
Toreador	John I Thornycroft & Co Ltd	Jan 1918	7 Dec 18	Apr 1919	Broken up 1937
Swordsman	Scotts Shipbuilding & Engineering Co Ltd	31 Mar 05	28 Dec 18	27 Jan 20	Sold Jun 1937 for breaking up
Tattoo	W Beardmore & Co Ltd	21 Dec 17	28 Dec 18	7 Apr 19	Sold Jan 1937 for breaking up
Spindrift	Fairfield Shipbuilding & Engineering Co Ltd	1918	30 Dec 18	2 Apr 19	Sold Jul 1936 for breaking up
Sesame	Wm Denny & Bros Ltd	13 Mar 18	30 Dec 18	28 Mar 19	Sold May 1934 for breaking up
Saladin	Alex. Stephen & Sons Ltd	10 Sep 17	17 Feb 19	11 Apr 19	Sold Jun 1947 for breaking up
Tuscan	Yarrow & Co Ltd	Jun 1917	1 Mar 19	24 Jun 19	Sold Aug 1932 for breaking up
Tourmaline	John I Thornycroft & Co Ltd	Nov 1917	12 Apr 19	Dec 1919	Sold Nov 1931 for breaking up
Stronghold	Scotts' Shipbuilding & Engineering Co Ltd	May 1918	6 May 19	2 Jul 19	Bombed and sunk, 4 Mar 42
Sardonyx	Alex. Stephen & Sons Ltd	25 Mar 18	27 May 19	12 Jul 19	Sold Oct 1945 for breaking up
Turbulent	R & W Hawthorn, Leslie & Co Ltd	14 Nov 17	29 May 19	10 Oct 19	Broken up 1936
Stormcloud	Palmer Shipbuilding & Iron Co Ltd	May 1918	30 May 19	28 Jan 20	Sold Jul 1934 for breaking up
Sturdy	Scotts' Shipbuilding & Engineering Co Ltd	Apr 1918	25 Jun 19	Oct 1919	Wrecked 30 Oct 40
Tyrian	Yarrow & Co Ltd	Jun 1917	2 Jul 19	23 Dec 19	Sold Feb 1932 for breaking up
Shikari	Wm Doxford & Sons Ltd	15 Jan 18	14 Jul 19	16 Sep 19	Sold Sep 1945 for breaking up
Spear	Fairfield Shipbuilding & Engineering Co Ltd	1918	9 Nov 19	17 Dec 18	Sold Jul 1926 for breaking up
Thracian	R & W Hawthorn, Leslie & Co Ltd	17 Jan 18	5 Mar 20	21 Apr 20	Bombed & beached 24 Dec 41, salved IJN, sold Feb 1946 for breaking up

APPENDIX L

FLOTILLA LEADERS – by type and completion date

NAME	BUILDER	LAID DOWN	LAUNCHED	COMPLETED	DAYS TO COMPLETE	WW2 USE	FATE
THORNYCROFT LEADERS – *SHAKESPEARE* CLASS							
Shakespeare	John I Thornycroft & Co Ltd	2 Oct 16	7 Jul 17	10 Oct 17	373	nil	Handed over in part payment of SS *Majestic* in 1936. Scrapped at Inverkeithling.
Spenser	John I Thornycroft & Co Ltd	9 Oct 16	22 Sep 17	*12 Dec 17*	429	nil	Handed over in part payment of SS *Majestic* in 1936. Scrapped at Inverkeithling
Wallace	John I Thornycroft & Co Ltd	15 Aug 17	26 Oct 17	14 Feb 19	548	WAIR	Sold to BIS Corp 20 Mar 45 and scrapped by Sep 1947
Broke (ex-*Rooke*)	John I Thornycroft & Co Ltd	*1 Nov 18*	16 Sep 20	20 Jan 25	2,272	SRE	Heavily damaged by shore batteries, Algiers 8 Nov 42 and sank under tow next day
Keppel	John I Thornycroft & Co Ltd	*1 Oct 18*	23 Apr 20	15 Apr 25	2,388	SRE	Sold for scrapping in July 1945
ADMIRALTY LEADERS – *SCOTT* CLASS							
Scott	Cammell Laird & Co Ltd	19 Feb 17	18 Oct 17	16 Jan 18	331	nil	Sunk 15 Aug 18, possibly torpedoed by *U-71* or struck mine
Bruce	Cammell Laird & Co Ltd	12 May 17	26 Feb 18	29 May 18	382	nil	Used as target for aerial torpedo trials off Isle of Wight, 22 Nov 39
Douglas	Cammell Laird & Co Ltd	30 Jun 17	8 Jun 18	30 Aug 18	426	SRE	Sold to BIS Corp 20 Mar 45 and scrapped at Inverkeithling May 1945–Sep 1946
Montrose	Cammell Laird & Co Ltd	4 Oct 17	10 Jun 18	14 Sep 18	345	SRE	Sold to BIS Corp 31 Jan 46 and scrapped by Apr 1946
Campbell	Cammell Laird & Co Ltd	10 Nov 17	21 Sep 18	21 Dec 18	406	SRE	Sold to BIS Corp 18 Feb 47 and scrapped at Rosyth Oct 1948
Stuart	Cammell Laird & Co Ltd	18 Oct 17	22 Aug 18	21 Dec 18	429	SRE	Sold to T Carr & Co Feb 1947 and scrapped in Sydney
Mackay	Cammell Laird & Co Ltd	5 Mar 18	21 Dec 18	19 May 19	440	SRE	Sold to BIS Corp, 18 Feb 47 and scrapped at Charlestown Feb 1949–Feb 1950
Malcolm	Cammell Laird & Co Ltd	27 Mar 18	29 May 19	14 Dec 19	627	SRE	Sold to BIS Corp July 1945 and scrapped at Barrow

Notes: Dates in italics are presumed since exact dates are not known
Sources: Preston, *V & W Class Destroyers*; Friedman, *British Destroyers*; Lenton and Colledge, *Warships of World War II*.

APPENDIX M

'V & W' DESTROYERS – by type and by completion date

NAME	BUILDER	LAID DOWN	LAUNCHED	COMPLETED	DAYS TO COMPLETE	WW 2 USE	FATE
'V' CLASS LEADERS							
Valkyrie (ex-*Montrose*)	William Denny & Brothers Ltd	25 May 16	13 Apr 17	16 Jun 17	387	Not converted	Scrapped in 1936
Valentine	Cammell Laird & Co Ltd	7 Aug 16	24 Mar 17	27 Jun 17	324	WAIR	Bombed and abandoned in the Scheldt Estuary 15 May 41; broken up Belgium 1953
Valhalla	Cammell Laird & Co Ltd	8 Aug 16	22 May 17	31 Jul 17	357	Not converted	Scrapped in 1932
Valorous (ex-*Malcolm*)	William Denny & Brothers Ltd	25 May 16	8 May 17	21 Aug 17	453	WAIR	Scrapped 1947–8
Vampire (ex Wallace)	J Samuel White & Co Ltd	10 Oct 16	21 May 17	22 Sep 17	347	Not converted	Transferred to RAN in 1933. Bombed and sunk by Japanese, Bay of Bengal 9 Apr 42
THORNYCROFT 'V' CLASS							
Viceroy	John I Thornycroft & Co Ltd	15 Dec 16	17 Nov 17	5 Feb 18	417	WAIR	Sold for disposal 1948
Viscount	John I Thornycroft & Co Ltd	20 Dec 16	29 Dec 17	4 Mar 18	439	LRE	Sold for disposal 1945
ADMIRALTY 'V' CLASS							
Vanoc	John Brown & Co Ltd	20 Sep 16	17 Jun 17	15 Aug 17	329	LRE	Wrecked, salvaged and scrapped 1946
Vimiera	Swan, Hunter and Wigham Richardson Ltd	*1 Oct 16*	22 Jun 17	19 Sep 17	353	WAIR	Mined and sunk 9 Jan 42 off the Nore, Thames Estuary
Vanquisher	John Brown & Co Ltd	27 Sep 16	18 Aug 17	2 Oct 17	370	LRE	Sold for disposal 1947
Vehement	William Denny & Brothers Ltd	25 Sep 16	6 Jul 17	16 Oct 17	386	Not converted	Sold for disposal 1945
Vendetta	Fairfield Shipbuilding & Engineering Ltd	*1 Nov 16*	3 Sep 17	17 Oct 17	350	Not converted	Transferred to the RAN – scuttled off Sydney 2 Jul 48
Violent	Swan, Hunter and Wigham Richardson Ltd	*1 Nov 16*	1 Sep 17	*1 Nov 17*	365	Not converted	Handed over for disposal 1937
Verdun	R W Hawthorn Leslie & Co Ltd	13 Jan 17	21 Aug 17	3 Nov 17	294	WAIR	Sold for disposal 1946.
Venturous	William Denny & Brothers Ltd	9 Oct 16	21 Sep 17	29 Nov 17	416	Not converted	Handed over for disposal in 1936
Vega	William Doxford & Sons Ltd	11 Dec 16	17 Nov 17	1 Dec 17	355	WAIR	Sold for disposal 1947
Vivacious	Yarrow & Co Ltd	*1 Jul 16*	3 Nov 17	*1 Dec 17*	518	SRE	Sold for disposal 1947
Vectis	J. Samuel White & Co Ltd	7 Dec 16	4 Sep 17	5 Dec 17	363	Not converted	Sold for disposal 1936
Verulam	R W Hawthorn Leslie & Co Ltd	8 Feb 17	3 Oct 17	12 Dec 17	307	Not converted	Mined and sunk, Gulf of Finland 1919
Venetia	Fairfield Shipbuilding & Engineering Ltd	2 Feb 17	29 Oct 17	19 Dec 17	320	Not converted	Mined 19 Oct 40 and sank in the Thames Estuary
Vivien	Yarrow & Co Ltd	*1 Jul 16*	3 Nov 17	28 Dec 17	545	WAIR	Sold for disposal 1947
Vortigern	J. Samuel White & Co Ltd	17 Jan 17	15 Oct 17	25 Jan 18	373	Not converted	Torpedoed by E-Boat off Cromer, 1942
Versatile	R W Hawthorn Leslie & Co Ltd	31 Jan 17	31 Oct 17	11 Feb 18	376	LRE	Sold for disposal 1946
Vesper	Alexander Stephen & Sons Ltd	27 Dec 16	15 Dec 17	20 Feb 18	420	LRE	Sold for disposal 1947
Vanessa	William Beardmore & Co Ltd	16 Mar 17	28 Dec 17	9 Mar 18	358	LRE	Sold for disposal 1947
Vimy(ex Vancouver)	William Beardmore & Co Ltd	15 Mar 17	28 Dec 17	9 Mar 18	359	LRE	Sold for disposal 1947
Velox	William Doxford & Sons Ltd	*1 Jan 17*	17 Nov 17	1 Apr 18	455	LRE	Sold for disposal 1947
Vidette	Alexander Stephen & Sons Ltd	1 Feb 17	28 Feb 18	27 Apr 18	450	LRE	Sold for disposal 1947
Vittoria	Swan, Hunter and Wigham Richardson Ltd	*1 Feb 17*	29 Oct 17	*1 May 18*	454	Not converted	Torpedoed and sunk by Bolshevik submarine Gulf of Finland 1919
Vanity	William Beardmore & Co Ltd	28 Jul 17	3 May 18	21 Jun 18	328	WAIR	Sold for disposal 1947
ADMIRALTY 'W' CLASS OR REPEAT 'V' CLASS							
Wakeful	William Beardmore & Co Ltd	17 Jan 17	6 Oct 17	*1 Nov 17*	288	Not converted	Torpedoed and sunk during the Dunkirk evacuation
Watchman	William Beardmore & Co Ltd	17 Jan 17	2 Nov 17	26 Jan 18	374	LRE	Sold for disposal 1945
Walker	William Denny & Brothers Ltd	26 Mar 17	29 Nov 17	12 Feb 18	323	Not converted	Sold for disposal 1946
Walrus	Fairfield Shipbuilding & Engineering Ltd	*1 Feb 17*	27 Dec 17	8 Mar 18	400	Not converted	Stranded in Filey Bay 12 Feb 38 and written off
Whirlwind	Swan, Hunter and Wigham Richardson Ltd	*1 May 17*	15 Dec 17	15 Mar 18	318	Not converted	Torpedoed and sunk by *U-34* SW of Ireland 5 Jul 40
Winchelsea	J. Samuel White & Co Ltd	24 May 17	15 Dec 17	15 Mar 18	295	LRE	Sold for disposal 1945
Warwick	R W Hawthorn Leslie & Co Ltd	10 Mar 17	28 Dec 17	18 Mar 18	373	LRE	Torpedoed and sunk by *U-413* off Trevose Head 20 Feb 44
Westcott	William Denny & Brothers Ltd	*30 Mar 17*	14 Feb 18	12 Apr 18	378	SRE	Sold for disposal 1945
Waterhen	Palmers Shipbuilding & Iron Co Ltd	*1 Jul 17*	26 Mar 18	17 Apr 18	290	Not converted	Transferred to the Australian Navy in 1933. Bombed and sunk off Libya 30 Jun 41
Westminster	Scotts Shipbuilding & Engineering Co Ltd	*1 Apr 17*	25 Feb 18	18 Apr 18	382	WAIR	Sold for disposal 1947
Wolfhound	Fairfield Shipbuilding & Engineering Ltd	*1 Apr 17*	14 Mar 18	27 Apr 18	391	WAIR	Sold for disposal 1948
Winchester	J Samuel White & Co Ltd	*12 Jun 17*	1 Feb 18	29 Apr 18	321	WAIR	Sold for disposal 1946

Wessex	R W Hawthorn Leslie & Co Ltd	28 May 17	12 Mar 18	11 May 18	348	Not converted	Sunk by Luftwaffe off Calais 24 May 40
Wrestler	Swan, Hunter and Wigham Richardson Ltd	*1 Jul 17*	25 Feb 18	15 May 18	318	LRE	Mined off Juno Beach on 6 June 44 and written off
Voyager	Alexander Stephen & Sons Ltd	17 May 17	8 May 18	24 Jun 18	403	Not converted	Transferred to RAN. Bombed by Japanese aircraft and beached 1942
Walpole	William Doxford & Sons Ltd	*1 May 17*	12 Feb 18	7 Aug 18	463	SRE	Mined North Sea 6 Jan 45, written off and sold for disposal
Windsor	Scotts Shipbuilding & Engineering Co Ltd	*1 Apr 17*	21 Jun 18	28 Aug 18	514	SRE	Sold for disposal 1947
Whitley (not *Whitby**)	William Doxford & Sons Ltd	*1 Jun 17*	13 Apr 18	14 Oct 18	500	WAIR	Bombed by the Luftwaffe and beached off Ostend Belgium 19 May 40
Wryneck	Palmers Shipbuilding & Iron Co Ltd	*1 Jul 17*	13 May 18	11 Nov 18	498	WAIR	Bombed and sunk by Luftwaffe on 27 Apr 41 during evacuation of Crete
THORNYCROFT 'W' CLASS							
Wolsey	John I Thornycroft & Co Ltd	28 Mar 17	16 Mar 18	14 May 18	412	WAIR	Sold for disposal 1945
Woolston	John I Thornycroft & Co Ltd	25 Apr 17	27 Jan 18	28 Jun 18	429	WAIR	Scrapped in 1947
ADMIRALTY MODIFIED 'W' CLASS (1st Group)							
Venomous (ex-*Venom*)	John Brown & Co Ltd	31 May 18	21 Dec 18	*1 Jun 19*	366	Front boiler removed	Sold for disposal 1947
Verity	John Brown & Co Ltd	17 May 18	19 Mar 19	17 Sep 19	488	LRE	Sold for disposal 1947
Wanderer	Fairfield Shipbuilding & Engineering Ltd	7 Aug 18	1 May 19	18 Sep 19	407	LR	Sold for disposal 1946
Vansittart	William Beardmore & Co Ltd	1 Jul 18	17 Apr 19	5 Nov 19	492	LRE	Sold for disposal 1946
Volunteer	William Denny & Brothers Ltd	16 Apr 18	17 Apr 19	7 Nov 19	570	LRE	Sold for disposal 1947
Wren	Yarrow & Co Ltd	*1 Jun 18*	11 Nov 19	27 Jan 23	1,701	Not converted	Sunk by Luftwaffe off Aldeburgh, North Sea 27 Jul 40
Whitehall	Swan, Hunter and Wigham Richardson Ltd	*1 Jun 18*	11 Sep 19	9 Jul 24	2,230	LRE	Sold for disposal 1945
ADMIRALTY MODIFIED 'W' CLASS (2nd Group)							
Whitshed	Swan, Hunter and Wigham Richardson Ltd	3 Jun 18	31 Jan 19	11 Jul 19	403	SRE	Sold for disposal 1947
Witherington	J. Samuel White & Co Ltd	27 Sep 18	16 Apr 19	10 Oct 19	378	SRE	Sold for disposal 1947 but wrecked en route to breakers
Veteran	John Brown & Co Ltd	30 Aug 18	26 Apr 19	13 Nov 19	440	SRE	Torpedoed and sunk by *U-404* SW of Iceland 26 Sep 42. Lost with all hands
Wild Swan	Swan, Hunter and Wigham Richardson Ltd	*1 Jul 18*	17 May 19	14 Nov 19	501	Not converted	Bombed and sunk by the Luftwaffe in Bay of Biscay 17 Jun 42
Wivern	J Samuel White & Co Ltd	19 Aug 18	16 Apr 19	23 Dec 19	491	SRE	Sold for disposal 1947
Wolverine	J Samuel White & Co Ltd	8 Oct 18	17 Jul 19	27 Jul 20	658	SRE	Sold for disposal 1947
Worcester	J. Samuel White & Co Ltd	20 Dec 18	24 Oct 19	20 Sep 22	1370	SRE	Mined 23 Dec 43, written off & used as accommodation hulk
THORNYCROFT MODIFIED 'W' CLASS							
Wishart	John I Thornycroft & Co Ltd	18 May 18	18 Jul 19	*1 Jun 20*	745	SRE	Sold for disposal 1945
Witch	John I Thornycroft & Co Ltd	13 Jun 18	11 Nov 19	*1 Mar 24*	2088	SRE	Sold for disposal 1945

Notes:
Dates in italics are presumed since exact dates are not known.
*Due to a spelling mistake, *Whitby* was called *Whitley* and the name never changed.

SHIPS CANCELLED

ADMIRALTY 'MODIFIED W' CLASS (1st Group)

	Date Cancelled
Vimy (ex-*Vantage*)	Sep 1919
Votary	12 Apr 19
Warren	Sep 1919
Welcome	12 Apr 19
Welfare	12 Apr 19
Whitehead	12 Apr 19
Wye	Sep 1919

ADMIRALTY 'MODIFIED W' CLASS (2nd Group)

	Date Cancelled
Vashon	26 Nov 18
Vengeful	26 Nov 18
Vigo	26 Nov 18
Wistful	26 Nov 18
Virulent	26 Nov 18
Volage	26 Nov 18
Volcano	26 Nov 18
Wager	12 Apr 19
Wake	26 Nov 18
Waldegrave	26 Nov 18
Walton	26 Nov 18
Whitaker	26 Nov 18
Watson	Sep 1919
Wave	Dec 1918
Weasel	26 Nov 18
Whitebear	26 Nov 18
Wellesley	26 Nov 18
Werewolf	12 Apr 19
Westphal	12 Apr 19
Westward Ho	12 Apr 19
Wheeler	12 Apr 19
Whip	26 Nov 18
Whippet	26 Nov 18
Whelp	Sep 1919
Willoughby	12 Apr 19
Winter	26 Nov 18
Wrangler	Sep 1919
Yeoman	12 Apr 19
Zealous	12 Apr 19
Zebra	12 Apr 19
Zodiac	12 Apr 19

Glossary

3in/50 cal Mks 20–22	These American 3in naval guns dated back to the First World War and were considered to be dual-purpose (anti-surface/anti-aircraft), although they were of limited effectiveness in either role. While the projectile was 13lbs, the bursting charge was only 0.3–0.74lbs, depending on type.
4in/50 cal Mark 9	This low-angle gun was used in the United States Navy's First World War emergency-build destroyers – the 'four-pipers' or 'flush-deckers' as they became known, fifty of which were transferred to Britain in September 1940 in the Destroyers for Bases Agreement. Since many of these guns were removed to reduce topweight they found their way on to Defensively Equipped Merchant Ships (DEMS).
5in/38 cal	This dual-purpose gun was the main gun on United States Navy destroyers, most aircraft carriers, anti-aircraft cruisers and the secondary armament on most battleships and cruisers. It was extremely versatile, capable of a high rate of fire despite the projectile and charge being separate, and was probably the best gun of its size at the time.
AA	Anti-Aircraft.
'A' Position etc.	In British ships, main armament positions – almost invariably on the centreline of the ship – were given alphabetical designations starting with 'A' and 'B' at the bow and finishing with 'X' and 'Y' at the stern. Midships turrets usually had something like a 'Q' designation. The reason the designations did not follow the alphabet was to ensure that when giving orders, the names sounded sufficiently distinct so they would not be confused.
A-Scope	The original method of displaying a radar return on a cathode ray tube displaying amplitude of echo on the vertical axis and range on the horizontal axis.
ASDIC	This was the primary device for detecting submarines via echo-location. Called Sonar by the USN.
ATW	Ahead Throwing Weapon (such as Hedgehog or Squid) designed to project anti-submarine missiles ahead of an attacking ship's path.
AW	Air Warning – as in Air-Warning radar. Air-Search was another term used.
Cal/cal	Abbreviation for calibre, being either the ratio of the bore of the barrel of a gun to the length of the barrel (as in the USN 4in/50 cal meaning the barrel length was 50 times 4in or 200in) or, as in the case of the .50 cal Browning HMG, the bore, or calibre, was ½in.
Carley Float	A life raft made from a steel or copper inner tube, divided into watertight sections and covered in a buoyancy material such as cork in turn covered in painted canvas with a floor of webbing or slatted wood. They came in various shapes and sizes.
Charley/Charlie Noble	The easily identifiable 'H'-shaped smoke exhaust at the top of the stack from the warship's galley.
Commissioning	The act or ceremony of placing a warship into active service.
CTL	Constructive Total Loss: the cost of repair of a damaged ship is more than the value of the ship.
Bofors	The Swedish armaments manufacturer whose name was simply used to describe its famous 40mm anti-aircraft gun that was made under licence. The first models were simple single-barrelled air-cooled models but were developed by the licensees into two and four-barrelled water-cooled versions.
DC	Depth charge, a drum-shaped canister filled with high explosive detonated via a hydrostatic valve set at pre-determined depths.
DCT	Depth-Charge Thrower, hydraulic or explosively detonated projector to launch a depth charge clear of a ship. Called a Depth-Charge Projector in USN ships.
Decommissioning	The act or ceremony of taking a warship out of active service. Sometimes referred to as Paid Off.
Depth Charge Chute	A simple way of stowing one or two depth charges for dropping over the stern.
Depth Charge Rail	A frame for stowing a series of depth charges so that they can be released as and when required over the stern. In USN these were termed a Depth-Charge Rack.
DF	Direction Finder (more particularly MFDF or MF/DF for Medium Frequency Direction Finder to distinguish it from the later, HF/DF High Frequency Direction Finder) an electronic device for homing in on and thereby obtaining the bearing of a radio source. Sometimes called RDF or Radio Direction Finding/Finder. The square-shaped aerial was Type FM 12 or Outfit FM 12.
Displacement	By the Archimedes' Principle: the weight of the water displaced by the vessel when floating.
FIDO	The nickname for the Mk 24 mine – an air-launched acoustic anti-submarine torpedo.
Flag Superior	The letter that prefixes a pennant/pendant number indicating a flotilla or class or type of ship.
Flag Inferior	The letter that follows a pennant/pendant number indicating a flotilla or class or type of ship, usually of a minor nature.
Foxer	A decoy device consisting of two parallel pipes towed behind a ship to produce a noise sufficient to distract a GNAT torpedo from homing in on the noise created by the ship's propellers.
Full Load	That is, Full Load Displacement, the weight of the water displaced by the vessel when floating at its greatest allowable draft.
GNAT	An acronym for German Navy Acoustic Torpedo (more particularly the G7es T5 *Zaunkönig* or Wren) – a particularly deadly torpedo devised in service from 1943 that homed in on the noise created by a ship's propellers.
HA	High Angle, in effect anti-aircraft capable only.
HA/LA	High Angle/Low Angle, in effect capable of both anti-aircraft and surface action.

Hedgehog A 24-spigot anti-submarine mortar firing 7in diameter contact-fused projectiles with a 35lb charge. Spigots were arranged to give a 40yd diameter circle at approximately 200yds ahead of the ship.

HF/DF High Frequency Direction Finder – 'Huff Duff' – which was able to obtain the bearing of even very short transmissions. A 'game-changer' in the Battle of the Atlantic allowing escorts to home in on U-boats transmitting to base or each other. FM 3 was introduced in 1942, FM 4 in 1943 with a cathode ray display.

HMG Heavy Machine Gun, such as the .50 cal Browning or .5in Vickers.

IFF Identification Friend or Foe; an electronic system to establish via interrogation signals the identity of aircraft, ships etc. Type 242: sometimes called Outfit ASB Type 242. Often seen on top of the Type 271 radar lanterns. Type 253, sometimes called Outfit 252, a distinctive egg-timer shape.

LA Low Angle, in effect surface action-capable only.

Laid Down The term applied to the keel being laid down which was traditionally the first and major structural item on which the rest of the framework of the ship was constructed.

Launched Ships are seldom launched in a completed state – that is, fully fitted out. The slipways are needed for the next ship so ships are launched when they are substantially complete and moved to fitting-out berths.

LRE Long Range Escort.

MF/DF See DF.

MG Machine Gun.

mm Millimetre, in this case the calibre, the bore, of the weapon.

Montagu Whaler The standard rowing/sailing ships' boat in service for seventy years, 27ft long, highly seaworthy, double-ended and clinker construction.

Oerlikon A Swiss armament manufacturer but the name more commonly used to describe their high-velocity 20mm cannon made under licence in large numbers in Britain and the USA primarily as a light, short-range, anti-aircraft weapon.

P.P. Length Between Perpendiculars, is the length of a ship along the waterline from the forward surface of the stem, or main bow perpendicular member, to the after surface of the sternpost, or main stern perpendicular member. Also referred as LBP or BP.

PPI Plan & Position Indicator; Introduced in 1942 and what we think of as normal today by way of a circular radar screen showing the targets – that is, coastline, other ships, navigational marks, etc. – 'painted' as glowing marks on the screen. Prior to this invention, radar signals had to be interpreted on a cathode ray tube as blips in a straight line – an 'A' trace (or 'grass' as it was called) running across the tube.

Paid/Paying Off The process leading up to decommissioning when the ship is de-stored and the crew is 'paid off'.

Pendant Number Pronounced Pennant Number the numbers or letters or combinations of numbers and letters used to identify individual ships.

Pom-pom The name is derived from the sound the Vickers 40mm QF 2-pounder Mk II made when fired. It was, in effect, an oversized Maxim machine gun. The later Mk VIII model was made in single, quad and eight-barrel mountings and capable of a high rate of fire.

Proximity Fuse A miniature radar-like device embedded in the nose of a shell causing it to explode in the vicinity of aircraft, mainly, but could be used in bombardment for air-bursts.

Q Attachment This was an additional ASDIC set from 1943 which enabled contact to be maintained with deep targets at short ranges and also minimised the dead zone via a narrow fan-shaped beam.

QF Quick Firing guns use fixed ammunition where the projectile and propellant are in one piece offering a higher rate of fire as distinct from Breech Loading (BL) where the projectile and propellant are separate and slower to load.

QF 12-pounder 12 cwt This weapon dated back to 1894. Twelve pounds (12-pounder) was the weight of the projectile and 12 hundredweight (12cwt) the weight of the barrel and breech. It was not a Quick Firing gun in the true sense of the word in that the projectile and propellant were separate but they were loaded together on a special tray although it did achieve fifteen rounds per minute. The gun stayed in production throughout the Second World War with improvements, such was the demand for them.

QF 2-pounder Mk VIII A single-barreled, manually-operated and updated version of the QF 2-pounder Mk II commonly referred to as a pom-pom from the noise it made when firing. Usually replaced by the 20mm Oerlikon or, later, the 40mm Bofors.

Radar Originally called RDF – Range and Direction Finding – but the acronym came from RAdio Detection And Ranging. It is an object-detection system that uses °radio waves °to determine the range, angle, or velocity of objects via a °transmitter producing electromagnetic waves through an emitting antenna and a receiving antenna to capture any returns from objects in the path of the emitted signal plus a °receiver °and °processor °to determine the properties of the object.

RCN Royal Canadian Navy.

RDF Radio Direction Finder.

RN Royal Navy.

RNR Royal Naval Reserve; at the time of the Second World War it was a volunteer reserve force formed mainly from professional merchant seaman officers.

RNVR Royal Naval Volunteer Reserve; this was a 'hostilities only' force of officers formed mainly from volunteers with some form of seagoing experience, however slight.

R/T Radio Telephony.

SA A type of USN air-search/air-warning radar.

SC A type of USN air-search/air-warning radar.

SG A type of USN surface-warning radar. The antenna was a compact revolving dished rectangular plate.

Shark A specially developed anti-submarine projectile fired from 4in guns and designed to enter the water short of the submarine. The trajectory was maintained by special spoiler rings. A hardened nose-cone could pierce the submarine's pressure hull and allow the 24lbs of Torpex to explode internally.

SHP Shaft Horsepower: is the power delivered to the °propeller °shafts of a °steamship. This measure is not commonly used in the automobile industry, because in that context drive train losses can become significant.

Signal Projector	Signalling lamp, usually 6in or 10in diameter for signalling by light using Morse but the larger ones (20in, 24in) were primarily used as searchlights.
SL	A type of USN surface-search radar. The antenna was contained in a compact saucepan-shaped dome of about 4ft diameter.
Splinter Matting	A protection of limited value consisting, mainly, of a canvas envelope containing compressed coir (or similar material) designed to stop the penetration of shell splinters. Used to protect exposed gun positions, navigation bridges etc.
Squid	A three-barrelled anti-submarine mortar developed as a replacement for Hedgehog. Squid fired three much heavier depth charges (390lbs) about 275–300yd ahead of the ship and landed in a triangular pattern. The charges could be set to explode at a required depth, moments before firing with input direct from the ship's ASDIC, a Type 147.
SRE	Short Range Escort.
Staff Requirements	A design brief, in effect, which covered; Function, Speed/ Endurance, Armament/ Protection, Navigation, Manoeuvrability, Sensors (radar, ASDIC etc), Signals (visual, W/T, R/T) and any other special requirements such as might apply to a particular type of ship. Generally preceded by a Sketch Requirements which led to Draft Staff Requirements
Standard	That is, Standard Displacement, the weight of the water displaced by the vessel complete, fully manned, engined, and equipped ready for sea, including all armament and ammunition, equipment, outfit, provisions and fresh water for crew, miscellaneous stores, and implements of every description that are intended to be carried in war, but without fuel or reserve boiler feed water on board.
SW	Surface Warning – as in surface-warning radar.
SW1C/SW2C	A Canadian radar with an antenna characterised by a 'Y'-shaped antenna with a horizontal bar projecting forward over the top. Developed at the same time in ignorance of the parallel development of centimetric Type 271.
Sword	Another name for Type 147B ASDIC (see above).
TBS	Talk Between Ships; low-powered, line-of-sight VHF radio system.
Tumblehome	A term used to describe a ship's hull where the actual beam of the hull is wider than the deck in such a way that the sides of the hull slope inwards towards the deck. In the days of timber construction, it provided greater strength.
USCG	United States Coast Guard.
USN	United States Navy.
'Wheezers & Dodgers'	The Department of Miscellaneous Weapons Development, developers of, amongst other things, the Hedgehog.
W/T	Wireless Telegraphy.

Notes

2: Destroyer Types of the Late 1800s

1. Norman Friedman, *British Destroyers: From Earliest Days to the Second World War, An Illustrated Design History* (Barnsley: Pen & Sword Books, 2009), pp 39–40.
2. Ibid, p 40.
3. Ibid, pp 40 and 41.
4. Alastair Borthwick, *Yarrow and Company: The First Hundred Years* (Glasgow: The University Press, 1965), p 28.
5. Ibid, p 28.
6. Friedman, *British Destroyers*, p 48.
7. Ibid, pp 42–3.
8. Borthwick, *Yarrow and Company*, p 27; Friedman, *British Destroyers*, p 50.
9. Borthwick, *Yarrow and Company*, p 28.
10. Friedman, *British Destroyers*, p 190.
11. John Henshaw, *Town Class Destroyers: A Critical Assessment* (Marlborough: Crowood Press, 2018), p 78.
12. Dreadnought Project.org.
13. Ibid.
14. Friedman, *British Destroyers*, p 59.
15. David Lyon, *The First Destroyers* (London: Chatham Publishing, 1996), pp 49, 118.

3: The New Century: Evolution Not Revolution

1. Friedman, *British Destroyers*, pp 86–8.
2. Ibid, p 87.
3. Ibid, p 292.
4. dreadnoughtproject.com.
5. Edgar J. March, *British Destroyers: A History of Development 1892-1953* (London: Seeley Service & Co., 1966), p 75.
6. dreadnoughtproject.com.
7. Friedman, *British Destroyers*, p 90.
8. March, *British Destroyers*, pp 70–2.
9. Friedman, *British Destroyers*, p 282.
10. Ibid, pp 106–7.
11. Ibid, p 108.
12. Ibid, pp 293–4.
13. March, *British Destroyers*, p 93.
14. Ibid, pp 84–5.
15. Friedman, *British Destroyers*, pp 293–4.
16. March, *British Destroyers*, p 101
17. Friedman, *British Destroyers*, p 295.
18. March, *British Destroyers*, p 108.
19. Friedman, *British Destroyers*, p 113.
20. March, *British Destroyers*, p 109.
21. Friedman, *British Destroyers*, p 295.
22. March, *British Destroyers*, pp 116–17.
23. Ross Gillett, *Warships of Australia* (Adelaide: Rigby Ltd, 1977), pp 39, 128 and 141.
24. Ibid, p 153.
25. Friedman, *British Destroyers*, p 124.
26. March, *British Destroyers*, pp 124–5.
27. Ibid, pp 133–4.
28. Alan Raven and John Roberts, *'V' and 'W' Class Destroyers* (London: Arms and Armour Press, Lionel 29. Leventhal Limited, 1979), p 1; March, *British Destroyers*, p 151.
29. Ibid, pp 143–4.
30. Ibid, p 174.
31. Ibid, pp 183–9.
32. Ibid, p 190.

5: The Flotilla Leaders

1. Friedman, *British Destroyers*, p 76.
2. March, *British Destroyers*, p 152.
3. Friedman, *British Destroyers*, p 157.
4. Ibid.
5. Ibid.
6. Ibid, p 60.
7. Raven and Roberts, *'V' and 'W' Class Destroyers*, p 2.
8. Friedman, *British Destroyers*, p 151.
9. Ibid.
10. Raven and Roberts, *'V' and 'W' Class Destroyers*, p 2.
11. March, *British Destroyers*, p 194; Raven and Roberts, *'V' and 'W' Class Destroyers*, p 2.
12. David K Brown, *Atlantic Escorts: Ships, Weapons & Tactics in World War II* (Barnsley: Pen & Sword Books, 2007), p 18.
13. March, *British Destroyers*, p 194; Antony Preston, *V & W Class Destroyers 1917-1945* (London: Macdonald & Co, 1971), p 6.

6: The Benchmarkers

1. Raven and Roberts, *'V' and 'W' Class Destroyers*, p 3.
2. Friedman, *British Destroyers*, pp 158–9.
3. Ibid, p 162.
4. March, *British Destroyers*, p 205.
5. Ibid, p 206.
6. Ibid.
7. Ibid.
8. David K Brown, *Nelson to Vanguard: Warship Design and Development 1923-1945* (Barnsley: Pen & Sword Books, 2007), Appendix 9.
9. March, *British Destroyers*, p 206.
10. Ibid.
11. Raven and Roberts, *'V' and 'W' Class Destroyers*, p 4.
12. Ibid, p 4.
13. Ibid, p 6.
14. March, *British Destroyers*, p 206; Friedman, *British Destroyers*, p 163.
15. March, *British Destroyers*, p 208.
16. Ibid, p 208.
17. Raven and Roberts, *'V' and 'W' Class Destroyers*, pp 4–5.
18. 1Friedman, *British Destroyers*, p 164.
19. March, *British Destroyers*, p 208.
20. Raven and Roberts, *'V' and 'W' Class Destroyers*, p 7; March, *British Destroyers*, p 209
21. Raven and Roberts, *'V' and 'W' Class Destroyers*, p 14.
22. March, *British Destroyers*, pp 227–8.
23. Raven and Roberts, *'V' and 'W' Class Destroyers*, p 11.
24. March, *British Destroyers*, p 227.
25. Preston, *V and W Class Destroyers*, p 108.
26. David K Brown, *Atlantic Escorts*, p 18.
27. Ibid; March, *British Destroyers*, p 229.
28. Preston, *V & W Class Destroyers*, p 112.

7: The Big Leaders

1. Preston, *V and W Class Destroyers*, p 13.
2. Friedman, *British Destroyers*, p 166.
3. March, *British Destroyers*, p 196.
4. Friedman, *British Destroyers*, p 166.
5. Ibid, p 168.
6. Preston, *V and W Class Destroyers*, p 99.
7. Ibid.
8. March, *British Destroyers*, p 200.
9. Friedman, *British Destroyers*, p 167.
10. Preston, *V and W Class Destroyers*, p 99.

8: The First World War and the Baltic Campaign 1918–1920

1. Preston, *V and W Class*, p 22.
2. Ibid, p 26.
3. Ibid, p 27.
4. uboat.net/wwi/boats/?boat=UB+107
5. Preston, *V and W Class*, p 30.
6. Ibid, p 34.

9: Their Design Heritage

1. March, *British Destroyers*, p 133.
2. Angus Konstam, *British Destroyers 1939-45 Pre-War Classes* (Oxford: Osprey Publishing, 2017), p 6.
3. Friedman, *British Destroyers*, p 187.
4. March, *British Destroyers*, p 242.
5. Friedman, *British Destroyers*, p 190.
6. H T Lenton and J J Colledge, *Warships of World War II* (London: Ian Allan, 1964), p 95.
7. H T Lenton, *British Fleet & Escort Destroyers* (London: Macdonald, 1970), p 65.
8. Friedman, *British Destroyers*, p 190.
9. March, *British Destroyers*, p 239.
10. Ibid.

11. Les Brown, *British Destroyers, A-I and 'Tribal' Classes* (Barnsley: Seaforth Publishing, 2009), p 1; Lenton, *British Fleet & Escort Destroyers*, p 65.
12. Ibid, p 66.
13. March, *British Destroyers*, p 244.
14. Lenton, *British Fleet & Escort Destroyers*, p 66.
15. Ibid, p 68.
16. March, *British Destroyers*, p 250.
17. Ibid.
18. Ibid, p 247.
19. Friedman, *British Destroyers*, p 201.
20. Lenton, *British Fleet & Escort Destroyers*, p 79.
21. Ibid, p 75.
22. Ibid, p 83.
23. Ibid. p 99.
24. David K Brown, *Nelson to Vanguard*, p 107.
25. Norman Friedman, *U.S. Destroyers; An Illustrated Design History* (Barnsley: Pen & Sword Books, 2004), p 77.
26. Paul H Silverstone, *U.S. Warships of World War II* (London: Ian Allan, 1965), p 114.
27. www.navweaps.com/Weapons/WNUS_5-38_mk12.php.
28. March, *British Destroyers*, p 328.
29. Friedman, *U.S. Destroyers*, p 78.

10: The Second World War

1. Preston, *V and W Class Destroyers*, p 59.
2. Ibid, pp 60–1.
3. Ibid, pp 67–8.
4. John F. Moyes, *Scrap-Iron Flotilla* (Sydney: NSW Bookstall Co Pty Ltd, 1944), p 1.
5. March, *British Destroyers*, pp 213–14.
6. Konstam, *British Destroyers*, p 21.
7. Friedman, *British Destroyers*, p 230.
8. Preston, *V and W Class Destroyers*, pp 57–8.
9. Ibid, p 114.
10. Friedman, p 247.
11. David K Brown, *Atlantic Escorts*, p 19.
12. Preston, *V and W Class Destroyers*, p 62.
13. David K Brown, *Atlantic Escorts*, p 19.
14. Ibid, p 21.
15. Konstam, *British Destroyers*, p 25.
16. Friedman, *British Destroyers*, p 252.
17. Preston, *V and W Class Destroyers*, p 118.
18. Friedman, *British Destroyers*, p 249; David K Brown, *Atlantic Escorts*, p 21.
19. Ibid, p 250.
20. Ibid. p 248.
21. Ibid, p 21.

11: Miscellany

1. Norman Friedman, *Naval Radar* (Greenwich: Conway Maritime Press, 1981), pp 195–6.
2. Ibid, p 196.
3. Ibid, p 195.
4. Ibid, pp 192–3.
5. Ibid, p 192.
6. David K. Brown, *Atlantic Escorts*, Appendix IV.
7. The Dreadnought Project.

12: The Scoreboard

1. Captain Donald Macintyre, *U-Boat Killer* (London, Weidenfeld and Nicolson, 1956), p 38.
2. uboat.net/u205.
3. regiamarina.net.
4. uboat.net/u74.
5. uboat.net/u619.
6. uboat.net/u411.
7. uboat.net/u69.
8. uboat.net/u125.
9. naval-history.net/vidette.
10. uboat.net/u305.
11. uboat.net/u314.
12. Friedman, *British Destroyers*, p 170.
13. Paul Kemp, *The Admiralty Regrets: British Warship Losses of the 20th Century* (Stroud, Sutton Publishing, 1999), p 115.
14. Ibid.
15. Ibid.
16. Ibid, p 116.
17. Ibid, p 123.
18. Ibid, p 127.
19. Ibid, p 133.
20. Ibid, p 142.
21. Ibid, p 149.
22. Ibid, p 165.
23. Ibid, p 172.
24. Ibid, p 178.
25. Ibid, p 187.
26. Ibid, p 196.
27. Ibid.
28. Ibid, p 198.
29. Ibid, p 229.
30. Ibid, p 233.
31. Preston, *V and W Class Destroyers*, p 123.
32. Kemp, *The Admiralty Regrets*, p 248.

13: Conclusions

1. David K Brown, *Nelson to Vanguard*, p 107.
2. Preston, *V & W Class Destroyers*, p 19.
3. David K Brown, *Atlantic Escorts*, p 18.
4. Ibid, p 51.
5. Ibid, p 18.
6. Konstam, *British Destroyers*, p 6.
7. Lenton, *British Fleet & Escort Destroyers*, p 3.
8. David Goodey and Richard Osborne, *Destroyer At War: The Fighting Life and Loss of HMS Havock from the Atlantic to the Mediterranean 1939-42* (Barnsley: Frontline Books, 2017), p 253.
9. David K Brown, *Nelson to Vanguard*, p 86.
10. Ibid, p 98.
11. Preston, *V & W Class Destroyers*, p 126–7.
12. David K Brown, *Atlantic Escorts*, p 156.
13. John Terraine, *Business in Great Waters: The U-Boat Wars 1916-1945* (London: Mandarin Paperbacks, 1989), p 87.
14. William Y'Blood, *U.S. Escort Carriers in the Battle of the Atlantic* (Annapolis: Naval Institute Press, 1983), p 273.

Bibliography

Published Sources

Borthwick, Alastair, *Yarrow and Company: The First Hundred Years* (Glasgow: The University Press, 1965).

Brown, David K, *Atlantic Escorts: Ships, Weapons & Tactics in World War II* (Barnsley: Pen & Sword Books, 2007).

____________, *Nelson to Vanguard: Warship Design and Development 1923-1945* (Barnsley: Pen & Sword Books, 2007).

Brown, Les, *British Destroyers, A-I and 'Tribal' Classes* (Barnsley: Seaforth Publishing, 2009).

English, John, *The Hunts* (Cumbria: The World Ship Society, 1987).

Friedman, Norman, *British Destroyers: From Earliest Days to the Second World War, An Illustrated Design History* (Barnsley: Pen & Sword Books, 2009).

____________, *Naval Anti-Aircraft Guns & Gunnery* (Barnsley: Pen & Sword Books, 2013).

____________, *Naval Radar* (Greenwich: Conway Maritime Press, 1981).

____________, *U.S. Destroyers; An Illustrated Design History* (Barnsley: Pen & Sword Books, 2004).

Gillett, Ross, *Warships of Australia* (Adelaide: Rigby Ltd, 1977).

Goodey, David, and Osborne, Richard, *Destroyer At War: The Fighting Life and Loss of HMS Havock from the Atlantic to the Mediterranean 1939-42* (Barnsley: Frontline Books, 2017).

Haines, Gregory, *Destroyers At War* (London: Ian Allen, 1982).

Henshaw, John, *Town Class Destroyers: A Critical Assessment* (Marlborough: Crowood Press, 2018).

Hodges, Peter, and Friedman, Norman, *Destroyer Weapons of World War 2* (Annapolis: Naval Institute Press, nd).

Kemp, Paul, *The Admiralty Regrets: British Warship Losses of the 20th Century* (Stroud, Sutton Publishing, 1999).

Konstam, Angus, *British Destroyers 1939-45. Pre-War Classes* (Oxford: Osprey Publishing, 2017).

Lenton, H T, *British Fleet & Escort Destroyers* (London: Macdonald, 1970).

__________, and Colledge, J J, *Warships of World War II* (London: Ian Allan, 1964).

Lyon, David, *The First Destroyers* (London: Chatham Publishing, 1996).

Macintyre, Captain Donald, *U-Boat Killer* (London, Weidenfeld and Nicolson, 1956).

March, Edgar J, *British Destroyers: A History of Development 1892-1953* (London: Seeley Service & Co., 1966).

Marder A J, *From the Dreadnought to Scapa Flow, Vol IV, Years of Crisis* (Barnsley: Seaforth Publishing, 2013).

Moore, Robert J, *A Hard Fought Ship: The Story of HMS Venomous* (Privately published, 1990).

Moyes, John F, *Scrap-Iron Flotilla* (Sydney: NSW Bookstall Co Pty Ltd, 1944).

Preston, Antony, *V & W Class Destroyers 1917-1945* (London: Macdonald & Co, 1971).

Raven, Alan, and Roberts, John, *'V' and 'W' Class Destroyers* (London: Arms and Armour Press, Lionel Leventhal Limited, 1979).

Silverstone, Paul H, *U.S. Warships of World War II* (London: Ian Allan, 1965).

Terraine, John, *Business in Great Waters: The U-Boat Wars 1916-1945* (London: Mandarin Paperbacks, 1989).

Wright, Malcolm, *British and Commonwealth Warship Camouflage of WWII; Destroyers, Frigates, Escorts, Minesweepers, Coastal Warfare Craft, Submarines & Auxiliaries* (Barnsley: Pen & Sword Books, 2014).

Y'Blood, William T, *Hunter Killer, U.S. Escort Carriers in the Battle of the Atlantic* (Annapolis: Naval Institute Press, 1983).

Electronic Sources

navalhistory.net

navsource.org

uboat.net

INDEX